COMPUTER
BOOK SERIES
FROM IDG

Microsoft® Publisher 97 For Dummies®

W9-DHH-343

Navigation Keys

Home	Go to the beginning of current text line
End	Go to the end of current text line
Up arrow	Move up one text line
Down arrow	Move down one text line
Right arrow	Move right one character
Left arrow	Move left one character
Ctrl+Home	Go to the beginning of current text frame
Ctrl+End	Go to the end of current text frame
Ctrl+Up	Go to the beginning of current paragraph
Ctrl+Down arrow	Go to the beginning of next paragraph
Ctrl+Right arrow	Move right one word
Ctrl+Left arrow	Move left one word

If text is highlighted, pressing the left- or right-arrow key positions the insertion point at the beginning or end of that highlighting and then removes the highlighting.

Ten Design Tips

1. Design your publication for the right audience.

2. Talk to your printer early in the project.

3. Check with your print shop to be sure that you're using the right printer driver.

4. Use white space.

5. Use a simple design that highlights the important parts of your publication.

6. Add contrast to spice up your pages and keep readers interested.

7. Plan carefully for the number of copies that you need — don't print extra!

8. Try to substitute less expensive elements or processes to avoid going over your budget.

9. Be aware of copyright laws and follow them.

10. Scan graphics at the resolution you will use to print them.

...For Dummies: #1 Computer Book Series for Beginners

Microsoft® Publisher 97 For Dummies®

Cheat Sheet

Formatting Keystrokes

Ctrl+B	Bold selected text
Ctrl+I	Italicize selected text
Ctrl+U	Underline selected text
Ctrl+=	Superscript selected text
Ctrl+Shift+K	Change text to small caps
Ctrl+Spacebar	Change text to plain text and remove all styles
Ctrl+>	Increase the font size one half point
Ctrl+<	Decrease the font size one half point
Ctrl+Shift+P	Activate the Font Size list box in the Format toolbar
Ctrl+Shift+F	Activate the Font list box in the Format toolbar
Ctrl+Shift+S	Activate the Style list box in the Format toolbar
Ctrl+Shift+[	Decrease kerning in selected text
Ctrl+Shift+]	Increase kerning in selected text
Ctrl+Shift+"	Insert an inch mark and defeat smart quotes
Ctrl+Shift+'	Insert foot mark and defeat smart quotes
Ctrl+H	Hyphenate text
Ctrl+O	Remove space before a paragraph
Ctrl+1	Single space lines of text
Ctrl+2	Double space lines of text
Ctrl+5	$1\frac{1}{2}$ space lines of text
Ctrl+L	Left align text
Ctrl+R	Right align text
Ctrl+E	Center align text
Ctrl+J	Fully justify text
Ctrl+Q	Return paragraph to standard format
Ctrl+Enter	Insert a column or page break

Ten Questions for Your Service Bureau

1. Are you comfortable working with Windows files?

2. How do you want to receive my files?

3. What is your usual turnaround time?

4. What kind of imagesetter do you use?

5. What kind of equipment do you have in your shop?

6. Do you have the fonts in my publication?

7. Do you have the creator applications for the EPS graphics that I create?

8. How much do you charge?

9. Can you outsource the work that you can't do?

10. Can you give me some references?

References for the Rest of Us!®

COMPUTER BOOK SERIES FROM IDG

Are you intimidated and confused by computers? Do you find that traditional manuals are overloaded with technical details you'll never use? Do your friends and family always call you to fix simple problems on their PCs? Then the *...For Dummies*® computer book series from IDG Books Worldwide is for you.

...For Dummies books are written for those frustrated computer users who know they aren't really dumb but find that PC hardware, software, and indeed the unique vocabulary of computing make them feel helpless. *...For Dummies* books use a lighthearted approach, a down-to-earth style, and even cartoons and humorous icons to diffuse computer novices' fears and build their confidence. Lighthearted but not lightweight, these books are a perfect survival guide for anyone forced to use a computer.

> "I like my copy so much I told friends; now they bought copies."
>
> Irene C., Orwell, Ohio

> "Quick, concise, nontechnical, and humorous."
>
> Jay A., Elburn, Illinois

> "Thanks, I needed this book. Now I can sleep at night."
>
> Robin F., British Columbia, Canada

Already, hundreds of thousands of satisfied readers agree. They have made *...For Dummies* books the #1 introductory level computer book series and have written asking for more. So, if you're looking for the most fun and easy way to learn about computers, look to *...For Dummies* books to give you a helping hand.

7/96r

MICROSOFT®
PUBLISHER 97
FOR
DUMMIES®

MICROSOFT® PUBLISHER 97 FOR DUMMIES®

by Barrie Sosinsky, Christopher J. Benz, & Jim McCarter

IDG Books Worldwide, Inc.
An International Data Group Company

Foster City, CA ♦ Chicago, IL ♦ Indianapolis, IN ♦ Southlake, TX

Microsoft® Publisher 97 For Dummies®

Published by
IDG Books Worldwide, Inc.
An International Data Group Company
919 E. Hillsdale Blvd.
Suite 400
Foster City, CA 94404
www.idgbooks.com (IDG Books Worldwide Web site)
www.dummies.com (Dummies Press Web site)

Library of Congress Catalog Card No.: 97-72413

ISBN: 0-7645-0148-8

Printed in the United States of America

10 9 8 7 6 5 4 3 2

1E/TQ/QZ/ZX/IN

Distributed in the United States by IDG Books Worldwide, Inc.

Distributed by Macmillan Canada for Canada; by Transworld Publishers Limited in the United Kingdom; by IDG Norge Books for Norway; by IDG Sweden Books for Sweden; by Woodslane Pty. Ltd. for Australia; by Woodslane Enterprises Ltd. for New Zealand; by Longman Singapore Publishers Ltd. for Singapore, Malaysia, Thailand, and Indonesia; by Simron Pty. Ltd. for South Africa; by Toppan Company Ltd. for Japan; by Distribuidora Cuspide for Argentina; by Livraria Cultura for Brazil; by Ediciencia S.A. for Ecuador; by Addison-Wesley Publishing Company for Korea; by Ediciones ZETA S.C.R. Ltda. for Peru; by WS Computer Publishing Corporation, Inc., for the Philippines; by Unalis Corporation for Taiwan; by Contemporanea de Ediciones for Venezuela; by Computer Book & Magazine Store for Puerto Rico; by Express Computer Distributors for the Caribbean and West Indies. Authorized Sales Agent: Anthony Rudkin Associates for the Middle East and North Africa.

For general information on IDG Books Worldwide's books in the U.S., please call our Consumer Customer Service department at 800-762-2974. For reseller information, including discounts and premium sales, please call our Reseller Customer Service department at 800-434-3422.

For information on where to purchase IDG Books Worldwide's books outside the U.S., please contact our International Sales department at 415-655-3200 or fax 415-655-3295.

For information on foreign language translations, please contact our Foreign & Subsidiary Rights department at 415-655-3021 or fax 415-655-3281.

For sales inquiries and special prices for bulk quantities, please contact our Sales department at 415-655-3200 or write to the address above.

For information on using IDG Books Worldwide's books in the classroom or for ordering examination copies, please contact our Educational Sales department at 800-434-2086 or fax 817-251-8174.

For press review copies, author interviews, or other publicity information, please contact our Public Relations department at 415-655-3000 or fax 415-655-3299.

For authorization to photocopy items for corporate, personal, or educational use, please contact Copyright Clearance Center, 222 Rosewood Drive, Danvers, MA 01923, or fax 508-750-4470.

About the Authors

Barrie Sosinsky is the author or coauthor of 25 computer books on various aspects of personal computer technology. He is the author of *Macword Guide to Microsoft Works, dBASE 5 For DOS For Dummies Quick Reference,* and *Foundations of Microsoft BackOffice,* all published by IDG Books Worldwide, Inc. Among his interests are desktop publishing and print alternative. He was the Electronic Print columnist for *Techniques Magazine* in 1995-1996. His company, KillerApps, Inc., of Newton, Massachusetts, does database development and crossplatform workgroup software solutions for clients, as well as commercial vertical-market software. Barrie lives in Newton, Massachusetts with his wife, Carol Westheimer, and daughter, Alexandra.

Christopher J. Benz is the author or coauthor of eight retail-market computer books and a half-dozen computer courses. He has won two top awards for writing excellence from the Society for Technical Communication (STC), including Best of Show in STC's 1995 International Technical Publications Competition. In addition to his writing, Chris has trained hundreds of computer users on a variety of software applications and has desktop published dozens of publications. Chris currently works as a developmental editor and documentation project manager for a medical-software startup in Research Triangle Park, North Carolina, serves as public relations chair for the STC's Carolina Chapter, and brews his own beer. He lives in Carrborro, North Carlina (just outside Chapel Hill), with his wife, Kat (that's her real name!), his dog, Pippi, his cat, Nittin, and his invisible giant wombat, Igor.

Jim McCarter attended Webster University in Vienna, Austria, where he minored in foreign languages and graduated with a degree in computer studies. There he also launched his career as a computer consultant, which has now spanned 13 years and has included serving as technical reviewer for at least 30 books for IDG Books Worldwide, Inc. and other industry publishers. Jim is a partner in the business technology firm of 411 Technology, Inc., based in Indianapolis, IN.

ABOUT IDG BOOKS WORLDWIDE

Welcome to the world of IDG Books Worldwide.

IDG Books Worldwide, Inc., is a subsidiary of International Data Group, the world's largest publisher of computer-related information and the leading global provider of information services on information technology. IDG was founded more than 25 years ago and now employs more than 8,500 people worldwide. IDG publishes more than 275 computer publications in over 75 countries (see listing below). More than 60 million people read one or more IDG publications each month.

Launched in 1990, IDG Books Worldwide is today the #1 publisher of best-selling computer books in the United States. We are proud to have received eight awards from the Computer Press Association in recognition of editorial excellence and three from *Computer Currents'* First Annual Readers' Choice Awards. Our best-selling ...*For Dummies*® series has more than 30 million copies in print with translations in 30 languages. IDG Books Worldwide, through a joint venture with IDG's Hi-Tech Beijing, became the first U.S. publisher to publish a computer book in the People's Republic of China. In record time, IDG Books Worldwide has become the first choice for millions of readers around the world who want to learn how to better manage their businesses.

Our mission is simple: Every one of our books is designed to bring extra value and skill-building instructions to the reader. Our books are written by experts who understand and care about our readers. The knowledge base of our editorial staff comes from years of experience in publishing, education, and journalism — experience we use to produce books for the '90s. In short, we care about books, so we attract the best people. We devote special attention to details such as audience, interior design, use of icons, and illustrations. And because we use an efficient process of authoring, editing, and desktop publishing our books electronically, we can spend more time ensuring superior content and spend less time on the technicalities of making books.

You can count on our commitment to deliver high-quality books at competitive prices on topics you want to read about. At IDG Books Worldwide, we continue in the IDG tradition of delivering quality for more than 25 years. You'll find no better book on a subject than one from IDG Books Worldwide.

John J. Kilcullen
John Kilcullen
CEO
IDG Books Worldwide, Inc.

Steven Berkowitz
Steven Berkowitz
President and Publisher
IDG Books Worldwide, Inc.

VIII
WINNER
Eighth Annual
Computer Press
Awards ≥1992

IX
WINNER
Ninth Annual
Computer Press
Awards ≥1993

X
WINNER
Tenth Annual
Computer Press
Awards ≥1994

XI
WINNER
Eleventh Annual
Computer Press
Awards ≥1995

Authors' Acknowledgments

The authors wish to acknowledge the efforts of the many people who made this book possible. Kudos go first to our publisher, Dummies Press, and to Dan Gookin for creating a series of books that have captured the imagination of the entire computer world. These books have made many areas of technology palatable to a large number of readers, and many of the books in the series are the best books on that subject, bar none. To the many people at IDG Books Dummies Press, our publisher and editors, we say thanks. A particular thanks goes to Susan Christophersen for her work as the project editor on this book, and to Kevin McCarter, Jim's brother, for ensuring the book's technical accuracy.

Publisher's Acknowledgments

We're proud of this book; please send us your comments about it by using the IDG Books Worldwide Registration Card at the back of the book or by e-mailing us at feedback/dummies@idgbooks.com. Some of the people who helped bring this book to market include the following:

Acquisitions, Development, and Editorial

Project Editor: Susan Christophersen

Acquisitions Editor: Michael Kelly, Quality Control Manager

Technical Editor: Kevin McCarter

Editorial Manager: Mary C. Corder

Editorial Assistant: Chris Collins

Production

Project Coordinator: Cindy L. Phipps

Layout and Graphics: Linda M. Boyer, J. Tyler Connor, Dominique DeFelice, Pamela Emanoil, Angela F. Hunckler, Heather Pearson, Brent Savage, M. Anne Sipahimalani

Proofreaders: Laura L. Bowman, Robert Springer, Karen York

Indexer: Joan Griffits

General and Administrative

IDG Books Worldwide, Inc.: John Kilcullen, CEO; Steven Berkowitz, President and Publisher

IDG Books Technology Publishing: Brenda McLaughlin, Senior Vice President and Group Publisher

Dummies Technology Press and Dummies Editorial: Diane Graves Steele, Vice President and Associate Publisher; Judith A. Taylor, Product Marketing Manager; Kristin A. Cocks, Editorial Director

Dummies Trade Press: Kathleen A. Welton, Vice President and Publisher; Stacy S. Collins, Product Marketing Manager

IDG Books Production for Dummies Press: Beth Jenkins, Production Director; Cindy L. Phipps, Supervisor of Project Coordination, Production Proofreading, and Indexing; Kathie S. Schutte, Supervisor of Page Layout; Shelley Lea, Supervisor of Graphics and Design; Debbie J. Gates, Production Systems Specialist; Tony Augsburger, Supervisor of Reprints and Bluelines; Leslie Popplewell, Media Archive Coordinator

Dummies Packaging and Book Design: Patti Sandez, Packaging Specialist; Lance Kayser, Packaging Assistant; Kavish + Kavish, Cover Design

◆

The publisher would like to give special thanks to Patrick J. McGovern, without whom this book would not have been possible.

◆

Contents at a Glance

Cartoons at a Glance

By Rich Tennant • Fax: 508-546-7747 • E-mail: the5wave@tiac.net

page 127

page 7

page 217

page 319

page 63

page 259

page 297

Table of Contents

● ●

Introduction

. . . .

Welcome to *Microsoft Publisher 97 For Dummies*. If you have never done desktop publishing and aren't really interested in becoming an expert at it, congratulations! This book that you hold in your hand is the right choice; it will help you get your current project done quickly — and with the least effort possible. That's our fervent intent.

In our busy, work-a-day life, who really has the time to master every intricacy of a rich computer software program? If using a software program is central to your work, then maybe you need this mastery. But most of us use computers as tools, and we simply don't need the level of detail (or useless trivia) presented by many computer books. If you want to know a simple answer to a single question about your Microsoft Publisher project, then this book is for you.

Microsoft Publisher 97, designed for Windows 95, is a low-priced desktop publishing program. You use this program to create printed materials. Even though Microsoft Publisher 97 is low priced, it is definitely not underpowered. You can do things with Microsoft Publisher 97 that two years ago would have made the big boys (you know, those expensive desktop publishing programs) sit up and whistle "Dixie." For example, you can create publications automatically through the PageWizards in Microsoft Publisher (something that you can't do with your Quarks and PageMonsters). We want to carry on with the . . .*For Dummies* tradition and help you have fun with Microsoft Publisher 97 as you use this book. Tastes great, less filling!

About This Book

You can read this book from cover to cover, but you don't have to; you can use it like a reference book. When you need to know something about something, just jump to the appropriate section and read about it. Most chapters are self contained. Typical sections that you may find include:

- ✔ You Want Fast? Well, Meet Mr. Wizard
- ✔ Things You Can Do with Files
- ✔ Keeping Good Margins
- ✔ Hide and Seek: Find and Replace
- ✔ Collecting and Using Type

   ✔ How Color Improves Your Page
   ✔ Printers and Output Quality

What you need to know is here in this book. Don't bother memorizing the contents, and don't even think about using this book to *learn* Microsoft Publisher 97. What you find in this book is only the information that you need to get your work done. Because we tend to babble on, from time to time we post a Technical Stuff icon (which features the *Dummies guy*) to forewarn you in case you want to ignore our rantings.

How to Use This Book

Because this book is a reference, you can look up a topic of interest in the table of contents or in the index at the back of the book. These tools refer you to the sections that talk about that topic. If you need to know something specific in order to understand a section's content, we tell you so. We know that computer technology is loaded with confusing words and phrases and technobabble. (Sometimes we can't avoid slinging this stuff about like a short-order cook in a cheap diner.) But in some cases, we may send you off elsewhere to help you figure out the confusing terms.

We like to give you examples of how to do something. Because Microsoft Publisher 97 is a Windows 95 program, most instructions tell you to *click here* or *click there,* to *choose File⇨Print* from the menu, or to *press Alt+F,P* on the keyboard. Notice two things about these instructions: First, we underline the *hot keys* that you can use to select menu commands from the keyboard; and second, we show that you actually press the *Alt* key at the same time that you press the *F* key by placing the + sign between them. Then you release both keys and press the *P* key. This keyboard combination produces the same action as using your mouse to choose the menu command. It's all standard Microsoft Windows fare.

If we want you to enter information from your keyboard, you may see a line that looks like the following (this comes up just a few times):

```
C:\>ENTER THIS STUFF
```

In the preceding example, you type the words **ENTER THIS STUFF** after the C:\> prompt and then press the Enter key. Notice that we don't use quotation marks around the text (that is, "ENTER THIS STUFF"), because we don't want you to enter quotation marks. We go on to explain why you do what we've told you to do and what happens after you do, so don't worry.

You've Been Warned

Desktop publishing is a complicated endeavor, with many things that you "may" want to know about. We include a few sections in the book on more advanced topics such as selecting paper, working with outside service bureaus, choosing color processes, and so on. Of course, if all you want to do is run the Airplane or Origami PageWizard and print the results from your ink jet printer, then you may not need to look at these topics. We try to warn you when a section tends toward the technical or is limited to specific interests. But you can read these sections, and doing so will earn you a gold star in the Desktop Publishing Hall of Fame (but that's not what this book is meant to do).

Our Foolish Assumptions

We make only three assumptions about you in this book. The first, we've already stated: You don't want to waste time studying useless trivia. You are in a hurry and you want to get your work done.

Our second assumption is that you have an IBM personal computer or compatible computer (that is, a clone) that has Microsoft Windows 95 installed. Maybe you have set up your computer, or maybe someone else has. But it's working, and you can get the help you need to keep it working.

Our third assumption is that you know your way around Windows 95 well enough to perform simple operations in that environment. You should know how to sling your mouse around and how to bang your keyboard. You should know how to select a menu command, know how to work with dialog boxes and windows, and be familiar with common Desktop items such as the Recycle Bin. We cover some of these topics (when the discussion is directly applicable to Microsoft Publisher 97), but not in detail.

By the way, if finding your way around your new computer or Windows 95 is still a mystery of life for you, we want to direct you to the following books:

- *PCs For Dummies,* 3rd Edition, by Dan Gookin and Andy Rathbone
- *Windows 95 For Dummies,* 2nd Edition, by Andy Rathbone
- *Real Life Windows 95,* by Dan Gookin

All are from IDG Books Worldwide, Inc.

How This Book Is Organized

Topics in this book are generally arranged as if we were directing you through a desktop publishing project from start to finish. In the progression of topics, we try to address those issues that you commonly tackle first, first; and the issues that you tackle last, last. Clever, eh? The book has seven major parts; each part has two or more chapters. (Our teachers taught us that each divided topic should have at least two subdivisions, and we slavishly follow their teachings.)

Aside from these considerations, you find that most chapters stand by themselves. You can start reading at any section. Great teachers also tell us, "Tell them (the audience) what you are going to tell them." So, we've outlined the entire book as follows.

Part I: Hey! Ya Say Ya Want a Revolution?

When you create a project in Microsoft Publisher 97 to print something, you are doing desktop publishing (DTP). Desktop publishing replaces technology of past centuries and decades with something new and special. For many folks, desktop publishing is a "killer app"; that is, a software program that you buy a computer to run. Part I tells you what desktop publishing is, how it came about, and where it's going. Also in Part I, we give you the skinny on design issues and provide the nickel tour on basic basics that you need to know to run and use the program.

Part II: Some Glue, Some Scissors, a Board, et Voilà

Microsoft Publisher 97, like most desktop publishing programs, uses the metaphor of a pasteboard. In this part, you work on how to create a page, define the layout, and then add things to your page. You add objects to Microsoft Publisher 97 pages inside frames, which we tell you how to work with in this part. "You framed me, you dirty rat! And you're gonna get it. . . ."

Part III: 10,000 Words, One Maniac

An important part of desktop publishing is marrying text and figures on a page. In this part, you discover how to work with text on your page; not just how to enter text into a text frame, mind you, but also how to select and work with type.

Part IV: Picture That

A picture is worth a thousand words. Microsoft Publisher 97 lets you enhance your page with all kinds of pictures: drawings, images, and other forms of art. In this part, we tell you what you need to know to create and work with different kinds of pictures — and where to get help if you need it. We also use a chapter to talk about the related topic of using color in your publication.

Part V: Just So Output

This part contains a cornucopia of important fruits of knowledge for you to nibble on. You see how to fine-tune your page: edit copy, hyphenate, add flourishes, and assemble your project. You also find a chapter in this part with a discussion on paper, printing, and working with a service bureau.

Part VI: Publishing on the Internet

Publishing on the Internet is the latest rage. In this part, you learn how to create and edit a Web page, including adding graphics and hyperlinks, and adding color and texture to the background. You also find tips on previewing your Web site. Finally, we tell you how to publish your Web site.

Part VII: The Part of Tens

Other people have their lists and we have our lists. In this part, our Part of Tens, you get lists of ten things on topics that you should know about. We give you lists on design issues, text and type, colors, printing, service bureaus, and other things. Have fun reading this part, and when you're done, we will part.

Icons Used in This Book

We don't use a lot of icons, but we do use a few. Here are our little nuggets of wisdom for you to savor:

Nerdy technical discussions that you can skip if you want to.

Shortcuts and insights that can save you time, money, and trouble.

Our friendly Design icon points out principles that you want to espouse.

 A friendly reminder to do something.

 Points out some of the little *gotchas* that life (or Microsoft Publisher 97) has to offer. (Hint: Don't do this!)

Where to Go from Here

You're ready to use this book. Start by reviewing the table of contents to find a topic of current interest to you. Then, dive right in and read about it. Try some of our suggestions in your work and experiment. Microsoft Publisher 97 is a very friendly and forgiving program. (If you save copies of your publication as you go, little can go wrong that you can't fix.)

When you find something that doesn't work quite right or something that you want to know more about, return to this book. Repeat the process. Finding out about Microsoft Publisher 97 and Windows 95 can and should be an exploration. Microsoft meant for these two programs to be a "discover-able environment" — that is, to be like a well-designed computer game that you can figure out as you play. We're here to get you past any bumps or tilts that you might encounter.

Desktop publishing is fun. That's why so many people do it. And Microsoft Publisher 97 makes it easier to do than any other program we know.

Part I
Hey! Ya Say Ya Want a Revolution?

The 5th Wave   By Rich Tennant

"FOR ADDITIONAL SOFTWARE SUPPORT, DIAL "9", "POUND," THE EXTENSION NUMBER DIVIDED BY YOUR ACCOUNT NUMBER, HIT "STAR", YOUR DOG, BLOW INTO THE RECEIVER TWICE, PUNCH IN YOUR HAT SIZE, PUNCH OUT YOUR LANDLORD,..."

In this part . . .

Everyone wants to produce things that people will read. The quality of your printed work directly influences your income, your job advancement, who shows up at your parties, and more. Good-looking résumés get people interviews; good-looking books get bought; good-looking birthday cards get sent more often; good-looking ads pull orders; and good-looking people get more dates. (No, Microsoft Publisher 97 won't make you more attractive.) It's fair to say that the way our designs look affects what people think of us as a person.

Some of us are born designers; most of us are not. Microsoft Publisher 97 lets you create professional-quality output easily, even if you do not have an artistic bent. You do need to know something about what separates good design from poor design, and enough about the technology to create publications or page layout documents in Microsoft Publisher 97. That is what Part I is all about. The chapters in this part provide an overview of desktop publishing, tell you what constitutes good design principles, and give you some basic information that you need to know to get started working in Microsoft Publisher 97.

Chapter 1

Own the Printing Press

● ●

In This Chapter

▶ When to use Microsoft Publisher 97

▶ What is desktop publishing?

▶ The design process

▶ Using PageWizards

● ●

*D*esktop publishing uses page layout software and a personal computer to combine text, type, drawings, and images on a page to create books, newsletters, brochures, flyers, greeting cards, and so on. Anything that you can print on a page can be put into a page layout program. Microsoft Publisher 97 lets you place elements on a page, precisely position them, modify them, and specify a print job using techniques that commercial printers require. Whether you print to your ink jet or laser printer, run down the street to the Quick Copy Shop, or send your files to a commercial printer, Microsoft Publisher 97 helps you prepare your work for that level of quality.

When Should I Use Microsoft Publisher 97?

Many programs let you design and print pages to various levels of sophistication. These programs include word processors such as Microsoft Word, WordPerfect, and Ami Pro; graphics programs such as CorelDRAW! and Windows Draw; and even low-end integrated packages such as Microsoft Works for Windows 95 or ClarisWorks. The program that we write in, Microsoft Word for Windows, enables us to type text, format the text, import pictures, create drawings, and even work with images.

If you can do all of that in Word, why do you need a desktop publishing or page layout program like Microsoft Publisher 97? The short answer is control. Microsoft Publisher 97 lets you control these elements with finer precision and offers you many special tools besides.

How Microsoft Publisher 97 measures up

Plenty of desktop-publishing programs are out there, all claiming to be the best, most popular, friendliest, newest, or least likely to cause your computer to burst into flames. If you cut through all the marketing hype, though, these programs fall into just two categories:

- Programs that are inexpensive and easy to learn

- Programs that are expensive and difficult to learn

Programs such as PageMaker, QuarkXPress, FrameMaker, and Ventura Publisher are expensive — about five times the cost of Microsoft Publisher 97 — and difficult to learn. These programs are designed for hard-core desktop publishers (usually in a commercial trade) for whom absolute precision is everything. These people are picky — *extremely* picky. Do you care whether you can nudge a graphic 1/1000th of an inch? Do you think that you'll need to change the size of an individual character by less than the width of a human hair?

Be prepared for weeks or months of dedicated study before you can master their intricacies. If you can use one of these programs to put together a decent publication within your first week of intensive learning, you'll be doing quite well.

Microsoft Publisher 97 is about as powerful as these more capable programs were two years ago. That's a long time in the computer industry, but except for professional features, this category of software hasn't changed all that much. Microsoft Publisher 97 gives you 80 percent of the capability of the more powerful programs by incorporating 20 percent of their features. That translates into projects that you can accomplish in Microsoft Publisher 97 two or three times faster than in other programs. The bottom line is this: If you're not sure what Microsoft Publisher 97 is missing that you need, it probably will be *plenty* good enough.

So, if you just want to stick your company's logo at the top of your letter and insert a copy of your scanned-in signature at the bottom, you don't need Microsoft Publisher 97 to do that. If you want to create a company logo by combining a couple of graphics from different sources, some text, and some color, and then separate the output to give to a commercial printer to print, Microsoft Publisher 97 is a better choice. If you want to create a four-page newsletter, mix three and four columns of text on each page, and have the text wrap around some graphics, Microsoft Publisher 97 is definitely the way to go. It does these things well.

How Desktop Publishing Works

Page layout software takes various parts and combines them into a single document, called a *publication*. The following list briefly covers the parts that you can meld together. Refer to Figure 1-1, in which we labeled sample elements. Nearly all objects on a page are in frames or blocks that are created when you import or create the object.

Figure 1-1:
A sample
publication
with labeled
objects.

✔ **Text:** Okay, we know that you know what text is. Text is the stuff that you type: all those individual characters that form words, sentences, paragraphs, and so on.

✔ **Type:** Man/Woman does not live by text alone. Type or typography are the various letter forms that you can use to make your text attractive. Microsoft Publisher 97 lets you access WordArt, a special type of manipulation program.

✔ **Pictures:** Computers make two kinds of pictures: drawn (vector, or object-oriented) and painted (raster, or bitmapped) images. You can import both types into a picture frame.

Microsoft Publisher 97 ships with a Picture Gallery of clip art, borders, and other images that you can use in your picture frames. The gallery is much larger on the CD-ROM version of the product than on the floppy disk version — a good reason to buy the CD-ROM. If you have the floppy disk version, you can download the missing images from the Microsoft Publisher 97 Web site at http://www.microsoft.com/publisher.

✔ **Drawn objects:** Microsoft Publisher 97 is not a drawing program, but some tools in its Toolbox enable you to create drawn images such as lines, ovals and circles, rectangles and squares, and a whole bunch of custom shapes.

✔ **Tables:** Although you can import tables from other programs as objects, either as drawings or as OLE (Object Linking and Embedding) objects managed by other applications, Microsoft Publisher 97 has its own Table tool.

You can create these elements by using Microsoft Publisher 97, or you can use other programs to create the objects and then use Microsoft Publisher 97 to place them in your publication.

The Design Process

Page design is a process. You can always find a better way to make a point with design, to use type and color, to refine a graphic, and so on. You can always return to a publication later and find something that you could have done better. Like all creative endeavors, a well-designed publication can be improved by planning before the fact, experimenting, and offering thoughtful criticism at all stages. The sections that follow describe some of the methods that designers use to make their pages stand out from the crowd.

Storyboarding

To get a good start on the process, you can block out the way that you want your publication to look. One block-out method is called *storyboarding*. Storyboards are like block diagrams. Cartoonists use storyboards to show a story's progression. Movie designers use storyboards to illustrate key frames in a movie, which enables them to present the movie in a preproduction form that others can view and understand. You can use this same technique.

Many people like to mock up their design projects with pencil and paper. They create a dummy of their publication, and when the publication spans several pages, they create storyboards. But this is all a matter of preference: the important thing is to plan your publication before you create it.

We find Microsoft Publisher 97 so easy to work with that we prefer to create our dummies inside the program. The tools for creating frames, lines, and boxes make these page elements easy to create and modify inside Microsoft Publisher 97. We also find that working inside the program forces us to think, right from the start, about how we'll break apart a sample design and implement it.

Shout OLE and watch the bull fly!

Microsoft Publisher 97 is a heavy user of Object Linking and Embedding, or OLE (pronounced *o-lay*). This means that you can insert, or embed, data created in another application inside your publication and maintain a live link between the two. For example, you can insert an object created in a drawing program in your publication. You also can choose to link the publication to the object's source by placing a reference to that file in Microsoft Publisher 97. This way, when the original object changes, you simply update the reference to have the changes reflected in your publication.

The advantage of embedding is that you have your object contained within your publication; the disadvantage is that your file size grows. The advantage of linking is that your publication's file size stays smaller; the disadvantage is that file management is required (Microsoft Publisher 97 needs to know where to find the source documents).

One hand giveth, the other hand taketh away.

Microsoft Publisher 97 has a collection of wizards called PageWizards that build dummy publications for you based on the answers that you give in a series of dialog boxes. You see the PageWizards in the Startup dialog box as the collection of sample documents that you can create. In effect, storyboarding is what the PageWizards do when they create a template for you. When you create a document by using the PageWizards, the result is a dummy of the document that you are creating. Figure 1-2 shows a four-panel brochure created with the Brochure PageWizard. The Wizard generates a sample document with a headline, graphics blocks, and empty text frames. Each element on the page can be modified, but the document's overall look is obvious from the result of the PageWizard. Your dummies or mock-ups should show similar use of text, graphics, and overall design.

Here's a trick that works well for many people. Try moving away from your design and looking at it from afar. Is its purpose obvious, or is clutter obscuring the purpose? If you have too many page elements, try eliminating some.

Assembling a page

After you have blocked out a page design, you can replace the dummy text, pictures, and other frames with the data that you want to include on the page. This is the assembly part of page composition. Depending on the type of object frame or tool selected, you can apply one of the Edit or Insert menu commands to bring the data into Microsoft Publisher 97. The basics of importing text are covered in Chapter 6. You find the related topic of importing tabular data in Chapter 6 as well. For details on bringing graphics into your publication, see Chapter 9.

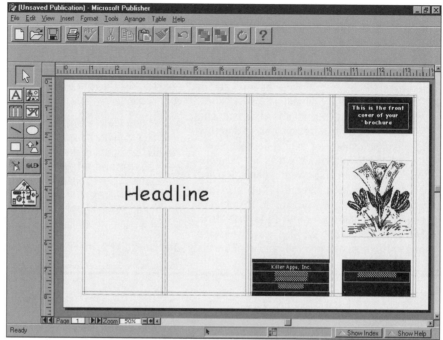

Figure 1-2:
A template
showing an
overall
design in
Microsoft
Publisher 97.

Chances are great that after you have all the frames composed and filled with real data, the page will require more tweaking. Microsoft Publisher 97 contains a number of specialized tools for repositioning, resizing, and fitting objects on a page. Chapter 11 details the final steps in the assembly process. You can also find information about preparing a publication for output to an outside printer in Chapter 12.

Don't be surprised if the assembly process is largely comprised of the tweaking phase of the project. Leave enough time to get this tweaking done the way you want it. (Think of the programmer who says that the program is 90 percent done when only 50 percent of the allotted time is spent.)

Outputting a page

After you have your page composed the way you want it, you are ready to print. You can choose to print files to local printers and select from any of the print drivers that came with Windows 95. Printing to a local printer is no different in Microsoft Publisher 97 than it is in any other Windows application; you simply choose File⇨Print. See Chapter 12 for detailed information about printing files.

Microsoft Publisher 97 also allows you to set up a print job for an outside printer. The process is only slightly different than printing to a local printer. When you specify that your publication is meant to print to an imagesetter or color printer, Microsoft Publisher 97 makes some selections for you that help your local print shop print your files correctly. Or you can use a disk file with your print shop's printer driver to compose your print job. Microsoft Publisher 97 also lets you print an InfoSheet, which you can give to your print shop to tell it what's in the publication. See Chapter 12 for details on having close encounters with printers of the third kind (human ones, that is).

How it was done in the old days

When we were young (okay, younger — it doesn't seem that long ago to us), designers composed pages by printing the elements of a page, cutting and pasting them on a large board called, appropriately enough, a pasteboard, and photographing the result. If the page layout involved full color, the designers took three or four photographs with colored filters to create the colored printing plates needed to combine colored inks into full-color prints. That was how it was done in the *old days*, as late as the early 1980s. We both have vivid memories of the difficulty and the time consumed by getting all elements to line up and work together properly.

Today, with Microsoft Publisher 97, you have it easy. Microsoft Publisher 97 takes the text that you type or import and lets you format it with type and spacing. You can place line art, scanned images, or any object that you can create in the computer on the page and make adjustments to have it all fit just so. You can change letter sizes and interletter spacing, word spacing, line spacing, and hyphenation to copyfit your text onto a page. Similarly, you can easily make text flow around graphics just the way you want it. You can resize your graphics as needed. You can do all this without resorting to sloppy cutting and pasting or trips back to a typographic print machine. That's

why this software is called page layout or page composition software. Heaven.

When you're done, Microsoft Publisher 97 replaces taking filtered photographs of your color pages with internal filters. The program includes an algorithm to *color separate* your pages. The effect is like looking at the world through a red, green, and blue plate of glass. What you see in each case is different. If you combined the three views, however, you see your color restored.

Print processes use three different colors to create colored pages. Each component of a color page (typically, for a printer, these components are Cyan, Magenta, Yellow, and Black — or CYMK) comes out as a printed page. Now the color plates are still made by preparing film from printed output, but it is typically done on a high-resolution printer called an *imagesetter*.

You can output a publication in several ways. You can print in black and white, *grayscale* (shades of gray), *spot color* (a single color appearing on the page in one or more places), and full color. A single publication can use any or all of these output options.

You can find related information on printing files in Chapter 12 and an explanation of how to work with color in Chapter 10.

You Want Fast? Well, Meet Mr. Wizard

Using a PageWizard is the easiest way to create a publication in Microsoft Publisher 97. A PageWizard is a set of dialog boxes that leads you through the creation of a project based on selections that you make. Starting and using PageWizard is pretty easy. Microsoft Publisher 97 always opens the Task Launcher to the PageWizard tab when you start the program. By the way, you can start Microsoft Publisher 97 in the following ways:

- ✔ Double-click the icon for the program on the Windows 95 Desktop.
- ✔ Choose the Start⇨Programs⇨Microsoft Publisher command, as shown in Figure 1-3. (Easy!)

Figure 1-3:
Opening
Microsoft
Publisher 97
from the
Start Menu.

If your computer is handy, you may want to try out the Airplane PageWizard described in the following section.

If you already have Microsoft Publisher 97 open on-screen, you can choose File⇨Create New Publication or press Ctrl+N to see the PageWizard tab, as shown in Figure 1-4. All the publication icons that you see on that tab open a PageWizard specific for that type of publication.

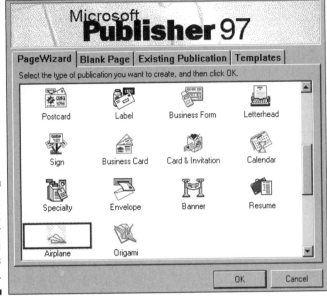

Figure 1-4:
The Task
Launcher
with
PageWizards
galore.

The Task Launcher is a modal dialog box, which means that you need to make a selection in it or dismiss it before you can go on. The cloudy section at the top of the dialog box is the title bar, and you can click and drag it about as you would any window's title bar.

Our favorite, the Airplane PageWizard

Microsoft Publisher 97 has some really neat PageWizards; you can see their document types in Figure 1-4. But for now, we want to show you a favorite of ours: the Airplane PageWizard. The first thing that Jim did after he got Microsoft Publisher 97 was to fire up this wizard and hand his two-year-old daughter, Rebecca, a great paper airplane.

The Airplane PageWizard is dedicated to the prospect that, if you put thousands and thousands of really bright people together in a place where the sun never shines and force feed them Jolt cola and high-octane candy, they produce genius for no apparent purpose. You rev up the Airplane PageWizard by

✔ Double-clicking the Airplane icon with the mouse pointer

✔ Highlighting the icon and clicking the OK button

✔ Using the arrow keys to move about, and pressing the Enter key

The preceding are all standard Windows 95 dialog box selection techniques that work universally throughout Microsoft Publisher 97. You can also start some PageWizards directly by clicking the PageWizards tool in the toolbox.

Generally, a PageWizard starts out with an introductory screen and runs you through several selections. Figure 1-5 shows the introductory screen. You can move to the next step in the PageWizard by clicking the Next button, or return to change a former selection by using the previous or first button. The Cancel button releases the PageWizard without creating a document; the Create It! button actually creates the document on-screen. Figure 1-6 shows you the resulting airplane inside a Microsoft Publisher 97 window.

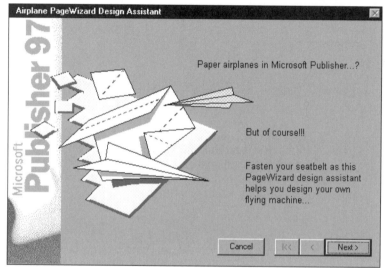

Figure 1-5: Steps in the Airplane PageWizard.

Facts about PageWizards

You need to know a couple important points about the PageWizards. First, although they appear to be dialog boxes, they are actually small programs that run on their own. PageWizards create new on-screen publications inside Microsoft Publisher 97.

Want to prove to yourself that the PageWizards are small programs? Try pressing the Alt+Tab key combination — the Windows 95 Cool Switch that switches between programs on-screen. The PageWizard is one of the program icons that you see in the Cool Switch, as shown in Figure 1-7. If you are in a program other than Microsoft Publisher 97 when you switch to the PageWizard, it appears by itself and without Microsoft Publisher 97.

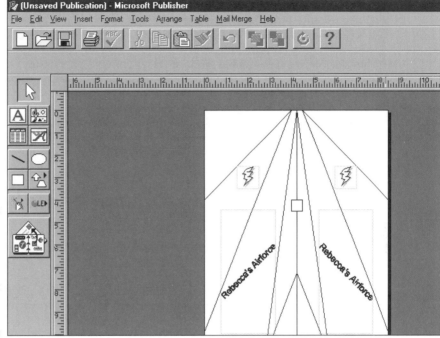

Figure 1-6:
The
resulting
airplane in
a Microsoft
Publisher 97
window.

Figure 1-7:
The
Windows 95
Cool
Switch.

Here's another fact for you to ponder. In Figure 1-6 (where you see the paper airplane), the screen looks like the Print Preview window in other programs (such as word processors). Because Microsoft Publisher 97 is designed to help you create printed output, it has only a single viewing mode for your publications, and it shows you what your printed document looks like. You never switch out of this view, although you can zoom in or out for a different perspective by using commands on the View menu or the Zoom control at the bottom-left corner of the window, next to the horizontal scroll bar.

The airplane created with the PageWizard is actually composed of a bunch of objects that are grouped so that they behave as a single object. If you click any part of the airplane, you select the entire airplane (refer to Figure 1-6). Resize or reshape handles (little squares on the edges) appear around the airplane, and an icon depicting two locked pieces of a jigsaw puzzle (called the Group Object icon) appears below the page. After you click the Group Object icon to ungroup the airplane, all component parts appear. Now you have fine control over the size, placement, color, and other properties of your airplane's component parts. If you use a PageWizard to create something in Microsoft Publisher 97, however, you have only scratched the surface of what you can do with the program. We are happy to present what's under the surface as you read through the book.

A page-layout program is really a specialized kind of draw program. If you are familiar with that kind of program, you find that many Microsoft Publisher 97 operations also are familiar to you.

Okay, now meet Mr. Wizard's family

Each PageWizard can generate several kinds of publications of the same class, depending on the selections you make. Microsoft Publisher 97 has 18 PageWizards:

- ✔ **Newsletter:** Some of these newsletters coordinate with paper from PaperDirect, a desktop publishing supply house. Phone: 800-A-PAPERS; Fax: 800-44-FAXPD.

- ✔ **Flyer:** Includes styles for handouts or flyers for Business, Personal, School, and Other needs.

- ✔ **Brochure:** Five different styles of brochures are offered: Classic, Modern, Flashy, Four–panel, and Two–panel. You can create self-mailers by using this wizard. Figure 1-8 shows you these styles.

- ✔ **Business Forms:** This wizard offers you the most choices: Customer refund, Expense report, Fax sheet, Invoice, Purchase order, Statement, Quote, Time billing, Employee time sheet, and some miscellaneous Other forms. As you click each radio button, a picture of the default form appears. Figure 1-9 shows you the Invoice form.

- ✔ **Letterhead:** The Letterhead PageWizard offers you six styles of letterhead (some are shown in Figure 1-10 near the end of this chapter). After you create a letterhead for your business or personal use, Microsoft Publisher 97 remembers the style that you used and asks whether you want to base your next letterhead on that style. Some of these styles match paper from PaperDirect.

- ✔ **Sign:** The Sign PageWizard creates single-page signs for Personal, Business, Public Information, and Other uses.

- ✔ **Business Card:** The Business Card PageWizard is similar to the Letterhead PageWizard in that it can create nine matching styles of cards. Microsoft Publisher 97 remembers the style that you used and asks whether you want to base your next business card on that style. Some of these styles match paper from PaperDirect.

✔ **Greeting Card:** This wizard is one of our favorites. It offers five categories of cards. Each of these categories offers you many choices. Some styles coordinate with paper from PaperDirect. Figure 1-11 shows you an example of different cards that you can create.

✔ **Calendar:** You can create a single specific month or year in any of five different styles by using this wizard.

✔ **Specialty:** The Specialty PageWizard enables you to create any one of nine items that don't easily fit into other categories: Menu, Catalog, Gift Tags, Poster, Address Postcard, 3-Fold Catalog, Certificate, Event Ticket, and Recipe Card. Figure 1-12 shows you the selection list for some of these styles.

✔ **Label:** You can create labels in any of the following styles: Audio Cassette Case; Audio Cassette; CD Jewel Case; $3^1/2$-inch Computer Disk; Jar, Bottle, or Box …; Return Address; Video Cassette - Face; and Video Cassette - Spine. Except when you select the Address Bulk Mailing option, this wizard often does not offer layout choices that match standards such as Avery labels; you need to go in and adjust the label sizes to suit your needs.

✔ **Envelope:** The Envelope PageWizard creates six styles of envelopes that match the Letterhead and Business Card PageWizards styles. Microsoft Publisher 97 remembers the style that you used and asks whether you want to base your next envelope on that style. The styles offered include Classic, Modern, Traditional, Jazzy, Fun, and Woodcut.

✔ **Banner:** The Banner PageWizard offers five styles of banners: Classic, Formal, Modern, Splashy, and Wild. You can set a height and width, or let the text that you type in your banner determine your banner's width.

✔ **Résumé:** This wizard creates three types of résumés: Chronological (experience and accomplishments by date), Entry-level (emphasizes skills and not job experience), and Curriculum Vitae (lists education, accreditation, and research). Each résumé type offers the styles Basic, Bold, Gray Flannel, and Linear.

✔ **Airplane:** This wizard creates four airplane types: Classic, Wing-tip Wonder, Stubby, and Wirligig.

✔ **Origami:** This wizard creates the Japanese style of paper figures. The four types range from easy-to-create (the Cup and the Boat) to hard (the Parrot and the Crane). Still, they're fun to give, and pretty when printed on a color printer or with colored paper. Figure 1-13 shows you these four figures (we're suckers for the exotic).

✔ **Postcard:** This wizard creates three categories of postcards: Business, Community, and Personal. Each category offers several types of postcards.

✔ **Web Site:** This wizard creates three categories of Web Sites: Business, Community, and Personal. Each category offers several types of Web Sites.

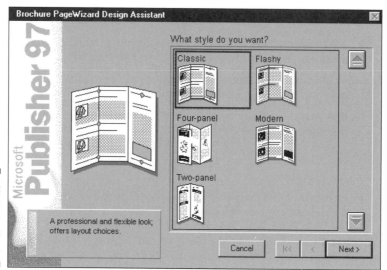

Figure 1-8:
The
Brochure
PageWizard's
styles.

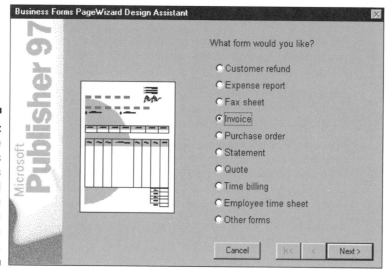

Figure 1-9:
The
Business
Forms
PageWizard
with the
Invoice
form
selected.

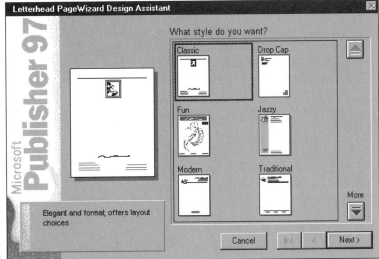

Figure 1-10:
The
Letterhead
PageWizard's
styles.

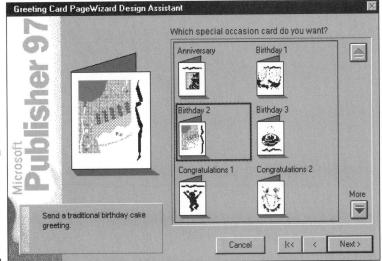

Figure 1-11:
A birthday
card in the
Greeting
Card
PageWizard.

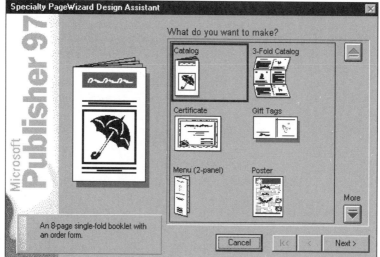

Figure 1-12:
The Specialty PageWizard's styles.

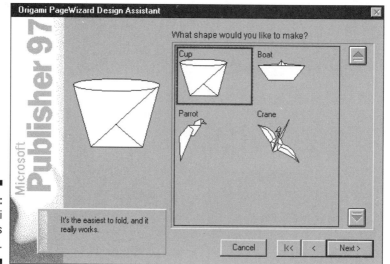

Figure 1-13:
The Origami PageWizard's choices.

You aren't limited to accepting whatever the PageWizards give you. You can replace one font with another, one picture with another, one border with another, and so on. Knowing Microsoft Publisher 97 well helps you quickly modify these wizards' output and makes the result something that you are proud to show to others.

Chapter 2
Designer Genes

- -

- -

*W*e live in a fast age. Before, you had time to read the occasional ad or brochure that appeared in your mailbox; now, you may receive ten or twenty mailings. We are bombarded with so much stuff that we tend to ignore almost everything.

So, here's the deal. Your publication has five seconds to get someone's attention. (Some design gurus claim that most pieces get about two seconds of review before being tossed.) If your published piece doesn't have something that interests your audience and makes them want to explore it further, *poof!* it's gone.

If you have only five seconds, you better make sure that your primary message is the first thing a reader sees. You have little room for error on this score. Consider any design device that you can use to repeat — and build on — the primary message.

This chapter shows you the design basics necessary to do your work in Microsoft Publisher 97 quickly and well.

Know Your Audience

The first step to creating a successful project is figuring out who your audience is and how they will interact with your work. Knowing your audience helps you refine your publication's look and feel. In addition, it helps you determine your writing style, which is essential for good communication.

You can learn a lot about successful design by studying the work of marketing gurus, particularly those who do advertising. Advertising combines a creative art form with statistically measured results based on large populations of target markets. One of our favorite books on this topic is *Successful Direct Response Marketing* by Robert Stone (published by Crain Books).

While you're designing your publication, show it to others so that you can figure out who your audience is and what they need.

When you know your audience, you can create a publication that has the correct "voice" or "tone" for that group. For example, a typeface that looks like lettering on a ransom note is inappropriate for business correspondence but might be perfect for birthday party invitations. Microsoft Publisher 97 classifies document styles according to the expected audience; the *gray flannel* style, for example, should appeal to a business audience.

Knowing your audience can help you decide which typeface to use on a page. Some vendors sell type in packages designed for specific uses. Their catalogs (which are works of art in themselves) describe the best use for many typefaces and also suggest typefaces that work well together.

The typeface that you use can flavor your publication for a particular audience.

Where Others Have Gone Before

When we first start the design phase of a publishing project, we try to collect the best examples of work in that area. We look at the overall design of a piece and look for style elements that we can use as a springboard to creating our own style. Keep file folders of ads that you like, marketing pieces that you get in the mail, and other publications. Then, when you're ready to create a piece, you can sit down and peruse your samples. Invariably, you'll find an idea or two to get you started.

Make sure that you do not copy too much from anyone's design when making your own work.

Any artwork, images, templates, or designs that you find in Microsoft Publisher 97 and its Design Gallery are there for your use. The Readme file states: "You are free to use Publisher clip art for any publication you print. You may not, however, sell or distribute Publisher clip art electronically as software, such as in a clip art library." Restrictions such as these are common for clip art. You should always check the license of any artwork that you use before incorporating it into commercial products.

When you use other people's work, you can adapt the designs that you collect, borrowing an idea here and an idea there. You cannot and should not copy an entire design or image from someone else, however. That's illegal. Most designs are copyrighted by the authors.

Sometimes a fine line exists between adapting an idea and copying one. You need to use good judgment. Note that the law in this area is volatile and subject to change. We recommend *The Desktop Publisher's Legal Handbook* by David Sitarz (published by Nova Press) as a good place to start learning about these issues.

Another resource to use when beginning the design phase is a study of before and after makeovers. You can find case studies in the design makeover columns in desktop publishing magazines and in some specialized books on desktop publishing. The following resources take this approach:

- *Desktop Publishing & Design For Dummies,* by Roger C. Parker (published by IDG Books Worldwide, Inc.).

- *BEFORE & After: How to design cool stuff*, 1830 Sierra Gardens Drive, Roseville, CA 95661; Phone: 916-784-3880 and Fax: 916-784-3995.

The Keys to Design Success

Most design gurus agree that you can apply certain principles to your designs to make them easier to understand and more attractive to the reader. The exact terminology for these principles may vary, but the set of principles is nearly always the same.

A list of these principles follows. When you begin to design a publication, you may not always analyze your work in terms of these principles, but you should at least keep them in mind:

- **Be consistent.** Elements on a page should be repeated in appropriate places. Consistency is particularly important in longer publications such as books. The more structured you make your design, the easier producing the piece will be.

The best way to enforce consistent design is to create a meaningful style sheet for your publication. Microsoft Publisher 97 can help you apply styles or formats to text, objects, tables, and other page elements. Just as word processor documents can have style sheets, Microsoft Publisher 97 can import or create text styles. You can put together your Microsoft Publisher 97 project more quickly and more consistently if you use a well-developed style sheet and template rather than simply develop on-the-fly.

✔ **Put things where people tend to see them.** People have a tendency to view a page in a diagonal from the top left to the bottom right. Elements in the center of the page get the most attention; elements at the bottom left and top right get the least attention.

Your design should treat a two-page spread as if it were a single page because the entire two-page spread is the unit of design that readers see.

✔ **Keep your message simple.** To make your reader focus on the content, consider the following:

- Use white space. Many well-designed pieces have a white space content of 50 percent.

- Limit yourself to no more than two fonts on a page.

- Be judicious with color — apply it as highlighting.

✔ **Keep related or similar information on a page.** Keep related information close together or aligned.

You can create a block of related elements by separating them from other elements on the page with rules (lines), frames (boxes), or white space. Likewise, if a graphic relates to a story, the graphic should appear close to the story. Any caption for the graphic should appear close to the graphic.

✔ **Align everything on a page with something.** Create a grid and place your page elements on that grid, as described in Chapter 4. Creating a *page grid* for a layout is akin to creating an outline for a written document.

The same page grid can produce order on pages *without* producing pages that look alike. For example, three- and four-column newspapers and newsletters are so common because you can produce many looks within those formats. You can have blocks in the grid that are not filled in, for example, and graphics that span multiple blocks. Figure 2-1 is a four-column grid with three rows. This layout generates 12 blocks and offers a lot of flexibility. Figures 2-2 through 2-4 show you three examples that use this grid layout.

✔ **Provide contrast to enliven your work.** Balance consistency by doing the unexpected.

✔ **Use a page hierarchy.** If you have a large headline, the reader will probably start reading the page there. You can use smaller headlines to divide a page into sections. You can also use vertical and horizontal rules to break your page into blocks and provide contrast. Emphasize what's important by making it look different, but don't emphasize parts of your page that have less importance.

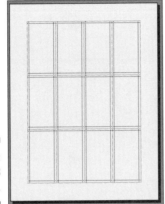

Figure 2-1:
A 4-x-3
page grid.

Figure 2-2:
The 4-x-3
page grid
with a 1:2:1
column
setup.

Figure 2-3:
The 4-x-3
page grid
with a 2:1:1
column
setup.

Figure 2-4:
The 4-x-3
page grid
with a 2:2
column
setup.

The columns in your page grid don't *have* to be the same width, and the pages in a two-page spread don't *have* to be balanced or symmetrical. *We think that balanced pages are boring.* We tend to vary the size and placement of graphics across columns. We also favor the use of sidebars, pull-quotes (short statements that summarize information on a page), large initial capitals, and column shadings to break up the page.

Desktop Style Resources

Desktop publishing has turned millions of people into typographers and typesetters. Using type and doing typography is not a skill that comes naturally to most people, however. The many rules and guidelines specific to page layout don't pertain to typewritten text or text prepared in word processors. The following resources can help you make the transition from text documents to desktop publications.

Two of the most accepted style guides for clear writing in the United States for the English language are the following:

- *The Elements of Style,* 3rd Edition, by William Strunk, Jr. and E. B. White (published by Macmillan)
- *The Chicago Manual of Style,* 14th Edition (published by the University of Chicago Press)

A number of texts specialize in the handling of type. In addition to *The Chicago Manual of Style,* the following books are worthy additions to your library:

- *Words into Type* (published by Prentice Hall)
- *Hart's Rules for Compositors and Readers* (published by University Press)
- *Pocket Pal* (published by International Paper Company)

The following two small texts are noteworthy for beginning users because they deal with typographical issues in a friendly way:

- *The PC Is Not a Typewriter,* by Robin Williams (published by Peachpit Press)
- *The Desktop Style Guide,* by James Felici (published by Bantam Computer Books)

Desktop publishing has its own language. Each typography reference work mentioned in this section helps you keep your picas separate from your points, your en dashes from your em dashes, and your verso from your recto.

Everything Costs Money

Your budget can play a prominent role in the design of your publication. You don't want to merrily design something only to be shocked by the sticker price when you arrive at the printer. A good designer always asks the question, "How much were you intending to spend?" straight out because it helps to ground the project in reality. Perhaps good designers ask the question also because it helps them set their pay scale.

Just because a project has a limited budget doesn't mean that the publication has to be poorly designed. It simply means that you must rely on techniques that not only enhance your work but also are within your budget. We have seen creative, effective, and attractive pieces produced on a limited budget, and we have seen expensively designed pieces that belong in the *Desktop Publishing Hall of Shame.* It takes experience and good judgment to get the most out of what you have to spend.

Establish a good working relationship with the staff at your print shop. They can help you in the early design phase by suggesting paper and color selections. Inquire about their price breaks for quantity printing. They can also supply you with the correct printer driver to install so that your design both formats correctly on your screen and prints correctly to their printer.

Chapter 3

Basic Housekeeping

● ●

In This Chapter

▶ Launching Microsoft Publisher 97

▶ Touring the Microsoft Publisher 97 interface

▶ Customizing your options

▶ Creating, finding, opening, and saving files

● ●

*W*e call this chapter "Basic Housekeeping" because we discuss things that you need to know to get on with your work in Microsoft Publisher 97. If you make a mess, this chapter tells you how to clean up after yourself.

If you know how to create, open, find, close, and save files, then you can probably get by without reading this chapter. Still, Windows 95 and Microsoft Publisher 97 offer you new ways to perform these tasks. Chances are that you'll discover methods you didn't know about by reading this chapter. A second saved here, a second saved there, and pretty soon you're talking about your entire life. We think that this chapter will repay your reading time with improved productivity.

Launch Time

When you install Microsoft Publisher 97 for Windows 95 on your computer, the Installer creates an entry on the Programs submenu of the Start menu. Using the menus is probably the easiest way to launch, or start up, Microsoft Publisher 97, but the following list contains other methods that you might want to know:

✔ Choose Start⇨Programs⇨Microsoft Publisher, as shown in Figure 3-1.

✔ Locate the program icon, shown in the margin, and double-click it.

The program itself was installed in the Microsoft Publisher 97 folder that is located inside the Program Files folder, which you can navigate to by using the Windows Desktop or the Windows Explorer.

✔ Drag the publication file icon (for the publication that you want to
    open) over the Microsoft Publisher 97 program or shortcut icon and
    then release the mouse button.

  ✔ Microsoft Publisher 97 is a drag-and-drop enabled program. You can
    navigate to and click the file icon for the publication that you want to
    open; then, you drag the file and drop it into Microsoft Publisher 97.
    The program opens with that publication on your screen.

Figure 3-1:
Starting
Microsoft
Publisher 97
from the
Start Menu.

What's All This on My Screen?

In this section, we show you the names and uses of all the buttons, bars, and
bows within Microsoft Publisher 97. We're not going to give you fine details
here about all interface elements that are standard fare for Windows 95. We
assume that you already know how to use the menu bar; title bar; scroll
bars; minimize, maximize, and restore buttons; and mouse pointer. If you are
not familiar with standard Windows 95 features, please refer to your
Windows manual or to a beginning text on Windows, such as *Windows 95
For Dummies,* 2nd Edition by Andy Rathbone (published by IDG Books
Worldwide, Inc.).

Microsoft Publisher 97 uses the term *workspace* to refer to the Microsoft Publisher 97 window and the customization options. Figure 3-2 shows a blank Microsoft Publisher 97 publication in a window with labeled interface elements.

Microsoft Publisher 97 places the following interface elements on your screen:

✔ **The Standard toolbar:** The toolbar contains icons that duplicate menu commands. When you move your pointer over each button, a Tooltip appears to tell you what the button represents. Looking from left to right in Figure 3-3, you see the following buttons on the toolbar: New, Open, Save, Print, Spelling, Cut, Copy, Paste, Format Painter, Undo/Redo, Bring to Front, Send to Back, Rotate, and Help (Microsoft Publisher 97's Help system, not Windows Help system). Depending upon your program's current status, some buttons may be disabled.

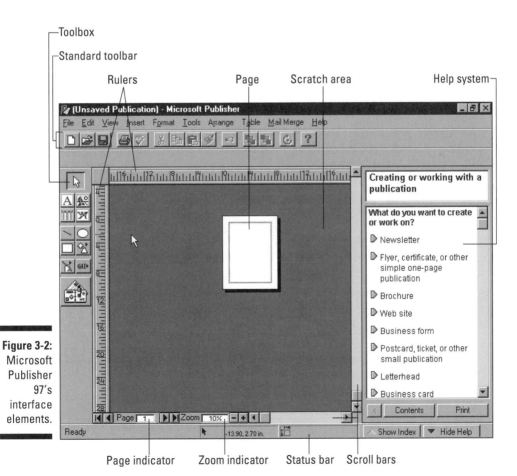

Toolbox

Standard toolbar

Rulers   Page   Scratch area   Help system

Figure 3-2:
Microsoft
Publisher
97's
interface
elements.

Page indicator   Zoom indicator   Status bar   Scroll bars

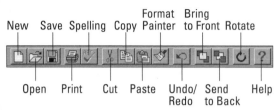

Figure 3-3:
The
Standard
toolbar with
buttons
labeled.

New Save Spelling Copy Format Painter Bring to Front Rotate

Open Print Cut Paste Undo/Redo Send to Back Help

If you have an object selected on your layout, you may see an additional Format toolbar for that object below the Microsoft Publisher 97 main toolbar (which is always on your screen). For example, when you have a line selected, you see a toolbar that lets you add arrowheads; flip and rotate the line; and change line weights, stroke (the outline), and fill colors.

You can turn off those pesky tippages and first-time Help dialog boxes by turning off the related options. To turn them off, choose Tools➪Options, click the Editing and User Assistance tab, and in the resulting dialog box, click the check boxes next to those options (to remove the check). Learn the interface first (before you do this) and don't turn off these options when you are working with other beginning users — they may find these features useful and won't know how to turn them back on.

You can also customize the toolbars and rulers that you see by right-clicking the toolbar, rulers, or toolbox and selecting the Toolbars and Rulers command from the context-sensitive menu. We talk about these in the following section.

✔ **The toolbox:** The twelve buttons in the toolbox (at the left of Figure 3-2) let you create objects or insert objects from other sources. These buttons also display Tooltips. The Pointer tool lets you select objects on a page. When you create an object on your layout, that object and the Pointer tool are automatically selected so that you can work with your new object.

Here's a good toolbox trick. If you plan to use the same tool repeatedly, hold the Ctrl key and click the tool. That tool stays selected until you click another tool.

✔ **The rulers:** The horizontal and vertical rulers aid in positioning objects on your screen. You can move the zero point of the rulers by clicking and dragging the intersection button or the ruler.

A guide is a dotted line used to position objects on your page. If you want to create a guide, hold down the Shift key when you click and drag a ruler. You can set a feature called Snap to Guides by choosing Tools➪Snap to Guides (or Ctrl+W). Objects that you create close to the guide align with the guide. You can also choose Tools➪Snap to Ruler Marks and Tools➪Snap to Objects for corresponding kinds of alignment. In the next chapter, we have much more to say about the rulers, guides, and methods that you can use for accurately positioning objects on a layout.

✔ **The Page indicator:** To the left of the horizontal scroll bar and the Zoom indicator is the Page indicator. The indicator's text box shows your current page. You can move to and fro between pages by using the double-arrow buttons next to the Page indicator.

✔ **The Zoom indicator:** To the left of the horizontal scroll bar but to the right of the Page indicator is the Zoom indicator. The indicator's text box shows your current magnification. You can click the word Zoom to open a pop-up menu that lets you change your magnification. You can also use the Zoom In (+) and Zoom Out (-) buttons next to the text box to change your view.

✔ **The scroll bars:** Click the arrows at the ends of the scroll bars to move incrementally, click the scroll bar itself to move a screenful, or click and drag the button (what some folks call the elevator) on the scroll bar to move your window view as much as you want.

✔ **The status bar:** Below the horizontal scroll bar is the status bar. It contains information that changes along with your changing activities on-screen. For example, if you have a layout object selected, the Current Position box shows the object's on-screen position; the Object Size box shows the object's dimensions; and the message on the left tells about your current activity. If you have not selected anything, the Current Position tracks your mouse pointer's position on-screen and the Object Size box indicates the size of any area that you've dragged around (a selection rectangle). Keep an eye on the status bar as you move about. It features other helpful messages and is a most useful positioning aid.

The dimensions that you see in the ruler and the status bar are in inches by default. You can set other units for dimensions and other program preferences by making selections from the Options dialog box. You open this dialog box by choosing Tools⇨Options.

✔ **The page:** The page is the white area where your page design appears, sometimes referred to as the *printable area*. Margins appear as blue dotted lines. The stuff that appears outside the margin box is the *nonprintable area*. Makes sense to us.

✔ **The work (or scratch) area:** Although the gray area surrounding your page looks dead and useless, it is not. The work area is a pasteboard that you can use to position objects that you want to use at a later date or to modify objects without having to disrupt your layout. You can think of the pasteboard as your scratch area, and you can use it for any purpose that comes to mind.

✔ **The Help system:** To the right of the main window is where the windows for the on-line Help system appear. The Help system's Contents screen is shown in Figure 3-2. The system also offers an index of topics based on keywords. You can show and hide these Help windows by using the buttons that appear below the Help system.

Microsoft Publisher 97's excellent online manual leads you to discussions on topics by using keywords. As you navigate tasks, you come to Help system screens called How To's. They give you step-by-step directions on how to perform a task. Microsoft is now using this technique to "write down" its manuals and save trees.

The Help menu has a number of features that you may want to check out including a short demo, keyboard shortcuts, technical support information, a connection to the Microsoft Publisher 97 Web site, and more.

If you are a person with a disability, Microsoft Publisher 97 has alternate methods for using the interface. Open and read the README.HLP file in the Microsoft Publisher 97 folder for more details.

Options and More Options . . .

We like to have it our way, so we like to mess around with the way our programs work. We used to think that this was due to having too much time on our hands. But now we have no extra time on our hands, and we recognize that, although sometimes entertaining, spending a lot of time playing with a program's options can be a real time waster. Microsoft Publisher 97 offers you options that you can set to have the program work differently. You make your choices in two tabs of the Options dialog box that you can view by choosing Tools⇨Options. The General tab of the Options dialog box, as shown in Figure 3-4, is the first of these tabs.

Figure 3-4:
The General
Tab of the
Options
dialog box.

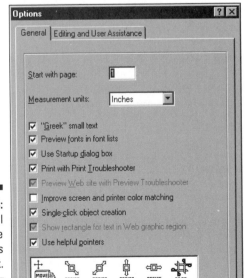

When you click the Editing and User Assistance tab of the Options dialog box, you view the dialog box shown in Figure 3-5.

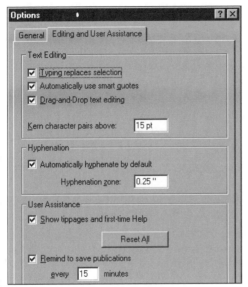

Figure 3-5:
The Editing
and User
Assistance
tab of the
Options
dialog box.

We refer to the selections in the Options dialog box throughout this book when the options that fit the features are being discussed. We want to draw your attention to the highlights. First, you can get a quick explanation of any option by right-clicking the option and selecting What's This? from the pop-up menu. Alternatively, if you click the Help button (?) at the right side of the dialog box title bar, you can left-click a feature to get the same explanation — standard Windows 95 behavior (and applause is heard from the peanut gallery).

Some of the more useful options in the General tab of Microsoft Publisher 97's Options dialog box that you may want to reset are as follows:

✔ **Measurement units:** Select Inches (the default), Centimeters, Picas, or Points from this drop-down list box.

Inches and Centimeters are probably familiar to most people. If you haven't worked with type before, the Points and Picas options may be unfamiliar. A *point* is a unit of measure based upon the smallest feature that a designer was supposed to be able to make in lead type for moveable type. There are 72 points per inch; you can convince yourself of this fact by drawing a 1-inch line on-screen and changing the Measurement units to Points. Then you can read the object's new size in the status bar.

The use of points has a practical application in the design of computer monitors. Most computer monitors create pixels at approximately 72 dots per inch so that type is represented well on-screen.

Picas are a somewhat larger unit of measurement in the typographical world. A *pica* is equal to 12 points, or approximately $1/6$ inch. Actually, a pica is 0.166 inch, making 30 picas equal to 4.98 inches. Most page-layout programs ignore this small differential, however, and set the pica to exactly $1/6$ inch, as is the case with Microsoft Publisher 97. (We're grateful that Microsoft Publisher 97 doesn't trouble us with Ciceros, Didots, and other arcane typographical measurements.)

✔ **Use Startup dialog box:** Turn this option off if you don't want the Startup dialog box to appear every time you launch Microsoft Publisher 97.

✔ **Single-click object creation:** If you want to click an object and have it appear at a default size, leave this option set on (checked). Otherwise, you must click and drag the object to create it. Whatever action you select, you can always resize any object later.

✔ **Use helpful pointers:** Whether the iconic mouse pointers are useful and helpful is a matter of preference. If you want to have more standard Windows-type pointers, click this option off. The small window below the check box shows the style of mouse pointers that you have selected.

Most of the selections in the Editing and User Assistance tab of the Options dialog box are text editing functions that you probably don't want to reset. (We explain text editing functions and hyphenation options in future chapters.) We think that you'll want to reset the options in the User Assistance section, though. These two options are as follows:

✔ **Show tippages and first-time Help:** Tippages? Well, that is a set of helpful hints and dialog boxes that pops up whenever you do something that Microsoft Publisher 97 thinks you may be able to do better. First-time Help pops up demonstrations the first time that you attempt a task.

For example, if you draw a straight line manually, Microsoft Publisher 97 pops up a dialog box telling you that you can constrain lines to the horizontal and vertical directions by holding down the Shift key. When you use the OLE tool from the toolbox for the first time, Microsoft Publisher 97 gives you a demo on OLE. If you want to view first-time Help again (after you have already done the procedures once), click the Reset All button.

✔ **Remind to save publications: every . . . minutes:** This check box and its corresponding text box tell Microsoft Publisher 97 to post a dialog box every so many minutes that you specify to remind you to save your work. We think that the default of 15 minutes is a reasonable one and recommend that you leave this feature set on. If you are more paranoid than we are (is that possible?), then set a lower number. Or live carefree and dangerously. It's your choice.

Some sticky details about customizing Microsoft Publisher 97

Microsoft Publisher 97 customization is hardly a straightforward thing. Some customization settings, such as Use helpful pointers, are *program-level settings*. Program-level settings are in effect every time you use Microsoft Publisher 97, or until you change them again. Other settings, such as the Microsoft Publisher 97 Help Topics command, are *session-level settings*. Session-level settings remain in effect for as long as you remain in Microsoft Publisher 97 without exiting. After you exit Microsoft Publisher 97 and reload it, these settings return to their original states. Still other settings, such as Start with page, are *publication-level settings*. Publication-level settings are specific to individual publications; they have no affect on other publications.

How do you tell one type of setting from another? We favor a Ouija board. If you don't have a Ouija board (and the spirit moves you), by the time you finish this book, you should know. The best thing to do in the meantime is to check your settings anytime you begin working with a publication. And it's not really all that important that your copy of Microsoft Publisher 97 works *exactly* as we describe — as long as you realize *why* it doesn't work that way and *how* you can fix it if you want to.

If you want to change your view of the interface elements that appear in Microsoft Publisher 97, right-click the rulers, toolbars, or toolbox to view the context-sensitive menu shown in Figure 3-6. If a check mark appears next to an element's name in the menu, that interface element appears in your view of Microsoft Publisher 97. To remove an element from view, click the interface element's name on the menu, thereby removing the check mark.

If you select the Toolbars and Rulers command from that menu, you view the Toolbars and Rulers dialog box, as shown in Figure 3-7. (This command is available on the context menu that appears anywhere you click in Microsoft Publisher 97.) In addition to removing elements from view, you can choose to turn off Color Buttons (view black-and-white ones) and Large Buttons (view small ones), and remove or Show Tooltips. We show you figures in this book with all these features turned on.

Figure 3-6:
The
toolbars
and toolbox
context-
sensitive
menu.

Figure 3-7:
The
Toolbars
and Rulers
dialog box.

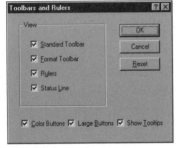

Help on Help

To begin with, the Help system in Microsoft Publisher 97 is not self-documenting. That's too bad, because to get instructions on the use of the Help system in other Microsoft programs (such as Works for Windows 95), the Help menu normally provides a command called "How to use Help." Not so in Microsoft Publisher 97. The best that Microsoft Publisher 97 can offer you is a set of topics in the index under the word *Help*. Figure 3-8 shows you the Help menu in Microsoft Publisher 97.

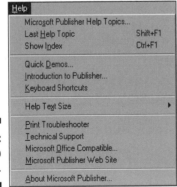

Figure 3-8:
The Help
menu.

Perhaps the most prominent difference between Windows help and Microsoft Publisher 97 help is that Microsoft Publisher 97 help is always available in the Help panel on the right side of your screen. You do not have control over either its size or its placement. Many reviewers really dislike this Help system, but Microsoft has found that beginning computer users prefer help to be obviously available.

To show the Help panel, do any of the following:

✔ Click the Show Help button at the extreme right of the status bar.

✔ Select the Last Help Topic command from the Help menu or press Shift+F1.

✔ Click the Help button at the right of the toolbar to view the contents page of the Help system and get an overview of its contents.

You can also jump back to the Contents page by clicking the Contents button below the Help panel.

The Help system also has a topic listing, which organizes the system by keyword. Figure 3-9 shows the Help system with both the Index and Help panels open. They take up a lot of real estate on your screen. You'll definitely want to hide the Help system when you don't need help.

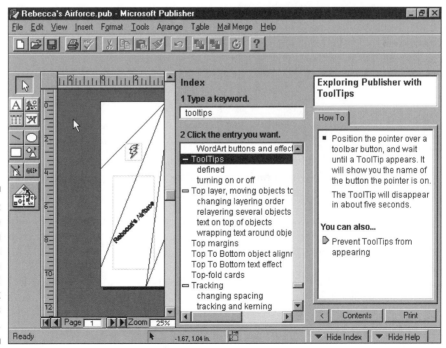

Figure 3-9:
The Help system open with both the Help and Index panels showing.

To hide the Help panel, do one of the following:

> ✔ Click the Hide Help button at the extreme right of the status bar.

> ✔ Choose the Help⇨Hide Help command from the menu bar or press Shift+F1.

The Help system is not context sensitive. That is, you don't simply jump to a topic of interest based on your current condition or selected feature when the Index panel opens. You can tell Microsoft Publisher 97 to jump to Help on a specific topic, however, by doing one of two things:

> ✔ Select a topic in the Index panel.

> ✔ Right-click an object in your window and select the Help command from the bottom of that context-sensitive menu.

Figure 3-10 shows you a sample context-sensitive menu for a text frame.

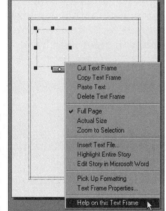

Figure 3-10:
A context-
sensitive
menu for a
text frame.

As you move from task to task in the Help panel, the Help system remembers your path through it.

To return to a previous Help panel, click the Back button (<), which appears just to the left of the Contents button. By doing so, you retrace your steps in the reverse order.

Don't forget that you can always return to an overview of the Help system by using the Contents button.

Finding a topic

If you know the topic you are interested in getting help with, searching the Help system's Index is easy to do. The Index panel contains keywords or phrase listings of topics that are in a searchable database. As you enter text into the "1 Type a keyword" text box, the program performs an incremental search and the Index panel and Help panel jump to that topic.

The manual contains a number of How To icons with keywords for you to search the Help system on. Enter those words into the "1 Type a keyword" text box.

To show the Index panel, use one of these three methods:

- ✔ Click the Show Index button at the right of the status bar.
- ✔ Choose the Help⇨Show Index command from the menu bar.
- ✔ Press Ctrl+F1.

Try a synonym to find related instructions and explanations.

When you click the menu or anywhere else in the Microsoft Publisher 97 window, the Index panel disappears. You can also click the Hide Index button to remove the Index panel from view.

Inch-by-inch; step-by-step

Each task described in the Help panel has an arrow-like bullet next to it. If you click a topic, you go either to a set of related topics or to a panel that has step-by-step help, which Microsoft Publisher 97 calls "How To" help. Figure 3-11 shows you an example of a How To panel.

Information related to the task described may be viewed in the More Info tab of the Help panel. Typically, these additional topics contain explanatory windows with descriptions of the topic. You can print these topics by clicking the Print button or dismiss them by clicking the Done button. Figure 3-12 shows one of these informational panels.

In How To help, colored text opens a pop-up window with an explanation, similar to the More Info topics.

Things You Can Do with Files

Files are what you use to store your work or your data in a computer. We like to look at our work, so we spend a lot of time staring at the Windows Explorer window. Microsoft Publisher 97 files are called *publications* and

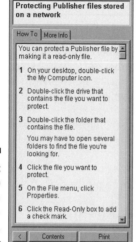

Figure 3-11: A How To procedure in the Help panel.

Figure 3-12: An informational panel in the Help panel.

have a PUB file extension. You can create files, open and close files, modify them, and save the changes that you make to your files. You need to do most file tasks that we've mentioned from within Microsoft Publisher 97. You can apply what you know about files in general to Microsoft Publisher 97 files, however.

Playing with files on the outside

Following is a short list of the tasks that you can do outside Microsoft Publisher 97:

✔ **To select a file(s):** Click the file on the Desktop or the Windows Explorer or click and drag a selection rectangle around a set of contiguous files. You can also hold down the Shift key and click additional files to extend or reduce your range of selected files.

✔ **To move a file:** On the Desktop or the Windows Explorer, click and drag the file to a new location.

✔ **To copy a file:** On the Desktop or the Windows Explorer, press Ctrl and click and drag the file to a new location.

Okay, we know that you can accomplish this same task inside Microsoft Publisher 97 by using the Save As command to copy a file. But this is much, much faster to perform in the interface.

✔ **To create a shortcut file:** On the Desktop or the Windows Explorer, press Ctrl and click and drag the file to a new location with the right mouse button. Select the Create Shortcut(s) Here command from the context-sensitive menu, an example of which is shown in Figure 3-13. (This menu is also a shortcut to copying and moving files.)

✔ **To delete a file:** On the Desktop or the Windows Explorer, click the file to select it and then press Delete. Or click-and-drag that file to the Recycle Bin.

Figure 3-13:
The context-sensitive menu for dragging a file in the interface.

One of the things that we love about Windows 95 is that these actions are now recoverable. If you think that you've made a mistake, you can choose Edit⇨Undo or press Ctrl+Z in your current Desktop folder or the Windows Explorer, and the action is reversed. Far out. If you make a mistake and delete a file that you didn't intend to delete, all is not lost. Open the Recycle Bin folder, select that file in the list, and choose File⇨Restore. Your file jumps back to its original location.

Your deleted file is not actually in jeopardy until you give the Empty Recycle Bin command or until the Recycle Bin fills up and needs the space. In that case, the first file in is the first one that is deleted (FIFO, or first in, first out). If the deletion was done through the menu command and not due to disk space requirements, you still may be able to recover your file. Restart your computer in MS-DOS mode and use the Recover command to try to get your file back. Or go out and get a file utility program such as Norton Utilities to provide you with the recovering function. The most important thing that you can do if you empty the Recycle Bin and need to recover a file is to perform no other operations in the meantime. That way, the file system is less likely to overwrite the disk sectors that contain the information from the deleted file.

You should never need to recover a publication from the trash. Always keep adequate copies and save your files by using the Backup option described later in this chapter, and you'll be fine.

Now that we've briefly described the things that you can do with files outside Microsoft Publisher 97 (that you don't want to or can't do inside Microsoft Publisher 97), we turn our attention to the operations that you want to do inside Microsoft Publisher 97.

Starting a publication

Microsoft Publisher 97 prompts you to create a publication every time you start a session — that is, launch the program. You see the Startup dialog box first (if you haven't turned that option off). If you are already in a Microsoft Publisher 97 session, you can get to the Startup dialog box (as shown in Figure 3-14) by choosing File⇨Create New Publication.

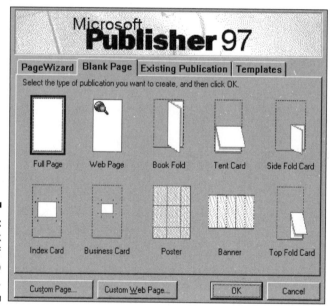

Figure 3-14:
The Blank
Page tab of
the Startup
dialog box.

In the Startup dialog box, Microsoft Publisher 97 shows you four tabs that give you four ways to create a new publication:

- **PageWizard:** Lets you create a new publication from a series of dialog boxes that builds your publication based upon selections that you make. Click the PageWizard tab, select the wizard that you want to use, and click OK.

- **Blank Page:** Lets you create a new publication from scratch with a generic or blank page format. On the Blank Page tab, click the type of blank page that you want to start with and then click OK. You can also click the button labeled Cus_tom page for advanced Page Setup options, which is discussed in detail in the next chapter.

- **Existing Publication:** Lets you create a new publication based upon a pre-existing publication. Click the Existing Publication tab, select from the available publications, and click OK.

- **Templates:** Lets you create a more canned publication that is based on a template. Click the Templates tab and select the template of interest. Then, click OK. We describe templates in more detail later in this chapter. You see the Templates tab only after you have created at least one template.

After you make your selections and click OK, Microsoft Publisher 97 opens the new publication in the window on-screen with the title "(Unsaved Publication) - Microsoft Publisher 97" in the title bar.

You can also open any Microsoft Publisher 97 publication and perform a Save As command (from the File menu) to create a new publication. Publications that you create in Microsoft Publisher 97 are retained in a preference file so that they are known to and listed by the Startup dialog box (on the Existing Publication tab). If you reinstall Microsoft Publisher 97, this list of known publications is lost.

Don't forget to perform a Save or Save As command to save your new publication to disk; otherwise, it may exist only in your memory.

Opening remarks

Microsoft Publisher 97's Open command works in a nonstandard way because it forces you to open files with the Startup dialog box rather than a standard Open file dialog box (as most Windows programs do or are supposed to do). Microsoft figures (and we think quite rightly) that showing you the files that you've already worked with is much friendlier than dumping you into the file hierarchy. Microsoft Publisher 97 is the "Happy Face" of page layout programs.

We note that Microsoft Works calls the Startup dialog box the Task Launcher. We wish that the various groups at Microsoft would talk to one another and get their terminology consistent. Still, we recognize the dynamic creativity that large groups of bright people have when no adult supervision is applied. The United States Congress operates in a similar manner.

When you open Microsoft Publisher 97 for the first time in a session, the program opens the Startup dialog box to the PageWizard tab. This is Microsoft Publisher 97 prompting you to create a new file. If you really want an existing publication, though, follow these steps:

1. **Click the Existing Publication tab of the Startup dialog box.**

   The Existing Publication tab is shown in Figure 3-15.

2. **Select the publication of interest (click it) in the Files in list box at the lower left.**

   You can look over the publication preview (that is, a thumbnail image of the first page of your publication) in the right pane of the Startup dialog box (provided that you checked the Save Preview option in the Save As dialog box — see the next section).

3. **Click OK to open the publication.**

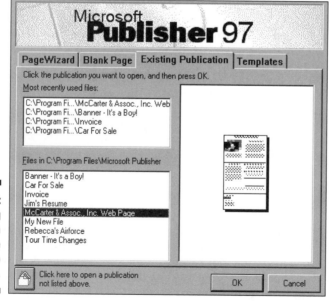

Figure 3-15:
The Existing Publication tab of the Startup dialog box.

After you are in a Microsoft Publisher 97 session, you need to choose File⊅Open Existing Publication from the main menu to see the Startup dialog box again. In this case, Microsoft Publisher 97 opens the Startup dialog box directly to the Existing Publication tab.

Are you smiling yet? What could be more friendly than this? Still, if you have reinstalled Microsoft Publisher 97 or are working with other peoples' publication files (that you didn't create), the Startup dialog box's Existing Publication tab won't help you. You need to see an Open file dialog box.

To open a file not found in the Existing Publications tab, do one of the following:

✔ Click the tiny little button tucked away in the lower-left corner of the Startup dialog box and labeled Click here to open a publication not listed above.

Tricky little devil. That button opens a standard file open dialog box that you expect to see come up directly when you choose the File⊅Open command from the menu bar of a typical Windows program. Did you spot it?

✔ Or, click the Open button on the toolbar (shown in the margin).

In either case, you see an Open Publication dialog box similar to the one shown in Figure 3-16.

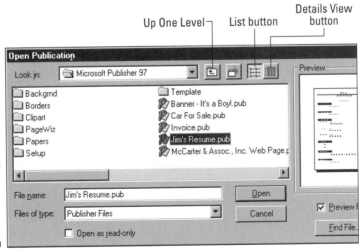

Figure 3-16: The Open Publication dialog box.

The Open Publication dialog box is a standard Windows interface element, only slightly altered to account for the capabilities that Microsoft Publisher 97 offers you. You locate files in the file hierarchy by clicking the Look in list box or by using the Up One Level button. The List button and Details View button let you change the way that the list box displays the file contents for your current folder.

You can filter your view of the File list box contents by selecting the appropriate filter from the Files of type list box. Click the Preview File check box if you want to preview the selected files. When you select a file (if it is a Microsoft Publisher 97 file with a preview), that preview shows up in the Preview section on the right of the Open Publication dialog box. The Open as read-only check box lets you open a file to view it without letting you make changes.

To open two publications simultaneously, you need to launch Microsoft Publisher 97 a *second* time. Then you can open one publication in each copy of Microsoft Publisher 97. To move between running copies of Microsoft Publisher 97, press Alt+Tab to view the Windows 95 Cool Switch and then press Alt+Tab again to move to the publication that you want to work in. You can also simply click the Taskbar buttons (at the bottom of the Windows 95 screen) to switch between your two running copies of Microsoft Publisher 97. You can have as many copies of the program running in memory as you have memory to run copies in.

In some cases, having multiple publications open on your screen can actually be useful. Because Microsoft Publisher 97 is drag-and-drop enabled, you can click an object or frame and drag it to another publication to create a copy of that object.

Finding files

Also tucked away in the Open Publication dialog box is a Find File utility. If you click the Find File button, the Find File dialog box appears, as shown in Figure 3-17. This dialog box lets you Find All Files Of This Type with `Publisher Files: *.PUB` on your hard drive as the default. You can also find a particular file by clicking the Find This File radio button and entering the filename (with or without wildcards) to search on. You initiate a search when you click on the Start Search button, and you open a selected file when you click the Open File button in the Find File dialog box.

This Find File utility is different from (and superior to) the general Find utility that comes with Windows because it actually lets you view the preview and open the file from within Microsoft Publisher 97. It is very fast and lacks only the ability to look inside at the contents of files to be complete — something that would make it very slow in comparison. We think that the Find File utility can satisfy most peoples' needs.

We want to tell you about a more advanced Find utility, though. To work with the Windows 95 find utility, choose the Start⇨Find⇨Files or Folders command. The Windows Find dialog box lets you search for files by: name and location, date modified, and Advanced searches. Advanced searches

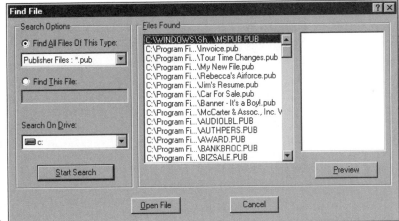

Figure 3-17:
The Find
File dialog
box.

includes searching by file type, text contained within, and file size. In the Windows Help system, the "finding, files or folders" topic tells you how to perform searches.

Saving your files means never having to say you're sorry

Microsoft Publisher 97 lets you save two kinds of files: Microsoft Publisher 97 publication (PUB) files and various forms of text files. For the most part, when you do page layout in Microsoft Publisher 97, you are interested in saving publications. Because you can create text in Microsoft Publisher 97 in the form of stories or stand-alone text frames, Microsoft Publisher 97 lets you save your text in a number of formats: plain text, interchange formats such as the rich text format (RTF), and any one of several word processor formats. This feature lets you move your text back and forth with agility between Microsoft Publisher 97 and any standard word processor.

File saving formats

A PUB file is Microsoft Publisher 97's proprietary format for saving layout information. Many page layout programs save to a PUB file — but they are not Microsoft Publisher 97's PUB files. To use a PUB file inside Microsoft Publisher 97, you have to save a page layout file in another program as a Microsoft Publisher 97 PUB file. To open a PUB file created in Microsoft Publisher 97 in another program, you need a mechanism to convert Microsoft Publisher 97's PUB file format during the file opening process. Generally speaking, you will not be able to work with PUB files between Microsoft Publisher 97 and other programs such as Quark XPress or PageMaker because page layout programs implement their page formatting in very different ways.

Start me up

Your computer has two chief places to keep information: *memory (random-access memory or RAM)* and *storage*. Memory exists within little chips buried deep inside your computer. Storage includes your hard disk, your floppy disks, and any CD-ROMs, tapes, or other such computer-information storage devices that you might have.

Memory is where all the work gets done. When Microsoft Publisher 97 is running, it's running in memory. When you work on a publication, it's also in memory. Memory is very fast and capable, but there's a big problem with it: It's not very good at remembering things. When you shut off your computer or when the power goes off for a moment (someone kicks your power cord or randomly flips circuit breakers in the basement), everything in memory gets wiped out. Similarly, when you close a publication, you lose everything in memory that had to do with that publication. So you see, keeping things *only* in memory is a dangerous thing.

Storage to the rescue! Although storage is incapable and slow compared with memory, it's very good at remembering things. Even when your computer's power is off, storage can keep track of information. That way, your computer can remember important things from day to day, such as how to run your programs, what publications you created yesterday, and the phone number of that cute laptop computer it met the other day. When you load Microsoft Publisher 97, your computer actually makes a copy of the program that's in storage, puts the copy in memory, and works with it there.

Saving is just the reverse process. When you save a publication, your computer takes a copy of what's in memory and places that copy in storage. That way, if memory gets wiped out for any reason, you still have a copy of your work. When you later want to look at your publication, you just ask your computer to reverse the process again, copying the publication back from storage into memory. This is called *opening*.

Windows 95 enables you to use long names with spaces and takes care of the translation to the previous convention (you know, eight-character names with a three-letter file type extension as a suffix, the dreaded *eight dot three*). Use this new capability and name your files something that you can recognize. Don't bother adding the PUB extension. Let Windows 95 handle that detail for you.

Publications — well, all computer files, actually — are quite unwilling to share their names with another file in the same folder. Multiple files with the same name can exist in different locations among your computer's disks, however. If you try to save a publication to a folder in which a publication of that same name already exists, Microsoft Publisher 97 opens a dialog box to warn you of the impending duel to the death. Click the Yes button in this dialog box to overwrite the first file with your new one. Click the No button to return to your publication.

Working with text is an entirely different matter. There's a way of getting text into and out of just about any word processor that you want to work in. You can save text to any one of the following text formats:

- ✔ **Plain text:** This format saves text only as lower ASCII characters in a TXT file. Plain text includes alphanumeric characters and a few common symbols. All formatting and font information is lost. All word processors open TXT files. This is your lowest common denominator, but saving in this format does not preserve all your work.

- ✔ **Rich Text Format:** The RTF format is an *interchange* format developed by Microsoft to let programs exchange text files that contain formatting information. In the files, instructions on how to format specific characters and paragraphs are contained in directions given as plain text characters. Most word processors support opening and saving RTF files.

- ✔ **Word Processor Filters:** Microsoft Publisher 97 contains some filters to save text to specific file formats. These formats include Word 2.x for Windows; Windows Write; Works 3.0 for Windows; Works 4.0 for Windows; WordPerfect 5.0; WordPerfect 5.1 for DOS; WordPerfect 5.x for Windows; WordPerfect 5.1 or 5.2 Secondary File; WordPerfect 5.0 Secondary File; Word 6.0/95; HTML Document; Word 4.0 for Macintosh; Word 5.0 for Macintosh; and Word 5.1 for Macintosh.

Microsoft Publisher 97 can open and import from most file formats to which it can save text; that is, it can bring text files from these other formats into your Microsoft Publisher 97 layout. We say more about this aspect of Microsoft Publisher 97 in Chapter 6. For the sake of completeness, though, here's the list of formats that Microsoft Publisher 97 can use to import text files: Plain Text; Plain Text (DOS); RTF; Word 6.0/95 for Windows & Macintosh; Word (Asian versions) 6.0/95; Word 2.x for Windows; WordPerfect 5.x; WordPerfect 6.x; Windows Write; Word for MS-DOS 3.x – 5.x; Word for MS-DOS 6.0; Works 4.0 for Windows; Works 3.0 for Windows; Lotus 1-2-3; Word 97; Word 4.0 – 5.1 for Macintosh; HTML Document; and Microsoft Excel Worksheet.

We must say that if you can't get your word processing files into and out of Microsoft Publisher 97 by using this list of formats, it's time to replace your word processor. Every word processor we know of can convert at least one of these formats.

File-saving mechanics

Here's the deal about saving your files:

- ✔ Anything that you see on your screen belongs to your computer.

- ✔ Anything that you save to disk belongs to you.

It's really that simple. If you forget to save your work, then anytime the power goes out, your work is lost. We wish, every so often, that we would remember this same sage advice that we give so freely to others.

Don't forget to save early and often. When you create a new publication, it doesn't really exist until you save it to disk.

To save your file, do one of the following:

✔ Choose the File⇨Save (or Ctrl+S) or the File⇨Save As command.

✔ Click the Save button (shown in the margin) on the Standard toolbar.

For a new publication, the Save command is identical to the Save As command. If you choose either command, the standard Save As dialog box (shown in Figure 3-18) appears. The dialog box prompts you to choose a Save in location and to specify a File name. After you save the file once, any subsequent Save command saves your changes without posting the Save As dialog box again. The Save As command enables you to create a new file or overwrite your old one.

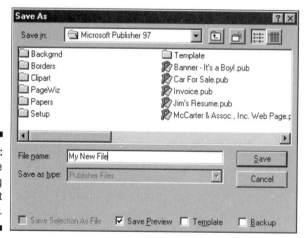

Figure 3-18: The Save As dialog box in List view.

The Save As dialog box is a Windows 95 feature that is only slightly modified to account for features that Microsoft Publisher 97 offers. If locating a file in the Windows 95 file system is new to you, you might want to read a basic Windows text such as Andy Rathbone's *Windows 95 For Dummies*, 2nd Edition from IDG Books Worldwide, Inc. or review the manual that came with Windows 95.

You can change how files look in the file list box by clicking the Details button just below the Help button at the right of the title bar. Figure 3-19 shows you the Save As dialog box in Details view.

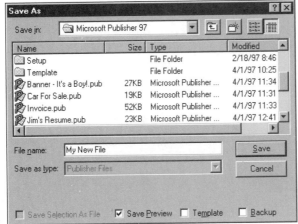

Figure 3-19:
The Save
As dialog
box in
Details
view.

If you want to locate a file in the file system, you can use the Up One Level button to move up the hierarchy or click the Save in drop-down list box to move about any distance. If you want to create a new folder, go to the folder that will enclose it, click the New Folder button, and enter the name of the folder in place of the highlighted name of "New Folder" that you see in the text box.

Here's a good trick for you to remember. If you right-click an item in a standard file dialog box, you generally get help. When you right-click a file or folder in the file list box, you get a fairly substantial context-sensitive menu that gives you file-maintenance selections. Figure 3-20 shows you an example of this menu for a file in the Save As dialog box. The good thing about Save As dialog box tricks is that they work in Open dialog boxes as well.

We want to draw your attention to the four save options available to you as check boxes at the bottom of the Save As dialog box:

   ✔ **Save Selection as File (or, Save All Text As File):** This check box allows you to save selected text (in a text frame) or all text in your publication (if nothing is selected) as a Microsoft Publisher 97 file, plain text file, RTF file, or any one of several popular word processing formats.

   When you select this check box, all other check boxes are dimmed and unavailable. Only this selection gives you the opportunity to save a file in a format other than a Microsoft Publisher 97 file. Use this option to create an export file that lets you use your text in other applications.

Figure 3-20:
A context-
sensitive
menu in the
Save As
dialog box.

To select an option in a dialog box that has an underlined letter, press Alt plus that letter as a keystroke combination.

✓ **Save Preview:** With this check box selected, Microsoft Publisher 97 creates a small image of the first page of your publication — called a *thumbnail* — that you see as a preview in the Open Publication dialog box or the Existing Publication tab. This feature adds very little overhead to the system and helps you figure out what's what. We always leave it selected.

✓ **Template:** A template is a special kind of file that you can use to create other files; we describe it in more detail later in this chapter.

✓ **Backup:** This option creates a duplicate file for you automatically, as described in the next section.

As you create a publication, save multiple copies of it as you progress. Then, if you decide that you like the publication better in a previous state, you can return to it. You can never be too thin, have too much RAM, or have too many backups.

Insurance, please

We have figured out that we can't always count on a hard drive working, so we back up to another hard drive, tape, or floppy disks. And we assume that our first backup is going to fail, so we back up anything important once again. Have we told you that we are paranoid? Well, just because we are paranoid doesn't mean that they are not out to get us.

The Backup option does two things for you. It allows you to return to your last previously saved state of the file — what other programs call a Revert — and it protects you from file corruption by giving you a backup to revert to. Publications can become large and complex, which makes them more susceptible to corruption than smaller files. (This is also true of files that are used frequently, such as font files.)

Backup files do not contain any changes that you made to your publication since you last saved the file. That is, if you save a publication three times during a session, the backup publication contains the file in the state that it was in after two saves.

You can recover from a computer disaster by saving a *backup* copy of a publication, one that contains the BAK extension. You don't see these files in the Existing Publication tab unless you have already opened them. You can search for backup files by using the phrase "backup of *" in the Find This File text box of the Find File dialog box (see discussion earlier in this chapter). Double-click on the backup file of interest. It opens, and you can work in that copy and save it out to a new file with a name of your choosing. From then on, the backup file is one of your choices in the Existing Publication tab.

A backup file takes the same name as your original publication but uses the BAK extension. The only drawback to using the Backup option is that it doubles your disk space requirements.

Unless you are in a tight disk space situation, hedge your bet and always select the Backup option.

If you create backups, you can safely tell the dealer, "Hit me."

Canning templates

You can think of a template as a piece of stationery containing all the content and formatting that was in it when you saved the file as a template. Templates provide a convenient starting place for your work and capture details that you want to make sure that you don't change. Template files are stored as PUB files, commonly in the TEMPLATE folder at: <drive>/ PROGRAM FILES/MICROSOFT PUBLISHER/TEMPLATE.

If you view a template's properties, you see that a template is a file with the Archive bit or file attribute set on. Different programs use this setting for different purposes. You are probably familiar with the use of the Archive bit to determine whether a file has been backed up. A backup program starts by turning off all the Archive settings and then turns them on individually as it performs a backup on that file. Microsoft Publisher 97 uses the Archive bit to determine that the file is a template and that it cannot be overwritten (changed) by a Save command.

From a practical standpoint, a template lets you create a publication based on that template. That file opens as an *Unsaved Publication,* without any name. When you use a template, the program prompts you to perform a Save As operation. After you have done this and created a new file, this file behaves as any publication would. If you try to save the file to the same location with the same name, Microsoft Publisher 97 posts a dialog box like the one shown in Figure 3-21. This dialog box warns that a publication already exists and you are going to overwrite the existing file. You can overwrite the file with another template or with a normal publication file.

Figure 3-21:
Overwrite
File
alert box.

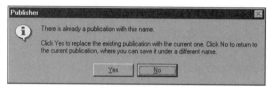

Nag me

Many programs *autosave* changes for you every so often. Page layout programs, being an artistic endeavor, do not, as a rule, do autosaves. You must manually save your file along with any changes that you make to it that you want to retain. Microsoft Publisher 97 (being a good dobee, for those of you who remember "Romper Room") does remind you, however, to save your work from time to time with a pop-up dialog box.

You can change this behavior by eliminating the prompt or changing the frequency of its appearance. Select the Tools⇨Options command and then click the Editing and User Assistance tab in the Options dialog box. You see the Editing and User Assistance tab of the Options dialog box. At the bottom of this dialog box, click the Remind to save publication check box off or enter a new number in the every text box. This "every" number sets the number of minutes that you work inside Microsoft Publisher 97 before it reminds you to save your publication again.

Another behavior that you might want to set while you are in the Editing and User Assistance tab of the Options dialog box is the Show tippages and first-time Help check box. This option posts helpful dialog boxes the first time that you do a particular operation. It also posts dialog boxes when it detects an operation that is causing you difficulty.

Close calls

If you have no changes to save in a file, you can close your publication without further bother by choosing the File⇨Close Publication command. If you made changes, Microsoft Publisher 97 posts the Save Changes dialog box (shown in Figure 3-22) to ask you to save your changes first before closing the file. Click on Yes to save your changes (the default), click No to discard them, or click Cancel to abort the Close operation and continue working in your publication.

Figure 3-22:
The Save
Changes
dialog box.
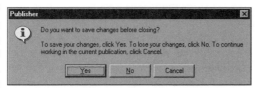

We know of only four methods that let you close a publication:

- ✔ Choose the aforementioned File⇨Close Publication command.
- ✔ Click the Close box of the Microsoft Publisher 97 window, at the extreme right of the title bar.
- ✔ Open another publication.
- ✔ Exit the program.

Shut Down without Crash Landing

You should close Microsoft Publisher 97 whenever you are finished using the program or when you are through with your session and want to shut down your computer. You use the Exit Microsoft Publisher 97 command on the File menu to perform this task. If you try to exit Microsoft Publisher 97 without saving changes made to a file, Microsoft Publisher 97 posts a dialog box asking whether you want to save your changes. If you have no changes to save, the program closes directly and the memory (RAM) used to store the program is released for use by other programs.

To close Microsoft Publisher 97, choose the File⇨Exit Publisher command or press Alt+F4. Also, you can automatically exit your various programs when you use the Shut Down command from the Windows Start menu.

So far, so good. You won't always be able to close Microsoft Publisher 97 in the correct way. You may have a program freeze your computer (yes, it still happens in Windows 95, although not as often), or your power may go out. In either case, *all your changes are lost.* Your file saved to disk is unaffected by the power outage. (Oh, did we mention that you should save your work early and often?)

Microsoft Publisher 97 writes temporary files to disk when it performs certain operations such as file or object insertions, saves, and spooling files to the printer. This protects you from file corruption but requires enough available disk space to complete the operation. The disk space required varies with the complexity of your file. If one of these operations fails, try deleting files and freeing up additional disk space before attempting them again.

Installation advice for the lovelorn

Microsoft Publisher 97 is one resource-hungry critter. You can get by with running Microsoft Publisher 97 on any machine on which you can run Microsoft Windows 95 — but you'll be sorry. Microsoft lists the system requirements as the following:

✔ An IBM PC computer or clone with a 386DX or higher processor; a 486 is recommended as a minimum, with a 75 MHz Pentium computer being more realistic

✔ Microsoft Windows 95 or the Microsoft Windows NT Workstation operating system version 3.51 or later; Microsoft Publisher 97 does not run on Windows 3.1

✔ 6MB of memory for Windows 95, with 8MB recommended

✔ 12MB of memory for Windows NT Workstation, with 16MB recommended

✔ 6MB for a minimum install where you run the program from files on the CD-ROM up to 32MB of available hard-disk space

✔ VGA or higher resolution video adapter (Super VGA for 256-color support recommended)

✔ CD-ROM drive for the CD-ROM version; 2X or greater recommended

✔ A mouse or other pointing device

A more realistic minimum memory allocation gives an additional 4MB of memory for every additional major program that you want to run while Microsoft Publisher 97 is running. Therefore, if you want to work in Microsoft Word at the same time that you work in Microsoft Publisher 97, a minimum for Windows 95 is 12MB of RAM. If you want to have Photoshop open as well, try and work on a Windows 95 computer with 16 MB of RAM. These are general guidelines, and you may get by with less RAM — but you won't like the experience.

Part II
Some Glue, Some Scissors, a Board, et Voilà

The 5th Wave   By Rich Tennant

"THE FUNNY THING IS, I NEVER KNEW THEY HAD DESKTOP PUBLISHING SOFTWARE FOR PAPER SHREDDERS."

In this part . . .

This part shows you how to work with pages and objects in ways that make your page layout both faster and more precise. You also see how your selected printer affects your design.

Microsoft Publisher 97 has many aids to help you design pages carefully, and many different page designs are already built into the program for you. This part also discusses *frames,* which are the containers for the various objects and elements that you place on a page.

Chapter 4
Working with Pages

. . . .

In This Chapter

▶ Looking at your publication from a new point of view

▶ Inserting and deleting pages

▶ Moving around in your publication

▶ Positioning objects precisely with guides and rulers

▶ Using backgrounds to create common page elements

▶ Changing the page layout for an existing publication

. . . .

*W*hen you start a publication, Microsoft Publisher 97 sets up the basic features of the publication for you — the number of pages, the page size, some margin guides, and so on. This default feature is all well and good if you like Microsoft Publisher 97's decisions, but what if you want to change things? You may need to change the margins, for example, to accommodate your design and the capabilities of your printer.

This chapter describes your publication's basic element — the page — and how to change your publication's basic structure, from things as minor as adjusting margins to something as major as converting a three-fold brochure into a 15-foot banner.

In the Beginning: The Page

The most basic element of a Microsoft Publisher 97 publication is the individual page. A page in the computer world is not that different from a page in the real world — it's just a chunk of words and pictures that, when printed, all fit on a single piece of paper.

Pages are designed singly or as part of a multipage spread. Microsoft Publisher 97 makes it easy for you to move between pages, look at pages in different views and magnifications, and add or delete pages as needed to fit your goals.

Moving from page to page

The *current page* is the active page — that is, the page on which your cursor is currently located. At any time, only one page in your document is the current page, even when you're viewing more than one page at a time. The current page is indicated in the Change Pages box at the extreme left side of the horizontal scroll bar.

After you have more than one page in your publication, you can move to another page in several ways:

✔ Select View⇨Go To Page and then type the number of the page that you want to work on in the Go To Page dialog box, shown in Figure 4-1.

✔ Press F5 to open the Go To Page dialog box; Shift+F5 to move to the next page; and Ctrl+F5 to move to the previous page.

✔ Click the Change Pages box to display the Go To Page dialog box.

✔ Click the Previous Page or Next Page buttons (next to the Change Pages box) to move backward or forward a page.

✔ Click the First Page or Last Page buttons to move to the beginning or ending pages of your document.

Figure 4-1:
The Go To
Page dialog
box.

If you try to move past the last page in your document, Microsoft Publisher 97 displays a dialog box like the one shown in Figure 4-2, asking whether you want to add an additional page after your last page. Click OK to insert the new page or click Cancel to dismiss the dialog box.

Figure 4-2:
The Add a
New Page
dialog box.

Scrolling within a page

You use the scroll bars, arrows, and boxes along the right side of your screen to view different parts of the current page. Here's what you can do with the various scroll bar parts:

- ✔ **Scroll arrows:** Click a scroll arrow to slide your view a little bit in the direction of that arrow. If you press and hold the mouse button down, the publication continues to scroll.

- ✔ **Scroll boxes:** Drag the scroll box (it slides like an elevator in a shaft) to slide your view any amount in that same direction.

- ✔ **Scroll bar:** Click above or below the scroll box in the horizontal or vertical scroll bar (the elevator shaft) to slide your view up or down a screenful.

These techniques affect only your view of the current page and do not move you between pages. They are standard Windows interface techniques that work in any Windows window.

In addition to using the scroll bars to move your view of a page in the window, you can use the following keyboard shortcuts:

- ✔ Press PgDn (Page Down) to move your view a screenful down.

- ✔ Press PgUp (Page Up) to move your view a screenful up.

- ✔ Press Ctrl+PgDn to scroll to the right.

- ✔ Press Ctrl+PgUp to scroll to the left.

With the last two shortcuts, you scroll an amount that varies, depending upon your current magnification and view.

If all this makes Microsoft Publisher 97 seem like a game of F19 or Microsoft Flight Simulator, that's all for the good. These keystrokes save you a lot of time.

Changing What You See On-Screen

In precise page layout work, you want to move quickly between different views and magnifications. You can work with a detail on your layout and then jump to a view that lets you get an overview of your document to see how the change looks in context.

If you are familiar with all the different views that you find in a word processor — for example, the Normal, Outline, and Page Layout views available in Microsoft Word — you may be surprised to find that Microsoft Publisher 97 offers only one kind of view: a *live* or editable page preview. Why does it offer just this one mode? Because the purpose of a page layout program is to create and display a page the way it will look when you print it.

Even so, Microsoft Publisher 97 does give you ways to change how your page looks on-screen. Most of these ways reside within the View menu. You can choose to see a single page or a two-page spread, and you can change the magnification of the page or pages that you're viewing.

Two-page spreads

Many publications, including this very book, are designed with pairs of pages that form *facing pages.* Facing pages, also known as a *two-page spread,* are what your reader actually sees — and what you, as a designer, design for.

If you are looking at a single page and want to see your layout as a two-page spread — that is, to see two facing pages side by side — choose the Two-Page Spread command from the View menu. Odd-numbered pages (1, 3, and so on) display on the right side of the Microsoft Publisher 97 screen, whereas even-numbered pages (2, 4, and so on) display on the left side (unless you've changed the Start with page option in the Options dialog box).

The standard setup for professional publications, such as this book, has the text beginning on a right-hand page. Therefore, if your publication has an even number of pages, the first page of the publication displays by itself on the right side of the screen and the last page displays by itself on the left side of the screen. If your publication has only one page, that one page displays by itself on the right side of the Microsoft Publisher 97 screen.

After you choose the Two-Page Spread command, the Single Page command replaces it in the View menu so that you can switch back to it if you want. Choosing this command displays a single page at your current magnification.

Your publication doesn't *have* to be a facing-page publication to take advantage of the Two-Page Spread view. Use this view at your convenience.

Full Page and Actual Size views

In addition to switching between one- and two-page views, you can view your pages at their actual size or view whole pages at once:

✔ Choose <u>V</u>iew⇨<u>F</u>ull Page to resize your current page or two-page spread so that it appears at the largest possible magnification to fill your screen. This view gives you an overview of your layout.

✔ Choose <u>V</u>iew⇨<u>A</u>ctual Size to switch to a 100% view of your document, whether you are in Single Page view or Two-Page Spread view.

✔ Press F9 to toggle between the current page view and Actual Size view.

If you select an object before you apply the <u>A</u>ctual Size command, that object is centered on your screen. If you do not select an object, the center of the page appears in the center of your screen. See Chapter 5 for information about objects.

Figure 4-3 shows a single-page document in Full Page view. Figure 4-4 shows the same document in Actual Size view.

Zooming around

The Zoom indicator box (shown in Figure 4-3) tells you your current magnification in a percentage, with 100% being Actual Size view. To enlarge and reduce the on-screen size of your publications — much as if you were

Zoom indicator box

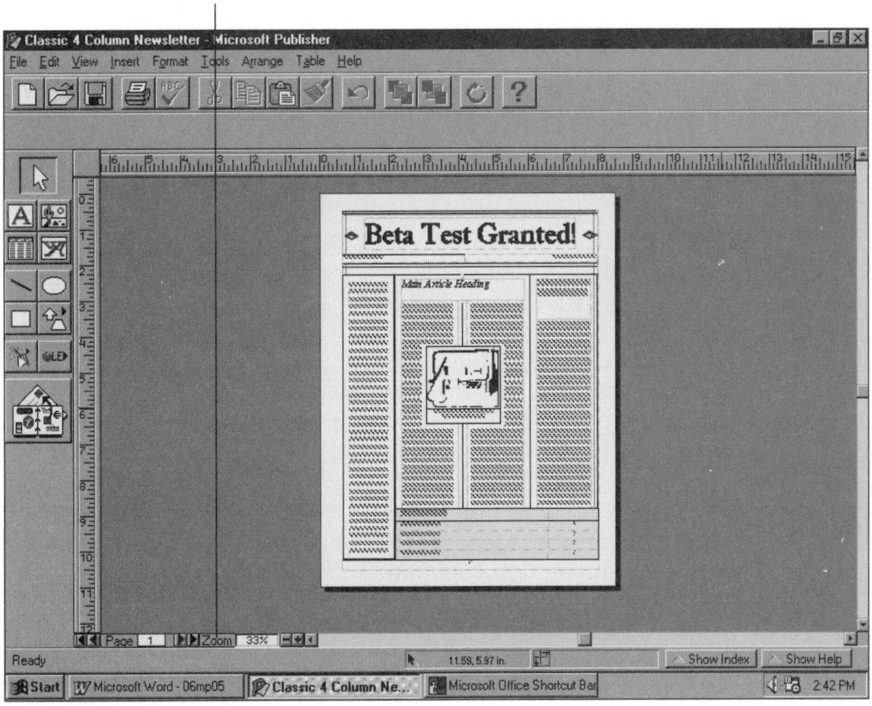

Figure 4-3:
A Full Page view with the Single Page mode selected.

Figure 4-4:
An Actual
Size view
with the
Single Page
mode
selected.

holding a magnifying glass to the screen and then removing that glass —
click the word *Zoom* to reveal the Zoom pop-up menu, shown in Figure 4-5.
The Zoom pop-up menu offers the following magnifications: Full Page, Actual
Size, Zoom to Selection, 10%, 25%, 33%, 50%, 66%, 75%, 100% (Actual Size),
150%, 200%, and 400%.

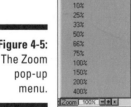

Figure 4-5:
The Zoom
pop-up
menu.

Full Page and Actual Size are the same as the Uiew menu commands. You see
the Zoom to Selection command on the Zoom pop-up menu only when you
have an object selected on the layout. This command magnifies the layout
to the largest view that still contains the object, and centers the object on
your screen. You also find these three commands in the context-sensitive
menu that appears when you right-click anywhere on the layout.

Lining Things Up

No matter how comfortable you are with your mouse, aligning things freehand is tough work. We know because we've been working with a mouse almost daily for many years now, and we *still* have trouble getting things to line up without some help. Fortunately, Microsoft Publisher 97's electronic guidance devices (not to be confused with any guidance devices developed for the military) can help to steady your trembling hands so that objects fall into perfect place with ease. This section looks at layout guides and ruler guides and then shows you how to activate the powerful Snap-to commands to get everything to line up neatly.

Margin and grid guides

Layout guides are an excellent way to determine where to place various objects on each page. Layout guides don't appear on your printout. On-screen, however, these blue or pink lines provide visual references on every page and, using Microsoft Publisher 97's Snap-to feature, can almost magically align other objects with themselves.

Microsoft Publisher 97 provides two types of layout guides:

- *Margin guides* define the boundary of your printable area.
- *Grid guides* let you set up a grid to make it easier to design your publication.

Margin guides appear automatically in every publication. Margin guides generally indicate where you should and shouldn't plop objects and help you align objects along the perimeter of each page. You're free to put objects anywhere you want, regardless of the margins, however. (Whether those objects look good there and whether they actually print are other matters altogether.)

Grid guides, like the lines on graph paper, are excellent tools for aligning any and all objects that you don't want to align to the margin guides. For example, you may want to set a graphic in the direct center of the page. Grid guides can help you do this.

Professional designers — whether they work on a computer or on paper — generally lay out pages according to grids. For example, when creating a three-fold brochure, they use a three-part grid to visually separate the three panels of each page where that brochure eventually will be folded. Or they may divide nonfolding pages into a grid of rows and columns to see how different parts of the page visually relate to each other and to the page as a whole. In this way, designers can ensure that their pages are readable, uncrowded, and visually appealing with appropriate spacing and correct alignment.

When you use certain PageWizards or templates to begin a publication, Microsoft Publisher 97 sets up grid guides automatically to save you the trouble of doing it yourself. Of course, you can always change them if you like. To set up or change layout guides, select Arrange⇨Layout Guides. The Layout Guides dialog box shown in Figure 4-6 appears.

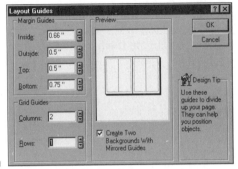

Figure 4-6: The Layout Guides dialog box for a two-page spread.

You set the margins for your printed page in the Margin Guides section of the Layout Guides dialog box. Different printers require different margin settings. If you set margins narrower than your printer will print, your page won't print properly. Text and/or figures will be cut off at the margins. (We discuss printing in depth in Chapter 12.)

In the Grid Guides section of the Layout Guides dialog box, enter the number of Columns and Rows that you want. Grid guides evenly divide the space contained by the margin guides.

If you can't see your layout guides after setting them, check the View menu to see whether the Hide Boundaries and Guides command is hiding your guides. If the Show Boundaries and Guides command appears on the menu, select that command or press Ctrl+Shift+O. To hide the guides again, reapply the Hide Boundaries and Guides command or press Ctrl+Shift+O once again. If you still can't see your guides, they may be covered by other objects, such as lines or a frame boundary.

Ruler guides

In addition to layout guides, you can also set *ruler guides* anywhere on your page. Ruler guides let you arrange elements on your page at any horizontal or vertical position that you want. You can create as many ruler guides as you need. Here's how ruler guides work:

In the gutter

If you want different margin guides for your left-facing pages than for your right-facing pages, be sure to select the Create Two Backgrounds With Mirrored Guides check box in the Preview section of the Layout Guides dialog box. This option is important for facing-page publications that will be bound, such as books. When you check this option, the Left and Right text boxes under Margin Guides change to Inside and Outside text boxes. Any change that you make to the Inside setting affects the right (inside) margin of left-facing pages, whereas the same setting affects the left (inside) margin of right-facing pages. The Outside setting does just the reverse.

It's typical for facing pages to have different *gutters* (internal margins) to accommodate the binding. If you're preparing facing-pages that will be bound, be sure to set different numbers in the Inside and Outside text boxes.

In general, the inside margins should be larger than the outside margins by the amount that the binding will consume. (Ask the person who will be doing the binding to provide this measurement.)

With this setup, you can easily create the extra room necessary on each page to accommodate the room lost due to the binding. Without this extra room, your pages can look lopsided and objects on those pages can get buried in the gutter.

When your gutters are properly set, you can spread objects across facing pages. Depending on your target printer's capabilities (its margins, for example), the object may not print completely. But for objects for which the cut-off doesn't matter — patterns, spot color, and fills — this is a valuable technique.

✔ To create a vertical guide, press and hold the Shift key and click and drag from the vertical ruler right to the desired position on your layout. Your cursor changes to include the word `adjust`; the tooltip says `Create Vertical Guide`; and a green dotted line appears when you release your mouse button.

✔ To create a horizontal guide, hold the Shift key down and click and drag from the horizontal ruler down to the desired position on your layout.

✔ To place a vertical guide in the exact center of your view, choose Arrange⇨Ruler Guides⇨Add A Vertical Rule Guide.

✔ To place a horizontal guide in the exact center of your view, choose Arrange⇨Ruler Guides⇨Add A Horizontal Rule Guide.

✔ To move a ruler guide, just click and drag it while holding the Shift key.

✔ To remove a ruler guide, hold the Shift key and drag the ruler off the page.

✔ You can remove all ruler guides by choosing the Clear All Ruler Guides command from the Ruler Guides submenu of the Arrange⇨Ruler Guides⇨Clear All Ruler Guides command.

Snap to it!

Guides would be interesting visual aids but not generally worth the bother if you couldn't automatically align objects to them. Microsoft Publisher 97 (like most layout and drawing programs) has a feature called Snap to Guides, which directly aligns objects that you place close to a guide.

The Snap-to commands make it appear as if the guides magnetically tug at your objects as those objects draw near, just as Batman might use a powerful electromagnet to suck the gun out of the Joker's hand. With these "magnetic" forces in place, you can be sure that any objects you draw or drag near a guide automatically align both with that guide and with each other. You can also make objects snap to the nearest ruler mark (increment) if you like.

Here's how you toggle the Snap-to commands on and off:

✔ Choose Tools⇨Snap to Guides (or press Ctrl+W) to align with your layout guides.

✔ Choose Tools⇨Snap to Ruler Marks to align with your ruler marks.

✔ Choose Tools⇨Snap to Objects to align with selected objects on-screen. See Chapter 5 for more about objects.

A check mark next to the command name means that the option is turned on; click it to turn it off. The absence of a check mark means that the option is turned off; click it to turn it on.

In our experience, the Snap to Guides command is ever so much more useful than snapping to ruler marks. That's why it gets the special Ctrl+W shortcut. We find this command more helpful, in part because you can set up your own guides (whereas you can't control the ruler marks) and in part because those rulers have so many darn marks.

 Microsoft Publisher 97 offers other commands that aid you in precise placement of objects on your layout. (We discuss these in Chapter 5.) In particular, you may want to explore the use of the Line Up Objects command to precisely align objects to your page. Microsoft Publisher 97 also has a Nudge Objects command that lets you move your objects a pixel at a time in any direction.

Using Virtual Rulers

You can use the status bar to determine an object's position and size, or you can use the on-screen rulers, located along the top and left edges of the scratch area. The current position of your cursor is indicated by a sliding dashed line that appears in each of your rulers. To do fine measuring with the rulers, you can enlarge them simply by zooming in on the page. As you magnify a page, the rulers also grow larger, and the tick marks (known in Microsoft Publisher 97 as *ruler marks*) become more numerous.

The unit of measurement on each ruler is determined by the <u>M</u>easurements setting in the Options dialog box, opened by choosing <u>T</u>ools➪<u>O</u>ptions. See the preceding chapter for option details.

If your rulers aren't showing, you can display them by selecting <u>V</u>iew➪ <u>T</u>oolbars and Rulers and clicking the Rulers check box. An even more convenient approach is to right-click and select that command from the context-sensitive menu.

To move a ruler, simply click and drag it to a new location. When you place your mouse pointer over a ruler, the cursor changes to a two-headed arrow that points up and down if you're pointing at the horizontal ruler, or right and left if you're pointing at the vertical ruler. As you drag, an outline of the ruler accompanies your pointer. When you release the mouse button, the ruler appears in its new location. To return a ruler to its original location, just drag it back in place.

You can move both rulers simultaneously by clicking and dragging the blank box at the intersection of the two rulers.

By default, the zero mark on each ruler is set to the upper-left corner of the page or two-page spread. You may find it convenient to *rezero* a ruler — that is, to change the position of its zero mark, as if you were sliding the ruler end-to-end over a page.

For example, if one object's right edge ends at the $2^{1}/_{4}$ mark on the horizontal ruler, and another object's left edge begins at the $5^{5}/_{16}$ mark, how much space is between those objects? Is this math class? Who knows, and who really cares? Wouldn't it be easier to measure this if the horizontal ruler's zero mark aligned with one of those edges?

To move a ruler's zero mark, simply point to a ruler, press and hold the Shift key, and click the *right* mouse button to drag the zero mark to a new location. As it does when you move a ruler, your mouse pointer changes to a two-headed arrow, pointing up and down if you're pointing at the horizontal ruler, or right and left if you're pointing at the vertical ruler. As you drag, the ruler stays in place but a solid line follows your pointer. When you release the right mouse button, the ruler rezeroes at that line.

To rezero both rulers to the upper-left corner of the page or two-page spread, double-click your left mouse button in that blank box at the intersection of the two rulers.

When you're working inside a text or table frame, a subsection of the horizontal ruler automatically provides a special zero mark just for that frame or current table column. (We discuss text and table frames in Chapter 5.)

Creating Background Pages

When you create a multiple-page publication, you may want certain objects to appear on all or most of the pages. These objects could include the publication's title, your name, page numbers, a company logo or some other graphic, a plea to send money . . . whatever. Microsoft Publisher 97 lets you create a *background* that appears on each page of your publication.

The benefits of using backgrounds are as follows:

- They eliminate the boring, repetitive work of placing and managing objects that appear on every page.
- They eliminate a source of bloated file sizes because information that needs to be repeated is entered only once.
- They enforce design consistency.

To understand Microsoft Publisher 97 backgrounds, imagine each regular publication *(foreground)* page as a piece of see-through tracing paper laid over a cardboard backing. You can see all the objects on the backing, along with the layer of objects on the tracing paper. As you move from page to page, the tracing paper changes but the backing remains the same. If you change something on the tracing paper, only the tracing paper changes. If you change something on the backing, however, that change affects the appearance of any tracing paper laid over that backing. Microsoft Publisher 97's backgrounds work just like that cardboard backing; the foreground pages work like the pieces of tracing paper.

Any objects on a background repeat on foreground pages throughout the publication. Those *background objects* that are not obscured by objects above them in the foreground print together with any *foreground objects* present on each foreground page. To work with the background or any object on it, you must first move the foreground pages out of the way, just as you would lift tracing paper from a cardboard backing.

From the background to the foreground and back again

To move to the background, select <u>V</u>iew⇨<u>G</u>o to Background or press Ctrl+M.

The Ctrl+M shortcut derives from the word Master. Most page layout programs let you create master pages, which work like Microsoft Publisher 97's backgrounds.

Rarely does anything radical happen when you move to the background. Any on-screen changes usually are very subtle, and the background may look like just another blank publication page, sporting the same layout guides as your publication's foreground pages. One way to tell whether you've moved to the background is to look near the bottom of your screen, to the left of the zoom controls. If the page controls are still there, you're in the foreground. If the page controls have been replaced with one or two *background buttons,* as shown in Figure 4-7, you've successfully moved to the background.

Figure 4-7: The background symbol replaces the page controls when you are working in the background.

Background buttons

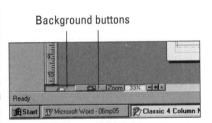

To return to the foreground pages, select <u>V</u>iew⇨<u>G</u>o to Foreground or press Ctrl+M. (This command is a toggle with the G<u>o</u> to Background command.) You return to the last foreground page that you were in, and the normal page controls return in triumph.

Working with multiple backgrounds

When you start a publication, Microsoft Publisher 97 sometimes creates just one background for you and other times creates two, based on the type of publication you create. To determine whether you have one or two backgrounds, move to the background and then observe the area usually occupied by the page controls. If you see only one background button, your publication has only one background. If you see two background buttons, your publication has two backgrounds.

One major difference between Microsoft Publisher 97 and more complicated layout programs is that the other programs let you create any number of *master pages* (backgrounds) and put them at any position in your publication. That flexibility adds additional complexity, but we think that not having the feature is a significant design loss.

To create a second background if you have only one, open the Layout Guides dialog box from the Arrange menu and click the Create Two Backgrounds With Mirrored Guides check box, as previously shown in Figure 4-6. When you create separate, mirrored layout guides for left- and right-facing pages, you automatically create a second background.

When you create a second background, three things happen:

- ✔ The original background becomes the right background.

- ✔ The new background becomes the left background.

- ✔ Microsoft Publisher 97 copies everything on the original (right) background — guides and objects — and places it in mirrored positions on the new (left) background.

If you have two backgrounds and delete one (by unchecking the Create Two Backgrounds With Mirrored Guides check box), the outcome depends on what view you're in at the time. If you're in Single Page view, Microsoft Publisher 97 simply hides all the objects on the left background. If you're in Two-Page Spread view, however, Microsoft Publisher 97 permanently deletes all left-background objects. (Fortunately, Microsoft Publisher 97 warns you of this before actually deleting the background.) Either way, every page in your document now uses the remaining (what was the right) background.

If you later return to using two background pages and are working in Single Page view, Microsoft Publisher 97 restores any hidden left-background objects. If you're working in Two-Page Spread view, Microsoft Publisher 97 copies everything from the single (right) background to mirrored positions on the new (left) background.

To move between background pages (if you have two of them):

- ✔ In Single Page view, click the background buttons to move back and forth from the right to the left master or background page.

- ✔ In Two-Page Spread view, you can see the two buttons, but they are not active. Just click directly on the page and element or object that you want to work on.

Two backgrounds are great for creating facing-page publications. Unfortunately, having twice as many backgrounds means twice as much work setting them up, so use only one background if that's all you need. You can return to a single background by unchecking the Create Two Backgrounds With Mirrored Guides check box. The left background page is eliminated. If any objects are on your left background, Microsoft Publisher 97 opens a dialog box to warn you that those objects will be hidden or deleted.

In addition to providing separate areas for different sets of layout guides, having two backgrounds enables you to set up separate sets of background objects — one set that repeats on left-hand foreground pages, and another set that repeats on right-hand foreground pages. Separate left- and right-hand repeating objects are quite common in facing-page publications. For example, look at the header text along the top of these two pages. On the left-facing page is a page number followed by the name of the current book part; this information is aligned along the page's left (outside) margin. On the right-facing page is the name of the current chapter followed by the page number; this information is aligned along the page's right (outside) margin.

Adding background objects

Adding objects to backgrounds is just like adding objects to foreground pages, which we describe in Chapter 6. Because background and foreground objects must share the final, printed page, however, you should consider a couple of things before you add a background object.

If you have only one background, any object that you put on that background repeats on every foreground page. If you have two backgrounds, any object that you put on the left background repeats on every left-hand foreground page, any object that you put on the right background repeats on every right-hand foreground page, and any object that you put on both backgrounds repeats on every left- *and* right-hand foreground pages. You can eliminate any and all background objects from specific foreground pages, however, as we explain later in this chapter.

You should place your background objects where they won't interfere with foreground objects. The easiest solution is to keep background objects near the margins. If you choose to put an object in the middle of a background instead, it might get covered up by a foreground object. Try to add all your background objects before you begin adding foreground objects. Otherwise, you may need to rearrange your foreground objects to make room for your background objects.

Creating headers and footers

To Microsoft Publisher 97, a *header* is stuff — text, graphics, or both — that repeats along the top of pages, whereas a *footer* is stuff that repeats along the bottom of pages. (You're probably already familiar with this concept from your word processor, and it's the same in Microsoft Publisher 97.) Headers and footers usually contain such boring and traditional information as the publication title, current chapter or other division title, author's name, company or publication-specific logo, and/or page number. Because headers and footers are supposed to repeat on most or all pages, the background is the perfect place to put them.

To create headers and footers, follow these steps:

1. **Select <u>V</u>iew⇨G<u>o</u> to Background or press Ctrl+M to go to the background.**

2. **Add an object(s) where you want your header or footer to appear.**

   The objects that you add could be frames or drawn objects such as lines or circles. The next chapter describes how to work with frames and drawn objects.

3. **If appropriate, fill and format the object and then format its contents.**

Headers and footers should line up with the top or bottom margin. Otherwise, they wouldn't really be headers and footers — they'd be "middlers"! To help your headers and footers line up perfectly, set a ruler guide for the bottom of the header and the top of the footer. Also, make sure that the Snap to <u>G</u>uides command (see the prior discussion in this chapter) is turned on before you add your object(s) to the header and footer.

If you're working on a facing-page publication, it's also a good idea to have the headers and footers align to the outside margins, as the headers in this book do. This design makes seeing those headers and footers easier for readers when flipping through your printed publication.

If your object is a text frame, you may want to type the text, add a fancy border around the frame, make the text larger and bolder, and right-align the text within the frame. To really make the header or footer stand out, you can add a drawn object, such as a rectangle that's filled with a color and has a thick border. You can even use the WordArt OLE server (see Chapter 9) to create special text effects that you can place in your headers and footers.

Here's a way to save some work if you need two backgrounds with similar headers and footers. Set up the headers and footers on one background, make sure that you're in Two-Page Spread view, and then create the second background. Microsoft Publisher 97 automatically copies your headers and footers to mirrored positions on the new background.

Inserting page numbers

One of the most common uses for headers and footers is to hold page numbers. Microsoft Publisher 97 is more than happy to number your pages for you. Nice program. Good program. Sit. Stay. Have a bone.

To number pages, all you need to do is add a semi-secret page-numbering code called a *page-number mark* to a header or footer text frame in the background. If your publication has two backgrounds and you want page numbers to appear on both left- and right-hand pages, you need to insert a page-number mark on *both* backgrounds.

Follow these steps to add page numbers to a header or footer:

1. **Choose View⇨Go to Background or press Ctrl+M.**

   You can't insert page-number marks on a foreground page, even if you want a number only on that one page. Even if you ask nicely.

2. **Click the text frame to which you want to add the page-number mark and position the insertion (I-beam) cursor in it.**

   A selected frame displays eight little black boxes, or *reshape handles,* along its perimeter.

   To create a text frame, click the Text tool in the toolbox and drag your frame on the layout.

3. **Type some identifying text, such as the word Page (optional).**

4. **Choose the Insert⇨Page Numbers command from the menu bar.**

   The page-number mark appears. Although this mark appears to be just a pound sign (#), it changes to the appropriate page number on each foreground page. Honestly!

5. **Format the page-number mark as you would any text (optional).**

   Formatting text is covered in Chapter 7.

Don't try to be sneaky and just type a pound sign from your keyboard to indicate where you want page numbers to appear. Although it looks just like a page-number mark, it produces only pound signs on your foreground pages.

In the foreground, each page proudly displays its own page number. Microsoft Publisher 97 uses only Arabic numerals (1, 2, 3, and so on) for page numbering. If you want to number your pages some other way, perhaps with small Roman numerals (i, ii, iii, and so on) for the introductory pages of a book, you have to number each page manually. Sorry.

Make sure that you leave enough room in your text frame to fit the longest page number in your publication. Otherwise, longer page numbers may get cut off. If you have this problem with an existing text frame, see Chapter 5 to find out how to resize a frame.

If you're desktop-publishing something that requires separate series of page numbers, such as several report sections that will be printed with other report sections, create each section of your publication in a separate file to accommodate those separate series. You can then set your page numbers in each publication to start at something other than 1. Choose Tools⇨Options and use the Start with page text box in the Options dialog box for this purpose. Microsoft Publisher 97 lets you use any number up to an amazing 16,766. This affects the page numbering only for the current publication.

Getting a date

Placing dates and times in your headers and footers isn't much different than putting page numbers there. Follow the procedure described in the preceding section, but substitute the Insert⇨Date or Time command from the menu bar in place of the Insert⇨Page Numbers command. Microsoft Publisher 97 opens up the Date and Time dialog box, as shown in Figure 4-8. Click the format of choice and then click the Update Automatically radio button (the default) if you want to create a placeholder that updates the date whenever you open or print your publication. The program cleverly uses the dates and times set in your Windows 95 Date/Time control panel. If you choose the Insert As Plain Text radio button instead, Microsoft Publisher 97 simply inserts the current date or time and doesn't update it.

Figure 4-8:
The Date
and Time
dialog box.

Suppressing background objects

Traditionally, headers and footers are left off a publication's first page. In larger publications, headers and footers are also usually left off the first page of each chapter or other major division. The headers in this book are a prime example. Go ahead: Flip through this book and you'll see.

To hide *all* background objects, move to the foreground page for which you want to hide background objects, and select the Ignore Background command from the View menu.

No ambiguity here. If you're viewing a single page, the background disappears. When you apply this command to a two-page spread, Microsoft Publisher 97 opens up the Ignore Background dialog box, shown in Figure 4-9, to ask you to select which page you want to ignore — the Left Page, Right Page, or both.

Figure 4-9:
The Ignore
Background
dialog box.

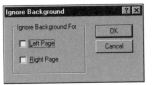

The Ignore Background command is one of those toggle commands: Issue it once to turn it on, issue it again to turn it off. If you're viewing two pages, the Ignore Background dialog box appears again. Just uncheck one or both boxes and then click OK.

Electronic masking tape

Sometimes, you may want to hide some, but not all, background objects. Perhaps you have a nice company logo that you want on every page, but you want to leave the page number off the first page. To do this, you can employ a trick that we like to call *electronic masking tape.* The secret of electronic masking tape lies in the fact that any opaque (non-seethrough) foreground object can cover up any background object.

Because text frames are one of the few Microsoft Publisher 97 objects that are opaque by default, they make a convenient choice for electronic masking tape. Simply move to the foreground page and draw a text frame (as explained in Chapter 5) over the background object that you want to hide. Or you can use just about any other object that you want. If the object is transparent, you can make it opaque by selecting it and then pressing Ctrl+T.

Adding and Deleting Pages

Microsoft Publisher 97 offers you several ways to add pages — perhaps more ways than you'll ever need. And if you end up with *too* many pages, you can, of course, delete them.

Adding pages

When you create a blank publication, Microsoft Publisher 97 generally gives you only one page to begin with. The Page Wizards give you a number of pages (sometimes you can select this number as an option) depending upon the document type. Regardless of how many pages Microsoft Publisher 97 creates by default, you can always add more blank pages if you need them.

Your new pages may not appear entirely blank. They may display the margin and other layout guides that you've set up to appear on every page of your publication. They may also display some background objects. We discuss background pages and objects in Chapter 5.

Microsoft Publisher 97 provides two ways to insert a blank page (or two) at the end of your document:

 ✔ Click the Next Page button to advance past the last page in your document, as explained previously in this chapter.

 ✔ Press Ctrl+Shift+N.

If you're in Single Page view, Microsoft Publisher 97 inserts one new blank page and moves you to that page. If you're in Two-Page Spread view, Microsoft Publisher 97 inserts two new blank pages and moves your view to those pages.

Oops. If you insert a page by accident, you can choose Edit⇨Undo Insert Page(s) or press Ctrl+Z to remove it.

You aren't limited to adding pages to the end of your publication. If you select the Page command on the Insert menu, you can insert any number of pages before the current page, after the current page, or, if you are in a two-page spread, between the current pages. You can add blank pages, add pages with a single text frame, or even duplicate the contents of a single page.

 Follow these steps to insert a new page or pages into your publication:

1. **Move to the page or spread that you want to immediately precede, follow, or flank your new pages.**

2. **Choose Insert⇨Page.**

   The Insert Page dialog box appears, as shown in Figure 4-10. This dialog box is one of the most useful ones you'll encounter, and its options for page creation can save you a lot of time.

   Although Ctrl+Shift+N is listed on the Insert menu as a shortcut for the Insert Page command, Ctrl+Shift+N does *not* open the Insert Page dialog box. Instead, it immediately adds one blank page (if you're in Single Page view) or two blank pages (if you're in Two-Page Spread view) after the current page or spread. No questions asked. We object to listing keystrokes that don't exactly call up a menu command, and we think it should be a bug (it quacks like a bug!), but the same behavior existed in the previous version of Microsoft Publisher 97.

3. **In the Number Of New Pages text box, type the number of pages that you want to insert.**

   The default is 1 for Single Page view and 2 for Two-Page Spread view.

   Inserting pages in even numbers is a good idea so that your left-hand pages don't become right-hand pages and vice versa. This rule of thumb isn't as important at the very beginning stages of a publication, but inserting pages in odd numbers can really wreak havoc if you insert them after having laid down some objects.

4. **Click the radio button that indicates where you want your new page(s) to be inserted.**

   Your choices are Before left page, After right page, and Between Pages.

5. **Under Options, click to indicate what kind of pages you want to insert.**

   - **Insert Blank Pages:** Inserts pages that have no objects of their own, just like those pages that are added when you insert pages using page controls.

   - **Create One Text Frame On Each Page:** Places a blank text frame on each new page that you create. Each text frame matches your publication's margin guides. This option is an excellent choice for publications such as books, which have page after page of primarily text.

   - **Duplicate All Objects On Page Number:** Makes a copy of whatever objects already exist on the page number you specify in the option box and places those objects on each of the new pages.

6. **Click OK.**

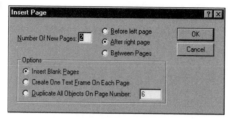

Figure 4-10: The Insert Page dialog box for a two-page spread.

If you accidentally insert pages, you can remove those pages by immediately choosing the Edit⇔Undo Insert Page(s) command from the menu bar.

You have to place the objects on the source page *before* you issue the Insert⇔Page command. If you copy text and table frames, you get copies of the frames themselves, not the text within them.

You may be tempted to use the Duplicate option to copy objects that you want on every publication page, such as headers, footers, and page numbers. Don't. Doing so creates larger file sizes. Use *backgrounds* instead. With a background, a single instance of an object serves all of your printed pages. See our discussion of backgrounds earlier in this chapter for more details.

If you're importing a great deal of text and you don't know how many pages you need to fit that text, you can have Microsoft Publisher 97 automatically add the necessary number of pages for you, create text frames on those pages, and then fill those frames with the text. Chapter 6 tells you more about this labor-saving feature.

Deleting pages

Deleting a page, especially from Single Page view, can be frighteningly easy — and shouldn't be taken lightly. When you delete a page, it's as if the page you deleted never existed. No mourning. No nothing. No kidding. (Have we mentioned backup recently? Like in the last page or two?)

When you delete a page, all the objects on that page are also deleted. Only objects off the page, on the scratch area, remain untouched. Microsoft Publisher 97 then automatically renumbers the remaining pages so that you don't end up with a wacky page sequence.

Follow these steps to delete a page:

1. Move to the page you want to delete.

2. **Choose Edit⇨Delete Page.**

   Note that this command is not available if you are currently viewing the background of your publication.

   If you are in the Single Page view, Microsoft Publisher 97 opens an alert box. Click OK to delete the page or Cancel to continue working without deleting the page. If you are in the Two-Page Spread view, Microsoft Publisher 97 opens the Delete Page dialog box, as shown in Figure 4-11.

3. **Click the radio button for the option you want: Both Pages, Left Page Only, or Right Page Only.**

4. **Click OK.**

Figure 4-11:
The Delete Page dialog box for a two-page spread.

If you accidentally delete pages, you can restore them and their contents by immediately choosing Edit⇨Undo Delete Page or by pressing Ctrl+Z.

We think that deleting pages, even with an alert box, is dangerous. Pay particular attention to page deletions, as they are an excellent method for losing work.

As with inserting pages, it's a good idea to delete pages in even numbers so that your left- and right-hand pages don't get fouled up. If you delete just a left- or right-hand page in the Two-Page Spread view, Microsoft Publisher 97 opens a dialog box asking you to consider deleting pages in even numbers instead.

Try as you might, and as much fun as it might be to do it, you cannot delete the only page in a single-page publication. If you try, Microsoft Publisher 97 simply deletes any objects on that page but leaves the page itself in place.

Modifying the Page Layout

Every publication you create, no matter how basic, already has a specific page layout that determines each page's physical size, orientation, and whether the paper requires special folding to create the individual publication pages. But just because the page layout is determined the moment you start a publication, that doesn't mean that you can't change it later through the Page Setup command on the File menu.

Do you get the feeling that there isn't *anything* that you can't change later on in a publication? We don't think that there is, but changing things — including page layouts — exacts a heavier and heavier toll as you go along. For example, if you lay down all the text and graphics in a 16-page pamphlet and then change the size of the pages, you may find yourself with plenty of work to do just to get your text and graphics to fit properly again. Making the correct choices early in your project saves you considerable time later on. The time that you spend fixing up your publication is time that you don't spend doing the creative work that makes desktop publishing fun.

Always select your target printer, as discussed in Chapter 12, before you spend any time adjusting the page setup.

To change the page setup of a document, Select File⇨Page Setup. The Page Setup dialog box, shown in Figure 4-12, appears.

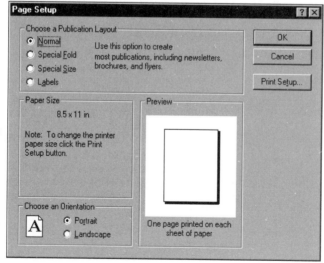

Figure 4-12:
The Page Setup dialog box for a Normal setup.

Microsoft Publisher 97 provides four major page-layout categories:

- **Normal:** Creates newsletters, brochures, flyers, and many other layouts.
- **Special Fold:** Creates greeting cards, tent cards, and book folds.

✔ **Special Size:** Creates posters, banners, business cards, and index cards.

✔ **Labels:** Creates mailing labels and full-page labels.

The sections that follow describe these categories and their myriad options. Regardless of what page-layout category you choose, however, you can also set an orientation for your paper:

✔ **Portrait:** The most common orientation, this prints your publication pages from top to bottom along the length of the paper — as you normally would if you were using a typewriter or word-processing program. In full-page publications, this option creates pages that are taller than they are wide.

✔ **Landscape:** This orientation turns the paper sideways so that your pages print from side to side along the width of the paper. In full-page publications, this option creates pages that are wider than they are tall. Spreadsheets, reports, and many graphs are often printed using this orientation.

Some printers, particularly the more ancient ones, don't enable you to change the paper orientation. If this is the case with your printer, the orientation options are dimmed.

By combining various layout categories, options within those categories, various custom settings, and paper orientation, you can get Microsoft Publisher 97 to print just about any publication conceivable, no matter how large or small.

The Normal layout

The Normal layout option consists of *full pages* — pages that match the size of the paper they're printed on — and requires little or no special handling.

Notice that the Paper Size area of the Page Setup dialog box displays the size of the paper that your target printer is currently set up to print on. Microsoft Publisher 97 lets you create layouts with dimensions ranging from 0.25 inches up to 240 inches (20 feet).

To change the paper size and the source of the paper, you need to make selections from the Print Setup dialog box. You can get to this dialog box directly from the Page Setup dialog box by clicking the Print Setup button. Or you can access this same dialog box by selecting File➪Print Setup. What's "normal" in terms of your printer's capabilities is determined by the print engine and the printer driver software that you have.

The Special Fold layout

The Special Fold layout option is for publications that require you to fold a single sheet of paper once or twice to create the individual publication pages. That is, one sheet prints with two or four publication pages on one side, and folding the sheet separates those pages. The advantage of special folds is that you end up with print on multiple sides of the publication while actually printing on only one side of the sheet of paper. Take a look at double-folded commercial greeting cards sometime to see what we mean.

When you select the Special Fold option, the Page Setup dialog box changes and appears as it does in Figure 4-13. Notice the new options in the Choose a Special Fold list box. It now offers you the following setups:

- ✔ **Book Fold:** Use this layout to create single-fold books and booklets. You fold the printed sheet in half with the two long edges touching to create two pages.

- ✔ **Tent Card:** Use this layout to create single-fold tent cards. You fold the printed sheet in half with the two short edges touching to get a free-standing tabletop card.

- ✔ **Side Fold Card:** Use this layout to create double-fold greeting cards. You first fold the printed sheet in half with the two short edges touching and then fold the sheet in half in the opposite direction to produce a card that opens along the side.

- ✔ **Top Fold Card:** This layout also creates double-fold greeting cards. In this case, though, you first fold the printed sheet in half with the two *long* edges touching and then fold the sheet in the opposite direction to produce a card that opens along the bottom.

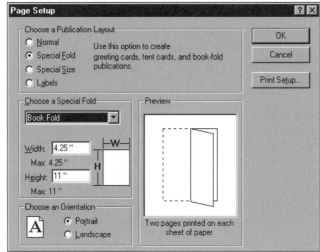

Figure 4-13:
The Page
Setup
dialog box
for a
Special Fold
setup.

By default, pages in a special-fold publication are exactly one-half or one-quarter of the paper size. You can manually adjust the Width and Height settings in the Page Setup dialog box to have each page take up less (but not more) than that amount of space. If you do change these settings, keep in mind that you then have to trim the extra paper off the sheet *and* fold it to produce the final publication. What a pain! A better solution is to set up your target printer to use a different paper size (assuming that you can get that size paper and that your printer supports that size). This strategy saves you both the trouble of changing the settings and manually trimming the paper.

By their very nature, special-fold publications contain either two or four pages. If you have something other than the appropriate number of pages in your publication, Microsoft Publisher 97 opens a dialog box after you click the OK button and offers to add or delete pages as necessary to give your publication the correct number of pages. Click Yes to let Microsoft Publisher 97 adjust your pages for you, or click No if you're feeling especially obstinate.

Not all folding publications (brochures, for example) require special-fold layouts. They may, however, benefit from appropriately set grid guides, as explained earlier in this chapter.

The Special Size layout

The Special Size layout option is for publications whose pages are either larger or smaller than the paper they are printed on. Publications that may be larger than the paper they're printed on include banners and posters; to create the final publication, you have to tape several sheets of paper together. Publications that may be smaller than the paper they're printed on include business and index cards; to create the final publication, you trim off the parts of the paper that you don't need.

When you select the Special Size option, the Page Setup dialog box looks as it does in Figure 4-14. Among the size options that you are offered in the Choose a Publication Size list box are the following:

- ✔ **Printer Sheet Size:** This selection is redundant. It's the same as choosing the Normal layout option in the box above, so ignore this option.

- ✔ **Index Card (5 × 3 in):** This selection creates index cards, with one card per sheet.

- ✔ **Business Card (3.5 × 2 in):** This option creates business cards, with one card per sheet.

✔ **Poster (18 × 24 in)** and **Poster (24 × 36 in):** These two options create posters by printing out several sheets that you tape together.

✔ **Custom:** This is a catch-all option. It creates publications in any size you want, just in case none of the other options does the trick for you.

✔ **Banner (5 ft), Banner (10 ft),** and **Banner (15 ft):** These options create banners by printing the publication over several sheets of $8^1/_2 \times 11$-inch paper that you tape together later.

✔ **Custom Banner:** This option is the catch-all option for banners. It enables you to set height and width to create banners in any size you want.

As you select these different options, watch the Preview box to get an idea of how your publication will print.

The whole point of a Special Size layout is that it can create a special size. Therefore, you will undoubtedly want to enter new settings in the Width, Height, Banner Width, and/or Banner Height text boxes, depending upon the layout you choose. If you do change any of these settings, Microsoft Publisher 97 changes your special-size option to Custom or Custom Banner accordingly.

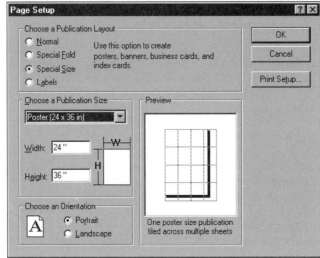

Figure 4-14:
The Page Setup dialog box for a Special Size setup.

Notice that, when you change the orientation for a Special Size layout, you are not changing the orientation of your publication, but rather the orientation of the sheet(s) of paper you're printing it on. If you'd rather change the orientation of the publication (for publications other than banners), instead use the Width and Height text boxes above the orientation section.

The Labels layout

The Labels layout option is for creating mailing labels or full-page labels. When you select the Labels option, the Page Setup dialog box looks as it does in Figure 4-15. You can choose from all the popular Avery label sizes.

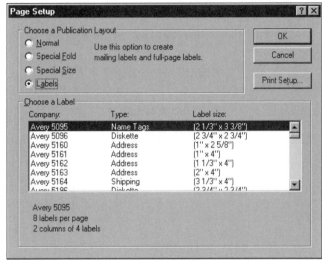

Figure 4-15:
The Page Setup dialog box for a Labels setup.

As you select these different label types, a description of the label appears at the bottom of the dialog box showing the label name, the number of columns, and the number of labels per column.

You can use the Labels layout options to create a mail merge using the commands on the Mail Merge menu, or to create labels manually.

Getting Your Pages Set to Print

Perhaps the most common design mistake that starting desktop publishers make is doing their page layout with the wrong printer driver. The mistake is easy enough to make, even for experienced desktop publishers who are aware of the problem. A change in printers, the service that you are using, or the specifications for the publication itself can result in changing printer drivers. And you may not have control over those situations.

If you lay out your pages using the wrong printer driver, many of the page setup options that you take for granted may not exist when you send your file out to be printed. After all your hard work of carefully nudging objects around the page, you may find that objects are cut off, blurry, or otherwise poorly printed. If you are having your publication printed through a professional printer or service bureau, talking about the printer driver before you initiate a design project can really help you out and save you time. See Chapter 12 for more detailed information about printing your publication.

Make sure that you are designing your page for the correct printer as early in the project as possible.

Chapter 5

Objects and Frames

● ●

In This Chapter

▶ Understanding frames (what they are and why you need them)

▶ Working with frames

▶ Creating and working with drawn objects

▶ Creating special effects with layers

▶ Using groups to speed up your work

● ●

*T*he preceding chapter discusses the basic elements of your publication's pages. It's now time to add structure to your pages with frames and drawn objects. In this chapter, we focus on how you use frames and drawn objects to create a design framework into which you can add the content that makes each publication unique.

In Microsoft Publisher 97's language, an *object* represents any publication design element: a text or graphic frame, a line, a circle, or other item on a page. Objects fall into different categories, and each category has a set of properties. After you know how one object in a category works, you can understand the behaviors and properties of related objects (in that same category). With a good set of objects, you can conquer the world.

This chapter focuses on two types of objects: those that are contained in frames and those that aren't. *Frames* are container objects into which you place the content of your publication. Text and graphics are two common examples of publication elements that require frames. You can also use frames to create tables and special text effects.

Not all objects on a layout use frames, however. Some objects — such as lines, circles, rectangles, ovals, and other shapes that you draw using the tools in Microsoft Publisher 97's toolbox — are complete, in, of, and by themselves. You find out how to create these types of objects in this chapter as well.

Working with Frames

As we mentioned, frames are *container objects* that hold your publication's content. Frames have properties that you can change. Frames have a size and shape, and they can be resized and moved. They can be transparent or opaque, have color or patterns applied to them, and have other properties common to *drawn* objects. Frames exist as separate objects, but you can associate frames together as a group by using the equivalent of electronic glue.

Frames also have special properties that are not common to objects in general. Frames can be linked so that the contents of one frame flow into the next frame. This is particularly valuable for text in a long document, when you may want an article to begin on one page and continue on another.

Microsoft Publisher 97 provides four frame types:

- ✔ **Text frames:** These frames are containers for text. Text frames can be linked to create what Microsoft Publisher 97 calls *stories*.

- ✔ **Table frames:** These frames are containers for tables. They help you arrange text in tidy rows and columns. Table frames are useful for creating graphic arrays or matrices, providing a dense representation of data, or creating things such as a table of contents in a publication.

- ✔ **Picture frames:** Microsoft Publisher 97 requires that you put pictures and other graphics inside picture frames. Picture frames have special properties that let you modify the way graphics look in them.

- ✔ **WordArt frames:** WordArt, a separate OLE server program, creates graphic objects based on type (you know, the characters and symbols that you make with your keyboard). By using WordArt, you can create many special text effects that are useful in headlines and other places.

Technically speaking, Microsoft Publisher 97 offers one other frame: the PageWizard frame. This frame, however, isn't really a frame type per se. It simply lets you specify an area in which the Calendar, Ad, Coupon, or Logo PageWizard operates to create that kind of object.

Each of the program's four frame types behaves a little differently. In addition to holding different sorts of objects, each type varies in how you create, delete, and otherwise manipulate it.

OLE! OLE!

A WordArt frame would be better termed an *OLE frame*, after the kind of object that fills that frame. Microsoft Publisher 97 makes good use of OLE (Object Linking and Embedding), a technology that enables you to incorporate into your layout many kinds of data that the program doesn't directly support or can't directly create. Although Microsoft Publisher 97 incorporates WordArt directly in its package, you can create frames by using any OLE server.

OLE is a special form of cut-and-paste and is implemented by using the Edit⇨Paste Special command on the menu bar. You can create either *embedded* OLE objects or *linked* OLE objects. When you create an embedded object, the object is placed and stored — that is, embedded — right in your publication file, as is the information that enables Microsoft Publisher 97 to link back to the program used to create the object. With a linked object, the only thing that's stored in your publication file is the data needed to link back to the original OLE server program.

Whether you create linked or embedded OLE objects, you make any changes to them in the OLE server program rather than in Microsoft Publisher 97. You can specify that you want the changed objects to be updated automatically in your layout or that you want to update objects manually, on a case-by-case basis. Also, you can choose to apply changes made to embedded data to the copy of the object that exists in your publication only.

The OLE tool in the toolbox enables you to select an OLE server program and create an OLE frame. Microsoft Publisher 97 ships with two other server programs, Microsoft Draw 1.01 and a picture browser for the Microsoft Clip Gallery. Select the OLE server from the pop-up menu to choose from those two programs. You can also use the More command to open up any other OLE server registered with Windows.

Although OLE is nice to use in other kinds of programs, it's an essential part of working in a page layout program such as Microsoft Publisher 97. If you understand this feature, it can save you time, disk space, maintenance, and grief. We revisit OLE throughout this book.

Creating frames

To create a frame, you select the appropriate tool in the toolbox and click and drag with the tool on your layout. Figure 5-1 shows you where each tool is located in the toolbox. The tool that you select determines the frame's type, whereas your drawing action determines the frame's size and position in the publication.

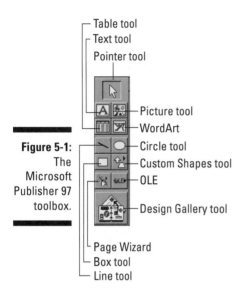

Table tool
Text tool
Pointer tool

Picture tool
WordArt
Circle tool

Figure 5-1:
The
Microsoft
Publisher 97
toolbox.

Custom Shapes tool
OLE

Design Gallery tool

Page Wizard
Box tool
Line tool

As soon as you click a tool, a Formatting toolbar appears underneath the main Microsoft Publisher 97 toolbar with buttons that let you change the format of your frame or the objects that you put in it. For the most part, these formatting buttons are duplicates of menu commands. Plenty of formatting tools are available for text and table frames, but just a few tools apply to WordArt and picture frames.

Follow these steps to draw a text or picture frame:

1. **Click the Text or Picture tool in the toolbox.**

   Your cursor changes to a crosshair. The status bar message area now tells you how to draw your frame.

2. **Move the crosshair over the publication page or scratch area.**

   The sliding ruler lines and the status bar's position box show your exact position.

3. **Click and drag to create the outline of your frame.**

   As you drag, the program draws a sample to show you the size and shape of your new frame. The status bar's size box indicates the frame's size.

To draw a frame from the center out, hold the Ctrl key as you draw. To draw a perfectly square frame, hold the Shift key. To do both, hold down the Ctrl+Shift keys together as you drag.

4. Release the mouse button to create the frame.

Microsoft Publisher 97 creates your text or picture frame and selects it (makes it active) so that you can work with it further.

Figure 5-2 shows you a selected text frame. A picture frame looks the same but lacks the Connect Frame button (used to link text frames together for automatic content flow control) that's shown in Figure 5-2.

Figure 5-2:
A newly created and selected text frame with the Connect Frame button indicated.

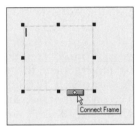

To draw a table or WordArt frame, the first four steps are the same as for creating a text or picture frame. But after you release the mouse button to create the frame, Microsoft Publisher 97 opens the Create Table dialog box, shown in Figure 5-3.

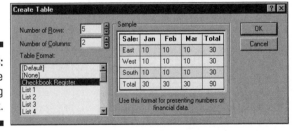

Figure 5-3:
The Create Table dialog box.

You then need to take the following additional steps:

1. Select the number of rows and columns that you want in your table.

2. Choose a format for your table (optional).

3. Click the OK button.

Your table frame is now complete. A sample table frame is shown in Figure 5-4.

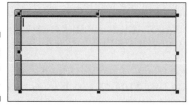

Figure 5-4:
A sample
table frame.

So far, so good. All three frames that we've just discussed behave similarly. The WordArt frame is somewhat different, though. WordArt is an OLE server, so when you draw a frame for that object type, the WordArt program opens, as shown in Figure 5-5.

You then have two choices: You can create your WordArt graphic or you can press the Esc key twice to close WordArt and complete the frame. You can always return to work with your WordArt object by double-clicking on the frame. When you do, WordArt opens up on your screen and you can make any changes without leaving Microsoft Publisher 97 (this process is called *editing in place,* in OLE lingo). You find out more about WordArt in Chapter 9.

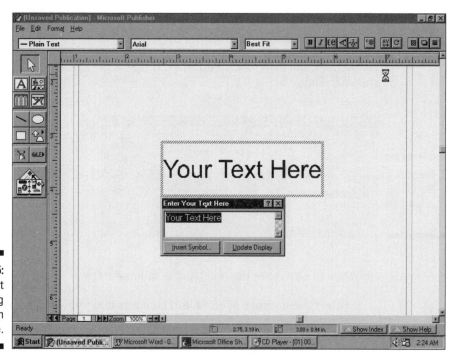

Figure 5-5:
A WordArt
frame being
edited in
place.

The first time that you work with a tool, the program offers to show you a Quick Demo that is part of its first-time Help feature. You can turn this option off or reset it with the Reset All button in the More Options dialog box to view the demos again. See Chapter 3 for details.

The PageWizard tool is even more fun. When you click that tool in the toolbox, a pop-up menu offering the Calendar, Ad, Coupon, and Logo PageWizards appears, as shown in Figure 5-6. Select the kind of wizard that you want to run and then click and drag the size of the frame that you want the wizard to fill. (If you don't select a wizard type, the frame is automatically filled by a calendar.)

Figure 5-6:
The
PageWizard's
tool menu.

After you make your selections, the program fills the frame with the contents that the wizard creates. If you examine a selected PageWizard frame closely, you find that it is really a grouped set of frames: For example, a calendar PageWizard frame contains a WordArt frame (for the title) and a table frame (for the dates). Also, PageWizards can create grouped sets composed of different elements, such as text and picture frames.

After you draw a frame, Microsoft Publisher 97 automatically deselects the frame tool and activates the Pointer tool so that you can manipulate your object. This feature is a pain if you want to draw several frames of the same type one right after the other. To get a frame tool to stay selected, press the Ctrl key and click the tool icon. When you're done drawing frames with that tool, deselect the tool by clicking any other tool in the toolbox. Or click outside of your frames to deselect them. These techniques work for any tool in the toolbox (for example, the Line, Box, and Circle tools), not just for frame tools.

Selecting things

In Microsoft Publisher 97, before you can change a frame or object, you have to select it. After you select an element, you can fill it, resize it, move it, delete it, or do whatever your heart desires. You can also select multiple frames or any set of objects on a page, thus enabling you to perform the same operation on a set of frames or objects simultaneously — provided that the operation is legal for the selected elements.

For example, if you have two text frames selected, Microsoft Publisher 97 lets you add borders to both of them at the same time. If you try to paste text from the Clipboard into two selected text frames simultaneously, however, the program gets confused and creates a third text frame with your text.

A frame is automatically selected after you finish drawing it, as shown back in Figure 5-2. You can tell that a frame is selected because it displays eight little black boxes, called *selection handles,* around its perimeter. Some selected frames display more than just selection handles. A text frame displays a Connect Frame button near its bottom-right corner, and a table frame displays two selection bars (Select Table Columns and Select Table Rows) along its top and left edges. (A table frame looks and acts like a miniature spreadsheet, which is what it is.) You find out how to connect text frames and work with tables in the next chapter.

Use the Pointer tool to select frames (and objects) in Microsoft Publisher 97. The following are selection techniques that you can use:

- ✔ **To select a single frame, just click it.**
- ✔ **To select additional frames, hold down the Shift or Ctrl key and click the frames.**
- ✔ **To deselect one frame from a range of selected objects, hold down the Shift or Ctrl key and click the frame.**
- ✔ **To select multiple frames that are close to one another, click and drag around the frames.** As you drag, Microsoft Publisher 97 shows you a *selection box* — a dotted line that indicates the area you're encompassing. When the selection box surrounds all the frames (or objects) that you want to select, release the mouse button.
- ✔ **To select everything on the current publication page(s) and the scratch area, choose the Edit⇨Select All command.** (You don't need the Pointer tool selected to perform this task.)

These same selection techniques work for all types of objects, not just frames.

Figure 5-7 shows you several frames and objects selected on a layout. The selected objects are, clockwise from top left, a shape, two text frames, and a table frame. Notice that you find a single *bounding box* (the rectangle that encompasses the selected items) around them, but each object still has its own set of selection handles. (The rounded arrow shape is not selected with this range of objects.)

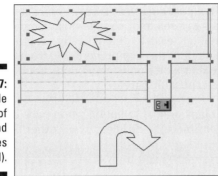

Figure 5-7:
A multiple
selection of
objects and
frames
(ungrouped).

You can tell that this multiple selection is *ungrouped* because the picture on the Group Object button so indicates (it looks like two unjoined puzzle pieces) and because each object retains its own selection handles. In the ungrouped condition, the objects and frames retain their individual identities. (Microsoft Publisher 97 handles the objects as independent entities unless they are *grouped;* you find out about grouping later in this chapter.) Because a multiple selection is not a single object, you cannot resize the selection or any individual component, but you can move the selection about and apply other commands, such as formatting. For example, if you apply a border to the multiple selection, each component of the selection takes on that border format.

Sometimes when you click a frame (or object), you can't select or modify it. If this happens, check out the following possibilities:

- ✔ **The frame or object may be a background object.** To select a background object, move to the background by choosing <u>V</u>iew➪<u>G</u>o to Background or pressing Ctrl+M.

- ✔ **The frame or object is grouped.** Figure 5-8 shows you the same set of objects shown in Figure 5-7, but this time they are grouped together. You can click the Group button to ungroup a group; look for more about groups later in this chapter.

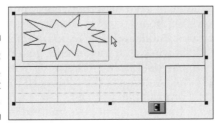

Figure 5-8:
A selected,
grouped set
of objects.

After you're done working with a particular frame or set of frames, deselect them so that you don't accidentally delete or change them in some way. Selected frames can be frighteningly easy to delete. Many programs offer a Lock command to freeze objects (and thereby prevent you from accidentally moving or deleting them). But Microsoft Publisher 97 does not have this handy feature, so you must be especially careful.

To deselect frames, click in a blank area of the publication page or scratch area. Or click a single frame (or object) to deselect every other frame and select just that one.

Editing frames

Because frames are container objects, you can make two types of deletions:

- ✔ You can delete the entire frame itself, which also deletes all of its contents.
- ✔ You can delete the contents of the frame and leave the frame intact.

To delete a frame, you select the frame and press Delete. In the case of a table frame, you have a container with many "drawers"; you can delete the contents of each cell in the table by selecting the contents of that cell and pressing Delete. When you have selected text in a text frame or an insertion point in a cell of a table frame, you must select the frame and press Ctrl+Del to delete the frame. Using only the Delete key in those cases deletes the selected text or the contents of the current cell in the table.

In these cases of text or table frames, you may notice that the commands Delete Text and Delete Text Frame (or Delete Table Frame) appear on the Edit menu. These Delete commands bypass the Windows Clipboard and simply remove the object from your layout. If you want to make use of the Windows Clipboard, you need to use the Cut, Copy, and Paste commands, which you also find on the Edit menu.

The Windows Clipboard is a piece of computer memory (RAM) that can store text, formatted text, graphics, and other objects. (It's sort of like a temporary holding tank where you can keep data that you want to use again.) You can use the Windows Clipboard to work with frames and the contents of frames within Microsoft Publisher 97. The operations that we outline in the following bulleted list work with frames and, generally, with objects of other types. When you use the Clipboard between Windows programs, you can transfer only the contents of the Clipboard that the receiving program understands. For example, you can't paste a Microsoft Publisher 97 frame into WordPad, but you can move formatted text between the two programs.

The Edit menu's Cut, Copy, and Paste commands work as follows:

- ✔ **Cut:** Choose Edit⇨Cut or press Ctrl+X to place the current selection onto the Windows Clipboard and remove it from your layout. The previous contents of the Clipboard are lost.

- ✔ **Copy:** Choose Edit⇨Copy or press Ctrl+C to make a copy of your selected element and place it onto the Windows Clipboard. The selection remains intact on your layout. The previous contents of the Clipboard are lost.

  Copying is a great timesaver and an ideal way to make exact duplicates of frames that you've already drawn. Here's a great shortcut: To quickly copy a selected frame or object, press Ctrl and drag it to a new location.

- ✔ **Paste:** Choose Edit⇨Paste or press Ctrl+V to place the contents of the Windows Clipboard on your layout at your current position. The previous contents of the Clipboard remain intact. You can apply the Paste command any number of times you want.

  Pasted text is placed at the insertion point. If it finds no insertion point, Microsoft Publisher 97 creates a text frame in the center of your screen and places the text in it. If a cut or copied text frame is on the Clipboard, the Paste command puts the frame back on the page at the position from which it came.

  If an object such as a line is on the Clipboard, Microsoft Publisher 97 pastes that object at a position that's offset slightly from the original selected object. If you move to a new page after you place an object on the Clipboard, the object, when pasted, is placed on the new page at the same position that it appeared on the original page.

  Depending upon your selection, the Cut, Copy, and Paste commands appear differently on the Edit menu to reflect what is selected: Cut Text Frame, Cut Picture Frame, Cut Table, Cut Text, and so on.

When you flush the contents of the Clipboard, either by replacing them (with another Cut or Copy command) or by restarting your computer, the contents are gone and cannot be restored.

The Cut, Copy, and Paste commands also show up on the context-sensitive menu that appears when you right-click a frame or object. Figure 5-9 shows you this menu for a text frame. You can select the entire contents of a page or publication and cut and paste it to another page or publication. You can also drag and drop text, frames, and other objects between publications if you have two copies of Microsoft Publisher 97 open on your screen.

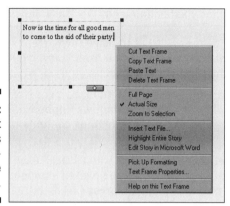

Figure 5-9:
A text
frame's
context-
sensitive
menu.

You should definitely explore the right-click menus for every frame and object that Microsoft Publisher 97 creates. They offer many editing and modification commands that provide useful shortcuts.

The Edit menu also offers another Paste command: Paste Special. Paste Special calls up objects that must be managed by outside programs through object linking and embedding, or OLE. Earlier in this chapter, in the section on creating WordArt frames, we discuss one example of OLE. Microsoft Publisher 97 can be an OLE client and use the services of any OLE server program that is recognized by Windows for a particular object's file type.

Filling frames

Frames are so important to creating publications that we devote some entire chapters in this book to them. Mourn the trees! The next two chapters offer more information about text frames, and Chapter 6 discusses table frames as well. Because WordArt frames create special text objects that are really graphics, we save the discussion of them for the chapter on type, where the lingo flies fast and thick — that is, Chapter 8. Chapter 9 covers picture frames.

Moving and resizing frames

For one reason or another, frames don't always end up the right size or shape or at the place where you want them to be. Nobody's perfect.

To move a frame (or object), move your pointer over the border or the shape itself until the pointer turns into a truck with the word *Move* on it. Then, click and drag the frame or object to a new location.

You can constrain a move to either the vertical or horizontal direction by holding down the Shift key.

As you drag, a dotted outline of the frame follows your pointer. When the outline is where you want your frame, release your mouse button.

If you want to move a frame or set of frames to a different page within your publication, drag the frame or set completely off the publication page and onto the scratch area. Then move to the destination page and drag the frame or set from the scratch area to that page.

Perhaps you need to make a graphic bigger or create more room for your text. Rather than delete the frame and any work you've done on it, use the frame's selection handles to resize the existing frame. As you move the cursor over the selection handles, the mouse pointer becomes a resize pointer and you should see the word *Resize.* After the resize pointer appears, you can do any of the following:

- Click and drag an edge handle (on a side of the bounding box) to resize a frame horizontally or vertically.

- Hold the Ctrl key and drag an edge handle to resize both horizontal or both vertical edges at the same time.

- Click and drag a corner handle (at a corner of the bounding box) to resize a frame both horizontally and vertically at the same time.

- Hold the Shift key down and drag a corner selection handle to resize a frame along its diagonal and retain the relative proportions of its height versus its width.

- Hold the Ctrl key down and drag a corner selection handle to have the frame's center retain its position on the page.

- Hold down the Shift and Ctrl keys together as you drag a corner handle to maintain a frame's proportion and resize it around its center.

You resize and move objects in the same manner as you do frames, using the selection handles that you find on each object's bounding box.

Many page layout programs offer features that enable you to resize a frame to a specific dimension or to reduce or enlarge a frame by a percentage. Unfortunately, you won't find such automatic features in Microsoft Publisher 97; you must resize your frames manually. If you need to modify a frame precisely, consider using guides and the Snap To commands on the Tools menu to align your frame. These features and the ruler are covered in detail in Chapter 4.

How resizing a frame affects the contents depends on the frame's type. Resizing a picture or WordArt frame changes the size of the picture or WordArt object within that frame. Resizing a text or table frame, however, merely changes the amount of area available for the text within the frame; the text itself doesn't change size but rearranges itself to fit the new shape of its home.

In addition to resizing frames, you can move a frame about as easily as you can slide a brand-new playing card across a freshly waxed table. Swoosh!

In the spirit of giving you more options than you could possibly use, Microsoft Publisher 97 provides four ways to move frames and objects: dragging, nudging, lining up, and the ubiquitous cutting-and-pasting (discussed in a prior section of this chapter). We cover the first three options in more detail in later sections of this chapter (after we dispose of the details of working with drawn objects). Each method for moving frames and objects has its own advantages, depending on where you want to move a frame and how adept you are with the mouse.

Working with Drawn Objects

If you read the first part of this chapter, you already know an awful lot about working with drawn objects. And if you've ever used a drawing program, these objects are more familiar still. Microsoft Publisher 97 is nothing more than a fancy drawing program.

Earlier sections in this chapter explain how to create objects, resize them, move them, and delete them. But the program offers six additional toolbox buttons for creating objects that we haven't discussed yet. Later, we move on to some of the general properties of objects, the various kinds of formatting commands that you can apply to them, and how you align, layer, and group objects. The following list describes the drawing tools in the toolbox; you find these in Figure 5-10.

- **Line tool:** Used to create lines on your layout. Click and drag a line from a starting point (where you click and begin dragging) to an ending point (where you release the mouse button).
- **Circle tool:** Used to create an oval. (Most drawing programs call it an Oval tool.) If you want to create a perfect circle, press the Shift key while you click and drag.

✔ **Box tool:** Used to create a rectangle. (Most drawing programs call it a Rectangle tool.) Press the Shift key while you click and drag to create a square.

Use the Shift key to constrain your shapes to the horizontal, vertical, or diagonal direction (45-degree angles). When you use the Shift key with the Circle and Box tools, you create perfect circles and squares — by necessity. Use the Ctrl key to draw shapes from their center point out and use the Ctrl+Shift keys together to combine these constraints.

In the language of *object-oriented* or *vector* programs — which is what techies like to call drawing programs when they don't want normal people to understand what they are saying — a basic shape is called a *primitive*. Lines, circles, and squares are primitives. More complex shapes that can be broken apart into unrelated line segments (such as the custom shapes) or that are a grouped set of shapes (such as those you see in the Design Gallery) are shapes that you can create for yourself in Microsoft Publisher 97. The Custom Shape and Design Gallery libraries exist to make your task in Microsoft Publisher 97 easier.

✔ **Custom Shapes tool:** Used to create more complex shapes. We're fond of this special tool because it lets you easily create interesting shapes that you can use for captions, callouts, product bursts, and many other purposes. Figure 5-11 shows you the pop-up menu for the Custom Shapes tool. Click to select the shape that you want from the menu and then drag to create your object on the layout.

✔ **Design Gallery tool:** Lets you select from a library of shapes. Click the Design Gallery tool to open up a browser, shown in Figure 5-12, that lets you select from a number of shapes in a library and inserts your selection into your publication.

You can think of the Design Gallery as a clip art collection of useful shapes. Use them as special elements in your publication for pull quotes, captions, and so on. Most Design Gallery shapes are groups of other shapes that you can modify for your own use. See Chapter 9 for more detail on this tool.

Figure 5-10:
The
drawing
tools.

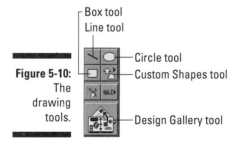

Box tool
Line tool
Circle tool
Custom Shapes tool
Design Gallery tool

Figure 5-11:
The Custom
Shapes
pop-up
menu.

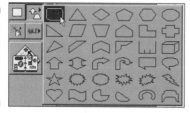

Figure 5-12:
The Design
Gallery.

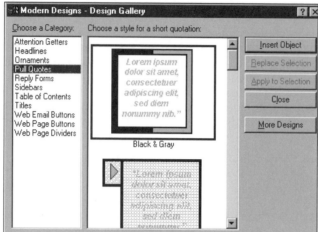

Microsoft included these drawing tools in the program specifically for their importance in page composition. In the desktop publishing game, lines are called *rules* and they are often used to separate headlines from body copy, one column from another, and so on. Boxes are important because they let you frame areas of the page, shade them, or apply spot color. Similarly, ovals can be used to frame pictures. Other shapes that you may see in general drawing programs are less useful to page layout and, therefore, aren't incorporated directly in the toolbox. You can use an OLE server program such as Microsoft Draw to access these other tools.

Understanding object properties

Objects have some basic properties that you probably already know about. This is head-banging stuff, but it lets us introduce some terms that are useful in discussions to come. If the italicized words in this section are familiar to you, you are not a pilgrim, and you should mosey on.

Size and shape

The first thing that you notice about an object is that it has a *shape*. (Strange, most people tend to notice that!) A shape is the actual defined area of the object and is indicated in Microsoft Publisher 97 by its border. When you select a shape, the shape is surrounded by the smallest rectangle that will encompass that object — called a *bounding box*. Figure 5-13 shows you a shape with its bounding box. The bounding box has the properties of a frame, and when the encompassed shape has right angles (like a rectangle), the shape's bounding box and border coincide.

Figure 5-13:
An object and its bounding box.

Use the selection handles on the bounding box to resize a shape or object. When a shape is irregular, you can see the bounding box and the border separately. If you look closely at Figure 5-13, you notice that the lower-left vertex of the trapezoid (the shape) displays a light gray diamond-shaped handle. That handle lets you reshape the trapezoid by changing its defining angle.

Borders, colors, and fills

Even if no border is applied to a shape, Microsoft Publisher 97 draws a dotted line so that you can see the shape and work with it. If you don't like this dotted line, you can apply a border — technically called a *stroke* — to the shape. A stroke can be as thin as a *hairline* ($1/2$ pixel wide) — which imagesetters can print but laser printers can't — or as thick as you want. Only the authors like to work with invisible shapes and write and talk to invisible people.

To apply a border to a shape, start by choosing Format⇨Border or by clicking the Border button (on the Format toolbar) and selecting More from its pop-up menu (see Figure 5-14). In either case, you get to the Border dialog box, as shown in Figure 5-15.

You can apply a weight to a shape's line or stroke. *Weight* is a term used by typographical folk to describe the thickness of the line. (Microsoft Publisher 97 keeps things simple by using the term *thickness* in the Border dialog box.) Usually, line weight is measured in *points*, which is a common unit of measurement used in publishing.

Figure 5-14:
The Border
button and
menu from
the Format
toolbar.

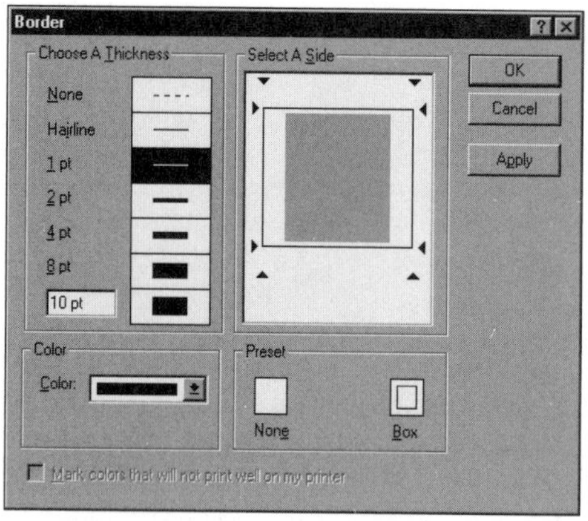

Figure 5-15:
The Border
dialog box.

You can also apply a color and even a pattern to a border stroke. Or, described another way, a stroke can have a *fill* and a *fill pattern.* Using the term
fill in this way can be confusing, though, because it's more commonly used
to refer to the interior of a shape — the part surrounded by the stroke. Like
a stroke, the interior of an object can have a color and pattern applied to it.

For some shapes, such as lines and boxes, Microsoft Publisher 97 doesn't let
you do anything more to a stroke than define its weight. It does let you
apply BorderArt (with patterns and colors) to frames and boxes, however.
We hold off telling you more about BorderArt until Chapter 9. Other, more
capable programs give you finer control and let you apply any attribute to a
stroke that you can apply to an object's fill.

Just to prove that there is an exception to every rule, one shape has a stroke
and no fill: a line. You can open the Line dialog box by choosing Format⇨
Line or by clicking the Border button on the Format toolbar and selecting
More from the pop-up menu. This dialog box lets you assign arrowheads,
line color, and line widths to a selected line. Figure 5-16 shows the Line
dialog box.

Color is a big subject and a very technical one for desktop publishers. We
tackle it in detail in Chapter 10. For now, remember it as one of an object's
basic properties. To apply a color to the fill of a selected shape, you need to
access the Colors dialog box. You can do this in two ways:

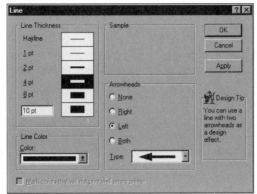

Figure 5-16:
The Line
dialog box.

▶ Click the Object Color button on the Format toolbar to reveal the pop-up selection menu, as shown in Figure 5-17. From this pop-up menu, access the Colors dialog box by clicking the More Colors button.

▶ Choose Format⇨Fill Color from the main menu. The much larger and more capable Colors dialog box, shown in Figure 5-18, appears.

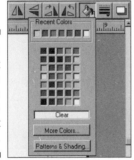

Figure 5-17:
The Object
Color button
and menu
on the
Format
toolbar.

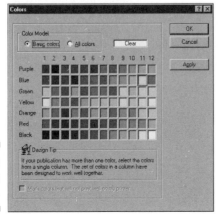

Figure 5-18:
The Colors
dialog box.

To apply a pattern, shading, or gradient to the selected object's fill, first access the Fill Patterns and Shading dialog box as follows:

✔ Click the Object Color button on the Format toolbar to reveal the pop-up selection menu, as shown back in Figure 5-17. From this pop-up menu, access the Fill Patterns and Shading dialog box by clicking the Patterns & Shading button.

✔ Choose Format➪Fill Patterns & Shadings from the main menu.

In the Fill Patterns and Shading dialog box, click the radio button for the Style of fill that you want to use. Figure 5-19 shows the options available when you select the Patterns radio button.

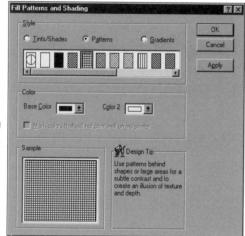

Figure 5-19:
The Fill
Patterns
and
Shading
dialog box.

In the vocabulary of color, a *Tint/Shade* is a mix of a color with white. Patterns use a base color for the lines or dots and a background color — normally black and white, respectively. *Gradients* are effects where the color is varied in some manner and in a specific direction (for example, from dark to light and outward from the center of the object). We think that the effects you can get with gradients are so cool!

Cool-looking gradients can take up a lot of memory and create challenges for your printer. Make sure that the printer you select can handle these large files. See Chapter 12 for more about printing.

Seeing through an object

Objects also have the property of being *transparent* (see-through) or *opaque* (not see-through). Many fancy drawing and page layout programs let you control the degree of transparency of an object and even the type of color that shows through. Microsoft Publisher 97 lets you assign a property of only *clear* or *transparent* to an object. A clear object lets other objects beneath it show through; for most desktop publishing purposes, this option is sufficient. Don't blink, though, or you'll miss the setting for clear. To locate it, click on the P̲atterns radio button in the Fill Patterns and Shading dialog box. The pattern all the way on the left — the one with a circle and a slash through it — is the clear setting.

To make an opaque object or frame transparent, press Ctrl+T. Press the keystroke again to make a transparent object or frame opaque — a technique that works less often because not all object types support it.

Relative positions

Another property that objects have in a layout is their position with respect to one another. When you create an object, it goes on top of all the other objects created before it. There is a strict order from back to front. You can change this automatic order — often referred to as the *layering order* or *stacking order* — by using a set of commands that we cover later in this chapter. Use these commands to send objects backward or forward in the stacking order. You can also align objects with each other and create groups of objects that behave like a single object. We talk about alignment and grouping later in the chapter, too.

Even this very basic set of properties allows you to create many special effects. For example, you can't apply BorderArt to a box, but you can create a text frame, apply BorderArt to that frame, and then place it behind the box to create the illusion of a box that has BorderArt applied.

Using the Format Painter

When you get an object's properties just so, you'd like to lock the object and prevent it from being changed. This very important command is unfortunately missing in Microsoft Publisher 97, which makes it imperative that you take care when you delete objects. The program does offer the Format Painter, however — a "just so" command that lets you apply the same set of formatting from one object to another object. The two objects don't even have to be the same kind of object.

You can copy an object's format in the following two ways:

✔ Select the object whose format you want to copy. Then click the Format Painter button (it's the Standard toolbar button that looks like a paintbrush). Finally, click the object that you want to format.

✔ Select the object whose format you want to copy and choose Format⇨Pick Up Formatting. This command "fills" the Format Painter's brush. To paint another object with the formatting, select the object and then choose Format⇨Apply Formatting.

The Format Painter's brush stays "loaded" with your format until you change it. You can find these commands on context-sensitive menus, too.

Aligning and positioning objects

The most natural method for moving an object or frame is to drag it. Dragging an object is the electronic equivalent of using your finger to slide a playing card across a table. In Chapter 4, we explain some of the tools used for precise positioning of objects and frames on a layout when you are dragging them into position: position measurements in the status bar, ruler marks, layout and grid guides, and ruler guides.

Ruler marks and guides work with Snap To commands, also covered in Chapter 4, to help you position objects precisely. When you get an object's border or center axis (either horizontal or vertical) close to a ruler mark or guide, it snaps into alignment with the mark or guide.

Three additional sets of commands, found on the Arrange menu, are also used for precise positioning or alignment:

✔ **Line Up Objects:** This command opens the Line Up Objects dialog box, shown in Figure 5-20. Selected objects are aligned using the Left to Right and Top to Bottom options that you choose. You can set either or both of these alignment options. The Sample section shows you an example of your choices.

You can also align objects to the page margin — one object must already be aligned to the page margin before you check the Align Along Margins check box for this option to take effect. We think that the Line Up Objects dialog box is clear cut and well implemented, and we doubt that it will give you any trouble. Use the dialog box's Apply button to see your changes before you dismiss the dialog box, and use the Cancel button to undo those changes. We just wish there were a keystroke that called this dialog box up quickly, because it is so useful.

✔ **Nudge Objects:** The Nudge Objects command opens the Nudge Objects dialog box, shown in Figure 5-21. *Nudges,* for those of you not in the know (nudge, nudge, wink, wink), are small movements of an object in one direction.

Most programs give you a nudge. Some programs give you a swift kick in the pants. Microsoft Publisher 97 gives you a dialog box. The traditional way of implementing nudges is to select an object and press the arrow keys. Each time that you press an arrow key, your object moves one pixel in that direction. Microsoft Publisher 97 requires that you hold the Alt key down and press the arrows keys to perform this action. You can also click the arrows in the Nudge Objects dialog box to perform this simple function — a technique that makes us, how shall we say this — nudgey.

Were it not for the ability to set the nudge distance in the Nudge Objects dialog box's Nudge By text box, we'd think that the Nudge dialog box was totally useless. Leave this box blank if you want each press of an arrow key to move your object one pixel. Or, enter a value of up to 2 inches. When entering your measurement, use the abbreviation *in* for inches. You can also use *cm* for centimeters, *pi* for picas, and *pt* for points.

✔ **Rotate/Flip Objects:** Microsoft Publisher 97 offers five commands to rotate and flip selected objects: Rotate L̲eft, Rotate R̲ight, C̲ustom Rotate, Flip V̲ertically, and Flip H̲orizontally.

The first two commands rotate your object(s) 90 degrees clockwise and counterclockwise with each application; the latter two commands reflect your selection through a vertical and horizontal mirror plane. The four Format toolbar buttons, shown in Figure 5-22, duplicate these four flip and rotate commands.

The Custom Rotate command is more interesting. You can also use the Rotate button (shown in the margin) at the right of the Standard toolbar to invoke the command. Either way, you open the Rotate Objects dialog box, as shown in Figure 5-23. In this dialog box, you can set an angle and rotate a selection in either direction.

To perform a free rotation, hold the Alt key and use the Pointer tool to click and drag on the object's handles.

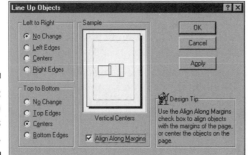

Figure 5-20:
The Line Up
Objects
dialog box.

Figure 5-21:
The Nudge
Objects
dialog box.

Figure 5-22:
The Flip and
Rotate
buttons on
the Format
toolbar.

Figure 5-23:
The Rotate
Objects
dialog box.

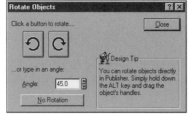

Working with layers

The position that an object has on a page is uniquely defined by its layer. In the natural creation order, the first object created is at the back and the last object created is at the front. It's like football players diving for a fumbled ball: Whoever gets there first ends up on the bottom. Fortunately for your publication, frames don't suffer from broken bones and torn ligaments. Both the background and foreground have separate layer orders, and they can't be mixed.

Grouped objects are considered to be in the same layer — that is, until they are ungrouped. Then they return to their natural relative order, one ungrouped object to another. You can defeat the natural layering by using a set of commands on the Arrange menu. Layers have some important implications. Opaque objects obscure the object(s) behind them. Text and table frames are opaque by default; picture and WordArt frames are transparent by default.

No matter what order you use to originally layer frames, however, you can rearrange these layers any way you want using the four layering commands on the Arrange menu:

- **Bring to Front:** Choose Arrange⇨Bring to Front, click the Bring to Front button on the Standard toolbar (shown in margin), or press F6 to bring the selected object(s) to the top layer.

- **Bring Closer:** Choose Arrange⇨Bring Closer to bring the selected frame(s) up one layer.

- **Send Farther:** Choose Arrange⇨Send Farther to send the selected frame(s) down one layer.

- **Send to Back:** Choose Arrange⇨Send to Back, click the Send to Back button on the Standard toolbar (shown in margin), or press Shift+F6 to send the selected frame(s) to the bottom layer.

No matter how far down you send a frame or other object on a foreground page, it always remains on top of any background object. And no matter how far up you bring a frame or other object on a background, it always remains below any foreground object.

Adjusting the layers and transparency of objects so that other objects either show through or are hidden is called *layering* by Microsoft Publisher 97. It is one of the most important design techniques you can apply to your publications. By using this technique, you can place text in front of a picture so that it appears to be part of the picture, apply fills and patterns that the object doesn't support by itself, wrap text around a graphic (another layering technique discussed later), and more. Figure 5-24 shows you an example of a labeled starburst with a transparent text frame on top.

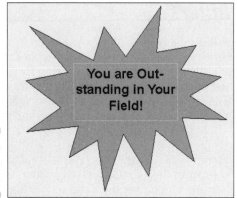

Figure 5-24:
An example
of layering.

Wrapping Text around Objects

Take a look at Figure 5-25, which shows you one of the most important types of layering — text wrapping. This is a special layer effect created with intelligent frame margins. Notice how the text makes room for the graphic, neatly wrapping around it? Is the text just being well-behaved or did the graphic forget to put on its deodorant this morning?

Figure 5-25:
Text
wrapped
around a
picture
frame.

Creating regular text wraps

Back in the bad old days of traditional publishing, wrapping text like this required painstaking hours of cutting, pasting, and rearranging individual lines of text. And pity the poor fool who suggested making a change to the text after the wrapping was complete!

In Microsoft Publisher 97, though, wrapping text is amazingly easy. Just place any type of frame — even another text frame — on top of a text frame, and the text underneath automatically wraps around the frame above.

Text doesn't wrap if one frame is on a foreground page and the other is on the background; both frames have to be on the same page, so to speak.

Although the program tries its best, it can sometimes wrap text too closely or too loosely around a frame. (We all get wrapped too tight from time to time.) Closely wrapped text can be difficult to read, whereas loosely wrapped text can waste space and create big gaps on the page. With all frames except table frames, you can easily change the amount of space between the wrapping text and the frame it wraps around by changing the margins of the wrapped-around frame.

To increase the margins of a text frame, click the text frame and then choose Format⇨Text Frame Properties from the main menu. Make your selections from the Text Frame Properties dialog box, shown in Figure 5-26. Turn text wrap on and off by checking or unchecking the Wrap text around objects check box. The Margins section changes the amount of space between the text in a frame and the border of the frame.

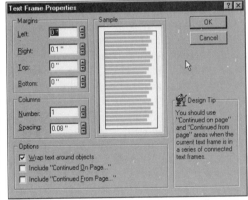

Figure 5-26:
The Text Frame Properties dialog box.

To increase the margins of a picture or WordArt frame and change the text wrap properties, do the following:

✔ Click (to select) a picture or WordArt frame and then choose Format⇨Object Frame Properties from the main menu. Make your selections from the Object Frame Properties dialog box (shown in Figure 5-27), which is the picture frame's equivalent of the Text Frame Properties dialog box.

> ✔ Just as you can adjust the margins in a text frame, you can change the margins that a picture has inside the picture frame. More important, you can adjust the way text wraps around a graphic so that it wraps around the entire picture frame or just the graphic contained therein — as shown by example in the Wrap text around section of the Object Frame Properties dialog box.

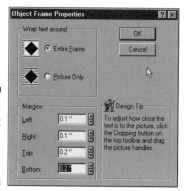

Figure 5-27:
The Object
Frame
Properties
dialog box.

Depending on the option set under Wrap text around, either one or four margin settings are available. Changing a frame's margins doesn't change the frame's overall size. Rather, it increases or decreases the amount of available space *within* the frame. When you change a picture or WordArt frame's margins, the graphic inside the frame grows accordingly smaller or larger. When you change a text frame's margins, however, the text in that frame stays the same size but rearranges itself according to the new space available.

Don't confuse *frame margins* with *margin guides*. Frame margins control the amount of space between a frame's perimeter and its contents. Margin guides mark the margins of an entire publication page. (We discuss margin guides in Chapter 4.)

If you set the margins of a picture or WordArt frame unequally, the graphic within that frame loses its original proportions, becoming squished in one direction or another. To return your graphic to its original proportions, either set the frame margins equally or resize the frame in the opposite direction of the squeeze.

Although you can set margins for individual cells within a table frame, you can't set margins for an entire table frame. If text wraps too tightly around one of your table frames, place an empty picture frame behind that table frame; the text now wraps around the picture frame. If you need to adjust the text wrap, just resize the picture frame accordingly.

By default, Microsoft Publisher 97 wraps text in a rectangular pattern around the perimeter of a frame, as shown earlier in Figure 5-25. If you're working with a picture or WordArt frame, however, you can have your text wrap to the actual shape of the graphic within that frame by selecting the Wrap Text to Picture button on the Format toolbar (or by selecting the Picture Only radio button in the Object Frame Properties dialog box). Figure 5-28 shows you an example of this. Very cool!

Figure 5-28: Text wrapped around a picture.

Fine-tuning your text wraps

Picky, picky, picky. Some folks like their text wrapped around their graphics just so. It is very important to them. Depending upon the justification that you use in your text, Microsoft Publisher 97 can do a poor job of wrapping text around a graphic to match its shape. This is particularly true when you use justified text. The program wraps text around most of its own clip art because the text boundaries are built in already. But Microsoft Publisher 97 can get mighty confused about the shapes of "foreign" graphics and can be especially pitiful when it comes to creating text boundaries for WordArt objects.

A couple of tools offer some help in this area. The first tool lets you create and adjust an irregular boundary on your graphic to control how text wraps around it. To create this kind of effect, select the graphic and make sure that the Wrap Text to Picture button on the Format toolbar is selected. Then click the Edit Irregular Text Wrap button, which is also on the Format toolbar. Both buttons have equivalent commands on the Format menu.

Notice that each graphic has reshape handles for text wrap. Click and drag these handles where you want them. You can also add a handle by holding the Ctrl key and clicking the outline of the graphic. To remove a reshape handle, press Ctrl+Shift and click it. Figure 5-29 shows you an example of this kind of text wrap. The topic "Irregular Text Wrap" in Microsoft Publisher 97's online help system gives you more information.

Figure 5-29:
Editing a
figure with
an irregular
text wrap
effect.

You can help the program out by manually adjusting the text boundary yourself for a graphic where the text is *wrapped around the frame.* To do this, first select the frame that contains the graphic and make sure that the Wrap Text to Frame button is selected on the Format toolbar. In that case, Microsoft Publisher 97 places a Crop Picture button on the Format toolbar. Cropping lets you shave off part of your frame, just as if you were cutting paper with a pair of scissors. (The command to do this is the Format➪Crop Picture command on the menu bar.)

Rather than eight selection handles, your graphic now displays any number of *adjust handles,* which look just like selection handles. Point to one of the adjust handles until the mouse pointer becomes a Crop pointer. This pointer has two scissors and the word *Crop* in it. Then drag to change the text boundary's shape. Repeat this as necessary with the other handles. Just be careful not to drag any handles too far inward, or you may block out portions of your graphic.

When you crop a graphic, you don't remove part of the figure. You only hide some of the figure from view. If you make a mistake, you can crop your figure again to enlarge it and return the missing piece. You can find out more about working with graphics in Chapter 9.

Grouping Objects

Some things in "the real world" just seem to go together: peanut butter and jelly, macaroni and cheese, death and taxes. In your publications, too, some things might belong together: Several drawn objects that comprise a logo, a graphic and its caption, a table frame and the picture frame that you stuck behind it to make text wrap the way you want, the assorted text and graphics that might comprise a company logo.

When you want different objects on your layout to stay together and behave like a unit, you can apply some electronic glue to stick them together in a *group*. There, they can share their most personal problems: "Hi, my name is Igor. I'm a picture frame trapped in a table frame's body."

Actually, grouping tells Microsoft Publisher 97 to treat the collection of objects as a single object. Thus, you can easily move or copy a group while keeping the objects in the same positions relative to each other. You don't have to worry about leaving one line, box, or frame behind accidentally. You can also resize a group while maintaining the same relative size and position of the frames within that group. (Trust us, this is a heck of a lot easier than resizing and adjusting the position of each object in a group individually and getting the same results.)

To group two or more objects, do one of the following:

- ✔ Select the objects that you want to include in your group and click the Group Objects button (that appears at the lower right of the selection's bounding box) to create the group. The button changes to resemble locked puzzle pieces. You can even group groups.

- ✔ Choose Arrange⇨Group Objects or press Ctrl+Shift+G.

To ungroup a group of objects, do one of the following:

- ✔ Select the group and click the Group Objects button again. The button changes to look like two unjoined puzzle pieces. Figure 5-30 shows you an example of the same figures grouped and ungrouped.

- ✔ Choose Arrange⇨Ungroup Objects from the main menu or press Ctrl+Shift+G.

What you can do to an object in a group depends upon that object's capability. Earlier in the chapter, you see how you can apply borders to several shapes at once in a group. You can also resize a group; if you do, each object resizes proportionally. You can type text in a text or table frame that is part of a group; just click the frame and start typing. You can modify a graphic, a WordArt object, or an OLE object by double-clicking it.

Figure 5-30:
Grouped
and
ungrouped
objects.

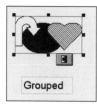

If you want to modify a single object in a group, you need to ungroup the group. For example, to resize a single frame or change one frame's margins, you need to ungroup the frames first. As you ungroup a group of groups, you need to successively apply the Ungroup command to release the objects. The PageWizards make good use of groups. Don't be surprised if you find yourself doing a lot of ungrouping to get at individual elements if you base your document on a PageWizard.

Part III
10,000 Words, One Maniac

In this part . . .

Fancy graphics and layouts can draw attention to your publication, but *words* usually comprise the core of your message. The three chapters in Part III cover working with the text in your publication: Where and how do you get it? What do you do to it once you have it? And how do you select type to convey the feeling of what you are trying to say? We don't tell you what to write here — that's up to you. (Who are we to put words in your mouth?) But after reading the chapters in this part, you'll be able to produce a publication that has better-looking text.

Chapter 6

Getting the Word

· ·

· ·

*I*n this chapter, we take a closer look at two frame types: text frames and table frames. You use *text frames* to place and manage text in your publication. Microsoft Publisher 97 has some special features to help you manage text frames across pages: the capacity to flow text automatically between linked frames, and *stories*, which are just blocks of text managed as a single entity. You can even place *continued on* and *continued from* notices in your publication to help your readers follow a story that begins on one page and continues on another.

In addition to regular text frames, Microsoft Publisher 97 provides two other types of frames for holding text: table frames and WordArt frames. If you've worked in a spreadsheet program such as Microsoft Excel or Lotus 1-2-3, or used a word processor that offers a table feature (such as Microsoft Word), the features in Microsoft Publisher 97's table frames will seem familiar to you. If not, you can find out what you need to know about table frames at the end of this chapter.

WordArt frames enable you to create fancy text by using the WordArt OLE server to manipulate type. We cover WordArt in Chapter 8, as these types of frames are more commonly used for short pieces of decorative text than for the longer text that comprises most people's publications.

More about Text Frames

If you're accustomed to creating text in other computer programs, you may find it odd that you can't just begin typing right away in a Microsoft Publisher 97 publication. You must first create a text frame to tell the program where to put your text. Chapter 5 shows you how easy creating a text frame is: You simply click the Text tool in the toolbox and then click and drag to create the frame.

After you create a text frame, you can fill it in three ways:

- ✔ You can type text directly into the text frame.
- ✔ You can paste text in from the Clipboard.
- ✔ You can import text from your word processor or text file.

Typing text

Microsoft Publisher 97 offers a complete environment for creating page layout, so you discover that you can write your text in text frames with little trouble. Microsoft Publisher 97 is not the most capable text creation tool, and it doesn't have all the bells and whistles that you would expect to find in your word processor, but it does enable you to handle such important tasks as spell checking.

If you're used to typing on a typewriter or in a word processor, you may be used to doing some things that you shouldn't do in Microsoft Publisher 97 — or in any page layout program — when you enter text.

Here are some highlights you need to keep in mind when entering text:

- ✔ **Turn on the Show Special Characters command.** Choose <u>V</u>iew⇨Show Special <u>C</u>haracters or press Ctrl+Shift+Y. Special characters are symbols that represent things such as spaces, tabs, line endings, and so on. These symbols help you figure out why your text appears the way it does. Figure 6-1 shows a text block with special characters turned on.

- ✔ **Don't press Enter to force a line ending.** Pressing Enter tells the program that you've reached the end of a paragraph. If you press Enter at the end of every line, you won't be able to format the lines of your paragraph together as a unit, which is a bad thing. When you get to the end of a line of text, let Microsoft Publisher 97 word-wrap the text to the next line for you (which it does automatically). Press Enter only to end a paragraph or a short, independent line of text (such as a line in an address).

✔ **If you need to force a line break without creating a new paragraph, press Shift+Enter.** This keystroke creates what is called a *soft carriage return*, and places the symbol ↵ at the end of the line.

✔ **Don't press the Enter key to create blank lines between paragraphs.** Microsoft Publisher 97 provides a much better way of creating spaces before and after paragraphs by choosing the Format⇨Line Spacing command on the menu bar.

✔ **Don't insert two spaces between sentences.** Use just one. It makes your text easier to read.

✔ **Don't use the Tab key to indent the first lines of paragraphs.** Instead, use the paragraph indent controls explained in Chapter 7. These controls offer much more flexibility than tabs.

✔ **Don't try to edit or format your text as you go.** It's much more efficient to do all your typing first, your editing second, and your formatting last.

If any preceding suggestion seems new to you, we recommend that you consider picking up a copy of one of the typographical style books mentioned near the end of Chapter 2. We are especially fond of *The PC is Not a Typewriter* by Robin Williams (published by Peachpit Press). If you are working in a specific word processing program, you may also want to pick up the *...For Dummies* book on that program.

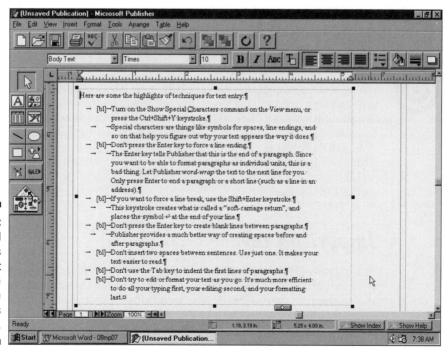

Figure 6-1: Special characters in your text frames help you figure out what's going on.

As you type, your text begins filling the text frame from left to right, top to bottom. If the text frame isn't large enough to accommodate all your text, you eventually reach the bottom of the frame. When you type more text than can fit into a text frame, the extra text moves into an invisible place called the *overflow area*. You can type blindly into that overflow area; the program keeps track of everything you type. If you're like most people, though, you probably want to see what you're typing as you type it.

The Connect Frame button tells you the condition of the overflow area. This button is located near the bottom-right corner of the frame. If the Connect Frame button displays a white diamond, the overflow area is empty. If the Connect Frame button displays three dots, the overflow area contains some text. Figure 6-2 shows you these two states. Although you can view the contents of a text frame's overflow area in several ways, the most straightforward method is to simply enlarge the text frame, as explained in Chapter 5. When you do, the text in the overflow area automatically appears. (You can also use the Connect Frame button to link text frames together for Autoflow, as described later in this chapter.)

Figure 6-2:
Connect
Frame
buttons.

 Overflow area

 Empty overflow area

Connect Frame

 The first thing that you may notice about text in a text frame is that in most views that provide an overview of your publication, you see squiggly lines in place of any text that you can actually read. Those squiggly lines are called greeked text, as in "that's Greek to me!" If you try to read greeked text, you are going to go crazy before your time. So do yourself a favor and press F9 to zoom right in to view your text as you type it into your text frame. (Microsoft Publisher 97 now recommends this approach to you in a Tippage.) You can turn the greeking feature off by deselecting the "Greek" small text check box in the Options dialog box. (See the discussion of options in Chapter 3.)

Importing text

Placing text created in another program into your Microsoft Publisher 97 publication, called *importing text*, can be an excellent time-saver — especially when you get someone else to do all the typing for you. In any case, you never want to type the same text into a computer more than once.

Using the Clipboard

You can paste text into a Microsoft Publisher 97 publication from the Windows Clipboard or import text from a disk file. Here's how:

1. **Highlight the text in the program containing the text that you want to use.**

2. **Select Edit⇨Copy or press Ctrl+C.**

3. **Open your publication, select the Pointer tool, and click to set the insertion point at the position where you want your text to be pasted.**

4. **Choose Edit⇨Paste Text or press Ctrl+V.**

   If you didn't set an insertion point in Step 3 or didn't have a text frame selected, the Paste Text command appears as the Paste command, and Microsoft Publisher 97 creates a new text frame and imports the copied text into that frame.

If you can copy formatted text successfully to the Windows Clipboard, the text should paste correctly into your text frame. For more information about using the Windows Clipboard, see Chapter 5.

If the text on the Clipboard can't fit in the text frame that you selected, the program performs an autoflow. First, it displays a dialog box informing you that the inserted text doesn't fit into the select frame, and asks whether you want to use an autoflow. We talk about autoflow in more depth later in this chapter.

Using the Text File command

The Text File command on the Insert menu provides a way to move text between your word processor and Microsoft Publisher 97 by using an intervening text file. If your computer has sufficient memory, you can also do editing-in-place by running Microsoft Word as an OLE server inside Microsoft Publisher 97.

Before you use the Text File command, you must save your text to a file in a format that Microsoft Publisher 97 can use. Fortunately, Microsoft Publisher 97 accepts many different file formats. The section on saving files in Chapter 3 covers these formats. Microsoft Publisher 97 uses the same filters to import text as it does to save the text in your publication. You can use this feature to export text out of Microsoft Publisher 97, as you find out later in this chapter.

The text file formats that Microsoft Publisher 97 understands include the following:

✔ Other Microsoft Publisher 97 files

✔ Plain text or plain text formatted for DOS (plain text is ASCII text)

Most programs should at least be able to save the text as plain or ASCII text. But ASCII is your last resort. If you save a text file in the ASCII format, you lose all your formatting. Any work that you did bolding, italicizing, underlining, and so on, is lost. Try to avoid this option at all costs.

✔ Rich Text Format (RTF) — Microsoft's text-based formatted text interchange format. In RTF, only normal characters are saved in your file. Any formatting such as bold, italic, and so on is indicated with a set of codes of plain text. No special symbols are used.

✔ Microsoft Word for Windows 2.x, 6.0/95, and Word 97

✔ Microsoft Word for the Macintosh 4.0 - 6.0

✔ Microsoft Works for Windows 3.0 and 4.0 word-processing files

✔ WordPerfect 5.x and 6.x

✔ Microsoft Windows Write

✔ Microsoft Excel Worksheet

✔ Lotus 1-2-3

✔ Windows Write

✔ HTML

If your word processor doesn't save to one of these file formats automatically, check to see whether it offers an Export command that can translate your word processor file into a form that Microsoft Publisher 97 understands.

To import a text file into Microsoft Publisher 97:

1. Position the insertion point in (click inside) the text frame into which you want to import the text.

2. Choose Insert⇨Text File.

The Insert Text File dialog box shown in Figure 6-3 appears.

3. Locate the file of interest, highlight it, and click OK.

After a moment, the text appears in your selected text frame.

If you can't find your text file, make sure that you selected the correct import filter from the Files of type list box. To see all files in a folder, type *.* into the File name text box and press Enter. If the file still doesn't appear, you're looking in the wrong place. Try clicking the Find File button to get Microsoft Publisher 97 to help you find your file.

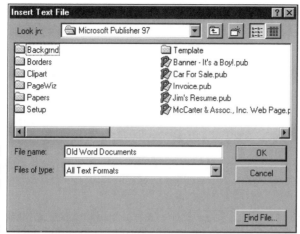

Figure 6-3:
The Insert
Text File
dialog box.

If all the imported text can't fit in the selected text frame, the program opens
a dialog box asking whether you want to autoflow the rest of your text into
other text frames. We present more information on autoflowing text later in
this chapter.

You can view the contents of a text file without importing the file into your
publication. Choose File⇨Open Existing Publication (or press Ctrl+O), click
the Click here to open a publication not listed here button, and select the
file of interest. Microsoft Publisher 97 opens the text or word processor file
as a full-page publication that offers the requisite number of pages filled
with full-page text frames.

As an alternative to using the menu commands, don't forget the context-
sensitive menus that you can get by right-clicking on a text frame, as shown
in Figure 6-4. We always find that using the context-sensitive menu for the
Insert Text File task is easier than mousing up to the top of our screen.

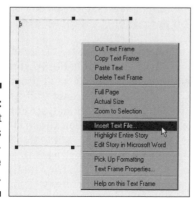

Figure 6-4:
A text
frame's
context-
sensitive
menu.

Exporting text

Hey! Here's something you already know how to do. Just as easily as you can bring text created elsewhere into Microsoft Publisher 97, you can also send text out of the program so that other computer programs can use that text. Just as bringing text into Microsoft Publisher 97 is called importing, sending text out is called *exporting*.

Microsoft Publisher 97 provides two ways to export text:

- ✔ Choose Edit⇨Copy to copy selected text from Microsoft Publisher 97 to the Windows Clipboard, and then choose Edit⇨Paste to paste it directly into another Windows program.

- ✔ Choose File⇨Save As to send the text of a selected text frame to a text or word processor file in one of the formats mentioned in the preceding section.

  Make sure to click the Save All Text as File check box at the bottom of the Save As dialog box.

  If no text frame is selected, all the text in your publication can be saved out to a text or word processor file.

It's probably unfortunate that Microsoft Publisher 97 doesn't have an Export command on its File menu, as other desktop publishing programs do. Then we could make believe that there was more to know about exporting text out of the program than there really is. It's almost too easy.

Let Me Tell You a Story

When you add large amounts of text to a publication, you often have text that doesn't fit in a single text frame. In such cases, the traditional publishing solution is to jump (continue) each article to other pages. Jumps are extremely common in newspapers and magazines: How often each day do you see lines such as "Continued on page 3" or "Continued from page 1"?

The capability of jumping a particular story between text frames and pages is one of the best arguments for using Microsoft Publisher 97 rather than a word processing program. Although most word processing programs prefer to deal with all the text in a file as one big story, Microsoft Publisher 97 excels at juggling multiple stories within a single publication. For example, you can begin four stories on page 1 and then jump half those stories to page 2 and the other half to page 3. At the same time, you can begin separate stories on pages 2 and 3 and jump each of those stories to any other page. If there's not enough room on a page to finish a story that you've already jumped from another page, you can jump the story to another page, and another, and another.

Forming, reforming, and deforming stories

In its simplest form, a Microsoft Publisher 97 story is a block of text that exists in a single, self-contained text frame. To enable a story to jump across and flow through a series or chain of several text frames, you connect those frames to each other in the order that you want the story to jump and flow. A chain of connected frames can exist on a single page or across multiple pages. You can even connect text frames that are in the scratch area and then later move those frames onto your publication pages.

Although you can use side-by-side connected text frames on a single page to create snaking columns, where text ends at the bottom of one column and continues again at the top of the next (as you find in a newspaper or magazine), you may find setting multiple columns within a single text frame on a page easier.

How and when you connect text frames depends on your situation:

- ✔ If you haven't yet typed or imported your text, you can manually connect empty text frames together to serve as a series of ready-made containers for that text. When you then type or import your text, it automatically jumps and flows between frames as water jumps and flows between the separate compartments in a plastic ice-cube tray.

- ✔ If you're typing your text in Microsoft Publisher 97 and don't know how much text you'll end up having, you can manually connect to new text frames as you run out of room in each current frame.

- ✔ If you're importing text and there's not enough room to fit it in the current frame, you can use the program's autoflow feature to help you connect your text frames. You can even have Microsoft Publisher 97 draw new text frames and insert new pages as needed to fit all that text.

The next few sections show you how to best handle each of these situations.

Connecting frames

Whenever you select a text frame, a Connect Frame button appears near that frame's bottom-right corner. This button serves as an indicator of whether any text is in the frame's overflow area, an invisible place where Microsoft Publisher 97 holds any extra text that can't fit in the frame. As you may recall, if the Connect Frame button displays a white diamond, the overflow area is empty. When the overflow area contains text, the Connect Frame button displays three black dots (refer to Figure 6-2).

The Connect Frame button isn't just an indicator. You also use this button to connect a frame to an empty, unconnected text frame or to an empty, connected frame that's the first frame in another chain.

Here's how to connect a text frame to another text frame:

1. **Click the Connect Frame button.**

   (If you accidentally click a Connect button, press the Esc key to get rid of the pitcher pointer.)

   Your mouse pointer changes from that accusing, hand-pointing pointer to a cute little pitcher pointer bearing a down-pointing arrow. As you move over an appropriate text frame, the pitcher tilts and the arrow points to the right. The metaphor that Microsoft Publisher 97 is using is that you've loaded the cursor with the text from your overflow area. The pitcher is a very '90s kind of icon — in earlier days, programs often used a loaded gun icon.

2. **Click the next text frame (even one on another page) to which you want to connect in the sequence.**

   The pitcher pointer now tips sideways, drains its text, and returns to its normal state.

The two frames are now connected; any text in the first frame's overflow area appears in the second frame. Also, as you type or enter additional text into the first text frame, it pushes extra text into the second frame. To create a chain of more than two connected frames, repeat the preceding steps. If a chain is empty, you can link another chain to its first frame to create the combination of the two chains.

As you might guess, you can connect text frames only. If you select another kind of frame, you don't see a Connect Frame button. Also, you can't connect a text frame that's already connected to some other text frame or a text frame that has some text in it already. If you try to do this, Microsoft Publisher 97 displays a dialog box to complain.

After you connect text frames together, extra buttons appear at the top and/or bottom of each frame when the frame is selected. Figure 6-5 shows an example of three connected text frames on a page in a sequence, with each frame selected. Think of Figure 6-5 as three separate figures, though, because if you tried to select all three text frames at the same time on your screen, you would see the frames selected as a group with only a single Group Objects button.

Don't worry too much about connecting frames in the proper order the first time around. After you connect frames, you can disconnect and rearrange them quite easily. Later in this chapter, the section on rearranging chains tells you how.

Figure 6-5:
Three
connected
text frames
— First
Frame (left),
Middle
Frame
(center),
and Last
Frame
(right).

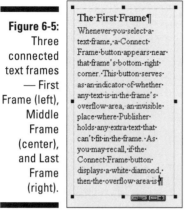

The·First·Frame¶

Whenever·you·select·a· text·frame,·a·Connect· Frame·button·appears·near· that·frame's·bottom-right· corner.·This·button·serves· as·an·indicator·of·whether· any·text·is·in·the·frame's· overflow·area,·an·invisible· place·where·Publisher· holds·any·extra·text·that· can't·fit·in·the·frame.·As· you·may·recall,·if·the· Connect·Frame·button· displays·a·white·diamond,· then·the·overflow·area·is¶

The·Middle·Frame¶

empty.·When·the·over- flow·area·contains·text,· then·the·Connect·Frame· button·displays·three· black·dots.·Figure·7.BB· showed·you·these·two· states.¶

The·Connect·Frame·but- ton·isn't·just·an·indicator.· You·also·use·this·button· to·connect·a·frame·to·an· empty,·unconnected·text· frame;·or·to·an·empty,· connected·frame·that's·the¶

The·Last·Frame¶

first·frame·in·another· chain.¶

Moving among the story's frames

One of the first things to consider when you work with multiple-frame story text is how best to move among the story's frames — and knowing which frame follows which! You can move easily and reliably between connected frames using either the mouse or the keyboard. Both techniques are easy.

To move between connected frames using the mouse:

1. **Click the Go To Previous Frame button to move backward in the sequence.**

2. **Click the Go To Next Frame button to move forward in the sequence.**

These two buttons are shown in the full-page, single text frame view shown in Figure 6-6. The button with an arrow at the top of the frame is the Go To Previous Frame button; the button with an arrow at the bottom of the frame is the Go To Next Frame button. The first frame in a chain has no Go To Previous Frame button, whereas the last frame has no Go To Next Frame button. That is, unless you live in the Twilight Zone.

To move between connected frames using the keyboard:

1. **Press Ctrl+Tab from a connected frame (that is selected) to move to and select the chain's next frame.**

2. **Press Ctrl+Shift+Tab from a connected frame (that is selected) to move to and select the chain's previous frame.**

If your connected frames are full of text, you can also use many of the keyboard shortcuts for navigating text (listed in Chapter 7) to move be-tween connected text frames. If your insertion point is in the last line of text in a connected text frame, for example, you can press the down-arrow key to move to and select the chain's next frame.

Go to Previous Frame

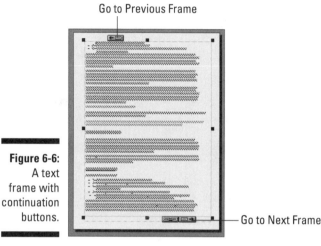

Figure 6-6:
A text
frame with
continuation
buttons.

Go to Next Frame

If the current text frame displays Continued notices, as described later in this chapter, you can't use the up- and down-arrow keys by themselves to move between connected frames. Instead, these keys move you into the Continued notices themselves.

Autoflowing text

Autoflowing text helps you fit long text documents into a series of linked text frames. This feature is handy for automatically managing the flow of text among pages of your publication. To autoflow text into a set of linked text frames, you need to select the first text frame in the chain. When you insert (or copy) text into the frame, Microsoft Publisher 97 fills your connected frames, beginning with the frame that you selected, with the inserted text. If the inserted text fits in the selected frame or chain of frames, you are done.

If all the text won't fit into the first text frame or the set of linked frames, Microsoft Publisher 97 posts the autoflow dialog box shown in Figure 6-7. Click Yes to Autoflow your text or click No to put the text into the overflow area of the first text frame. Microsoft Publisher 97 then proceeds to the next text frame in your sequence and posts yet a third dialog box to ask your permission to autoflow to that frame. Microsoft Publisher 97 continues posting this dialog box with every additional frame that it requires.

What happens if you don't have enough linked text frames to take care of the incoming text? The autoflow process continues: Microsoft Publisher 97 autoflows the extra text into the first empty or unconnected frame that it

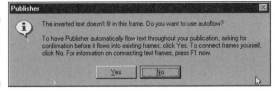

Figure 6-7:
An autoflow
dialog box.

can find, or, failing that, the first frame of any empty connected series of text frames that exist in your publication. At each new frame, the program asks your permission to use that frame. But wait, there's more!

If no empty frames are available, Microsoft Publisher 97 displays a fourth dialog box that asks whether you want to create additional pages at the end of your publication and fill those pages with full-page text frames until the imported text has been placed. If you click Yes, Microsoft Publisher 97 continues flowing the story to the end, creating new pages and full-page text frames as required. At the end of this process, the program displays a final dialog box that tells you the number of new pages created and your current page location (see Figure 6-8).

Figure 6-8:
Microsoft
Publisher 97
lets you
know how
many pages
it created.

Microsoft Publisher 97 looks for text frames from left to right, then top to bottom, and finally page to page. It even suggests empty text frames that it finds in the scratch area. If you want Microsoft Publisher 97 to connect your text frames in a different order, forget autoflow and instead connect the frames manually.

The process of autoflow is a lot more complex to explain than it is to do. We find it natural, efficient, and well thought-out; we doubt that it will give you pause or worry.

If text already exists in a text frame but you still want to take advantage of Microsoft Publisher 97's autoflow feature, use this little trick: Right-click in the frame that contains the text, choose Edit⇨Highlight Entire Story, and then cut and paste the story to your target text frame. Microsoft Publisher 97 treats pasted text just like it does inserted text, and initiates the autoflow process described in this section.

Rearranging chains

Rearranging a chain involves two parts: temporarily breaking the chain (disconnecting two frames in the chain) at the point at which you want to begin rearranging, and reconnecting frames in the desired order.

Here's how to rearrange a chain:

1. **Click the Connect Frame button for the frame that immediately precedes the point where you want to rearrange the chain.**

   The button changes from a set of three linked chains to a button with a white diamond or three dots in it. Your mouse pointer turns into the loaded pitcher pointer.

2. **Click the next frame you want to connect and continue clicking any additional frames you want to connect.**

3. **Click the Connect Frame button for the frame you want to connect.**

4. **Click the frame that follows the added frame.**

For example, if you have a chain A-B-C-D and you plan to add a frame X between frames B and C, click the Connect Frame button for frame B and click frame X. The pitcher tips as you click frame X, and you now have two chains: A-B-X and C-D. To end up with the chain A-B-X-C-D, just click frame X's Connect Frame button and then click frame C. Voilà! You're now ready to go into the chain-repair business.

If you continue to add new frames and don't reconnect C-D to your chain, eventually your story flows into your new additional frames. Frames C and D are still connected to each other; they just aren't connected to your linked chain.

Frame X in the example can be an empty, unconnected text frame or an empty, connected text frame that's the first frame in another chain. No surprise there. Because you're rearranging a chain, however, frame X also can be any empty frame that was but is no longer an original part of the current chain. For example, if you disconnect frames B and C in the chain A-B-C-D, you can then click frame D to make it the third frame in the chain. Click frame D's Connect Frame button and then click frame C to form the chain A-B-D-C.

If you try to type in an empty, connected text frame that isn't the first frame in a chain, Microsoft Publisher 97 opens a dialog box asking whether you want to begin a new story. Click OK to have the program disconnect that frame from the previous frame in the chain. Any frames farther down the chain are now part of the new story.

You can use this technique only when typing; it won't work when you're importing or inserting a text file. To insert a text file into an empty, connected frame that's not the first frame in a chain, you must first manually disconnect that text frame from the preceding frame in the chain, as described next.

After you know how to break a chain temporarily in order to rearrange it, permanently breaking a chain is easy. Just click the Connect Frame button of the last frame that you want to include in the sequence. Then, instead of clicking the next frame, click in any blank area of your publication or in the scratch area. All text that follows in the next frames disappears from those frames and becomes overflow for the last frame in your sequence. You can place the text where you want it at a later date when you connect this last frame to another frame.

Deleting stories

Connecting text frames makes accidental text deletions a little less likely. Unfortunately, it also makes intentional deletions a little more difficult. Life is full of trade-offs!

When you delete a story's only frame, the story text has nowhere else to go, so it gets wiped out along with the frame. When you delete a frame from a multiple-frame story, however, the story text does have somewhere it can go: into the other frames in the chain. Microsoft Publisher 97 is also nice enough to mend the chain for you. If you have the chain A-B-C and you delete frame B, for example, the program leaves you with the chain A-C.

If you really want to delete multiple-frame story text, follow these steps:

1. **Choose the Highlight Entire Story command from the text frame's context-sensitive menu by right clicking a frame or choosing Edit⇨Highlight Entire Story.**

2. **Press the Delete or Backspace key.**

   The entire story is deleted without deleting the frames.

Editing story text

Cutting and copying connected frames and the story text within them works similarly to deleting connect frames. If you cut or copy a connected text frame, pasting results only in an empty text frame; the story text in the original frame remains a part of the original story. To cut or copy multiple-frame story text, you must highlight the text itself.

Although editing and formatting multiple-frame story text is much the same as editing and formatting single-frame story text, you can suffer a stroke trying to highlight text in multiple text frames by dragging over it with the mouse. Save yourself a visit to the hospital: Use the Shift key together with the keyboard-based movement techniques listed in Table 7-1 in Chapter 7. For example, use Shift+Ctrl+End to extend your selection to the end of the current frame and then press Shift+right-arrow to extend your selection to the next frame in your publication. You also can select all the text in a multiple-frame story by using the Edit⇨Highlight Entire Story command from the menu bar, as mentioned in the preceding section.

If your connected frames are full of text, you can capitalize on the Highlight Entire Story command to zip to the beginning or end of a chain. Just choose Edit⇨Highlight Entire Story and then press either the left- or right-arrow key. Doing this is handy when you want to delete the entire text in a story. (Maybe you have a new version of the story that you want to place in your publication.) Or perhaps you want to edit your story in a word processor: You can export that story to a text or word processor file, open your word processor, open that file, and perform your edits.

Or, if you use Microsoft Word, choose Edit⇨Edit Story in Microsoft Word from the main menu. (The command also conveniently sits on the context-sensitive menu of the text frame.) This command launches the Microsoft Word OLE engine and opens the program with your story in a document window, as shown in Figure 6-9. When you are finished making your edits and close the Word window, you're automatically returned to Microsoft Publisher 97. Except for the title bar in Word, you would never know that

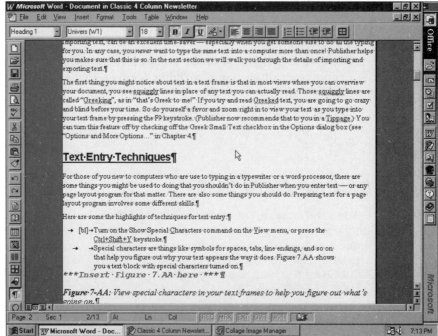

Figure 6-9:
Editing a
Microsoft
Publisher 97
story in
Microsoft
Word's OLE
server.

Microsoft Publisher 97 was the OLE client running the session. You just can't beat this kind of integration between these two programs.

Adding continuation notices

Microsoft Publisher 97 offers you a feature to help your readers locate the next and previous frames in a story in your publication: continued notices. Publishing professionals sometimes refer to these handy guidance devices as jumplines. They come in two types: a Continued from page notice tells readers where the story left off; and a Continued on page notice tells readers where the story continues.

Microsoft Publisher 97 manages continuation notices for you as an automated feature. To create a Continued notice, just right-click a linked text frame and select the Text Frame Properties command from the context-sensitive menu. Click the "Include Continued On Page..." and the "Include Continued From Page..." check boxes to turn the notices on (checked) and off (unchecked) for your selected text frame. When you click OK, the program places the notices on your text frame. Figure 6-10 shows you an example.

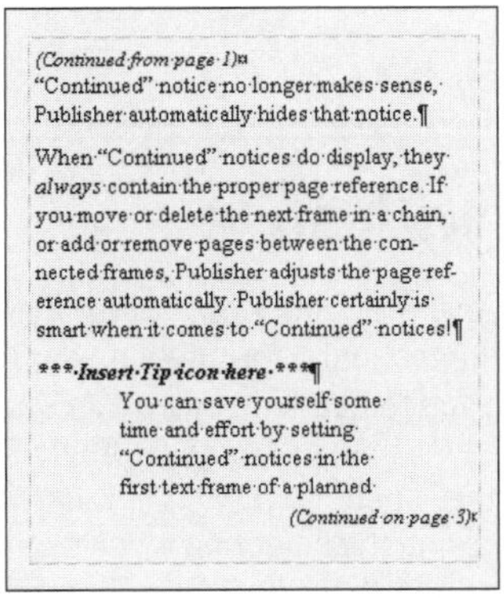

Figure 6-10:
A text frame with continuation notices.

(Continued from page 1)¤
"Continued" notice no longer makes sense, Publisher automatically hides that notice.¶

When "Continued" notices do display, they *always* contain the proper page reference. If you move or delete the next frame in a chain, or add or remove pages between the connected frames, Publisher adjusts the page reference automatically. Publisher certainly is smart when it comes to "Continued" notices!¶

****Insert Tip icon here***¶
　　You can save yourself some time and effort by setting "Continued" notices in the first text frame of a planned
*(Continued on page 3)*x

Microsoft Publisher 97 displays Continued notices only when it makes sense to display them. A Continued on page notice displays only if the current story jumps to another frame on another page. A Continued from page notice displays only if the current story jumps from a previous frame on another page. If you modify a story such that a Continued notice no longer makes sense, the program automatically hides that notice.

Story jumps are distracting, and after readers jump to a new page, they don't often come back to the page from which they jumped. Use story jumps as little as possible to increase reader comprehension.

When Continued notices do display, they always contain the proper page reference. If you move or delete the next frame in a chain or add or remove pages between the connected frames, Microsoft Publisher 97 adjusts the page reference automatically; it certainly is smart when it comes to Continued notices!

You can save yourself some time and effort by setting Continued notices in the first text frame of a planned chain before connecting the frames. When you later create the chain, Microsoft Publisher 97 automatically sets the same notices for every frame in that chain.

If you don't like the wording of a continuation notice, you can edit it as you edit any other text. For example, you can change a Continued on notice to read "See page" or "I ran out of room here so I stuck the rest of the story on page ...." Don't try to add a second line to a Continued notice, though. If you press Enter while in a Continued notice, your computer just beeps at you. If you add so much text to a Continued notice that it no longer fits on one line, some of the text disappears.

If you accidentally delete a Continued notice's page-reference number, you can replace it by choosing Insert⇨Page Numbers from the main menu. Or use the Text Frame Properties command to turn the Continued notice off and then use the command again to turn the notice back on. Your notice comes back as good as new.

Continued on ... with style

Microsoft Publisher 97 automatically formats Continued notices as italic text that's usually slightly smaller than the current frame's text. In addition, it left-aligns Continued from notices and right-aligns Continued on notices. If you don't like this formatting, you can reformat the text just as you would any other Microsoft Publisher 97 text. Chapter 7 tells you how to format text.

Don't enlarge the Continued notice text so much that it no longer fits on one line, however. If you do, some of the text disappears.

You can reformat each and every Continued notice one at a time, or you can reformat all notices by adjusting the Continued-On and the Continued-From Text style (styles are described in the next chapter). To change the style: Highlight and format a Continued on page notice to look the way you want. With the notice still highlighted, open the Style box at the left end of the top toolbar and select the Continued-On Text style. In the Change Or Apply Style dialog box that opens up next, click the Change the style using the selection as an example? radio button and then click OK. Then repeat these steps to format the Continued from page notice.

Unless you've already formatted some other Continued notices manually, every existing and future Continued notice in your publication takes on your new formatting.

In case you're bucking to become a true computer geek, what the preceding steps do is redefine the text styles that Microsoft Publisher 97 uses to determine the text formatting of Continued notices. (We discuss formatting text styles in the next chapter.)

Table Frames

As you discover in the next chapter, you can use tab stops and tabs in your paragraphs to create tables in your text frames. But a more elegant way is to use table frames to create a predefined grid of columns and rows that automatically align your text perfectly — and keep it perfectly aligned. Table frames are so easy to create and manage that it makes little sense not to use them throughout your publication whenever you need tabular displays.

Figure 6-11 shows how a plain, unformatted table frame may look after you create it. You can tell by the selection handles that the table frame is selected.

Select Column bar

Select All bar

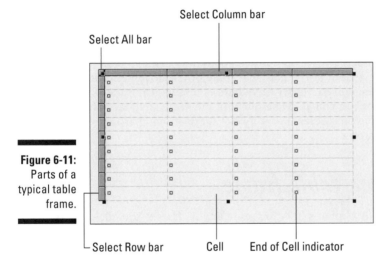

Figure 6-11:
Parts of a
typical table
frame.

Select Row bar   Cell End of Cell indicator

Here are some important things to know about table frames:

- ✔ A table frame's selection bars and gridlines display only when the frame is selected — and they never print.

- ✔ If you can't see the gridlines on-screen, choose View➪Show Boundaries and Guides or press Ctrl+Shift+O. You can hide the gridlines by choosing the Hide Boundaries and Guides command.

- ✔ If you choose a table format, what appear to be nonprinting gridlines in your table frame may be printing cell borders instead.

- ✔ If you choose to show special characters in your publication (which we recommend), each cell also displays an end-of-cell mark that looks like a small starburst. As with other special characters, end-of-cell marks display on-screen only; they don't print.

Moving around in tables

Microsoft Publisher 97 has only two navigation techniques specific to table frames:

- ✔ **Press Tab to move to the next cell (to the right).** If there's no cell to the right, the next cell is the first (leftmost) cell in the row immediately below. If you press Tab in a table frame's lower-right cell, however, you create an extra row of cells at the bottom of the table frame.

- ✔ **Press Shift+Tab to move to the previous cell (to the left).** If there's no cell to the left, the previous cell is the last (rightmost) cell in the row immediately above. If you press Shift+Tab in a table frame's upper-left cell, your computer just beeps at you.

If the cell that you move to contains any text, these movement techniques also highlight that text.

Although Tab and Shift+Tab can move you to any cell in a table frame, you may find it convenient at times to use some other movement techniques. As with text frames, you can move anywhere in a table frame simply by clicking at that position. You can also use many of the same keyboard shortcuts to move around in your tables. For information on moving around in text frames, see Chapter 7.

Creating a table frame

Chapter 5 briefly explains how to create a table frame: You click the Table tool in the toolbox and then click and drag your frame outline. Table frames are different from text frames in that after you create your frame outline, you have to make a selection from the Create Table dialog box that then appears, shown in Figure 6-12. You have three selections to make in this dialog box:

- ✔ Number of Rows
- ✔ Number of Columns
- ✔ Table Format

Microsoft Publisher 97 lets you create tables up to 128 x 128 cells large and offers you up to 23 different styles of tables, or formats. As you select a format, the program shows you a sample of the format in the Sample portion of the dialog box. The [Default] and [None] formats usually give you the same thing: a very plain, unformatted table frame. When you click OK in the Create Table dialog box, Microsoft Publisher 97 creates your table in the frame that you drew.

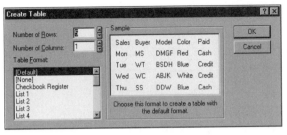

Each table format has a minimum default cell size. If you select a larger number of cells than can be accommodated, Microsoft Publisher 97 displays a dialog box asking your permission to resize the frame. If you click No, you return to the Create Table dialog box, where you can then reduce the number of rows and/or columns in your table. If you click Yes, you create a table with the number of rows and columns that you specified using the minimum cell dimensions.

Modifying tables

When a table is selected, the Table menu commands become active. This menu, shown in Figure 6-13, contains commands that you can use to modify the appearance of the table. If you choose the AutoFormat command, the Auto Format dialog box appears (see Figure 6-14). This dialog box is almost identical to the Create Table dialog box shown in Figure 6-12. The differences are that you can't change the number of rows or cells, but you can control some of the formatting options that you apply to your table.

Figure 6-13:
The Table
menu.

Although applying manual formatting is a good way to get your table frame to look just the way you want, it sometimes can mean plenty of work. Instead of manually formatting a table frame, use AutoFormat; it can do a lot of work for you. The AutoFormat feature not only applies character and paragraph formatting but also may merge cells and add cell borders and shading. Cell borders overlay table-frame gridlines and, unlike gridlines, actually print. Cell shading, a color or pattern that fills the interior of a cell, also prints.

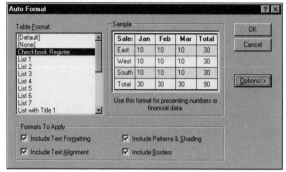

Figure 6-14:
The Auto
Format
dialog box.

Resizing tables, columns, and rows

The structure of a table frame is what really differentiates it from a text frame. Whereas a text frame is one, big rectangle into which you dump your text, a table frame is divided into a grid of separate text compartments (cells). After you create a table frame, you're not stuck with its original structure. You can resize the entire table frame; resize, insert, or delete selected columns and rows; merge multiple cells into one; and split a cell into separate cells. In short, you can restructure a table frame just about any way you want.

To resize a table frame:

- ✔ Click and drag any of its selection handles. Microsoft Publisher 97 automatically adjusts the height of each row to fit each row's contents.

- ✔ When you narrow or widen a table frame, thus decreasing or increasing the available horizontal area in each cell, Microsoft Publisher 97 often compensates by heightening or shortening some rows, thus heightening or shortening the overall frame.

- ✔ When you shorten a table frame, Microsoft Publisher 97 reduces each row only to the minimum required to display the text in each row.

- ✔ Regardless of whether your table frame contains text or not, you can't reduce any cell to less than $^1/_8$-inch square. You can heighten a table frame as much as you want, however; and Microsoft Publisher 97 heightens each row by the same proportion.

- ✔ If you choose Table⇨Grow to Fit Text, the table's rows will expand to accommodate the text that you enter.

To resize a column or row:

- ✔ Move your pointer to the edge of a column or selection-bar button until it becomes a double-headed arrow. Then click and drag until the column or row is the size that you want.

- ✔ You can't shorten a row to less than is required to display its text, and you can't shrink any cell to less than $^1/_8$-inch square.

✔ By default, when you resize a column or row, Microsoft Publisher 97 keeps all other columns and rows the same size. Columns to the right are pushed to the right or pulled to the left, whereas rows below are pushed down or pulled up. The table frame increases or decreases in overall size to accommodate the change.

✔ To keep a table frame the same size when resizing a column or row, hold down the Shift key as you resize. You now move only the border between the current column or row and the next. If you enlarge a column or row, the next column or row shrinks by that same amount. If you instead shrink a column or row, the next column or row enlarges by that amount. In either case, all other columns and rows remain the same size, as does the overall table frame.

✔ If you use the Shift key when resizing, you face even more limits. Unless you first lock the table frame, you can't shorten the row below the row that you're resizing to less than that lower row requires to display its text. And you can't shrink any adjacent column or row to less than $1/8$-inch. In addition, even if you lock the table frame, you can increase a column or row only by the amount that you can take from the next column or row.

✔ You can resize multiple columns or rows simultaneously. Just highlight those columns or rows, point to the right or bottom edge of the selection-bar button that borders the right or bottom edge of your highlight, and then click and drag. Note that if you use the Shift key to resize, however, the program ignores your highlighting. You resize only the rightmost highlighted column or bottommost highlighted row.

✔ If you resize an entire table frame after resizing individual columns and rows, Microsoft Publisher 97 resizes your columns and rows proportionally. For example, if your first column is 2 inches wide and your second column is 1 inch wide, and you then double the width of the entire table frame, your first column increases to 4 inches wide, and your second column increases to 2 inches.

Inserting and deleting columns and rows

You can insert and delete all the columns and rows you want. If you move to the last cell and press Tab, Microsoft Publisher 97 adds a new row at the bottom of the table frame and places the insertion point in the first cell of that row. You're now ready to type in that cell. How convenient!

To insert rows elsewhere, or to insert columns anywhere, you need to do only a little more work:

1. **Place the insertion point in the column or row adjacent to where you want to insert a new column or row.**

2. **Choose Table⇨Insert Rows or Columns.**

   Microsoft Publisher 97 opens the Insert (row or column) dialog box, as shown in Figure 6-15.

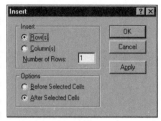

Figure 6-15:
The Insert
(row or
column)
dialog box.

3. **Select whether you want a Row or a Column inserted, type in the Number you want to insert, and select whether the new columns or rows go Before or After your current cell.**

   Even if your table frame is locked, the program increases the table frame's size to accommodate the new columns or rows.

4. **Click Apply and then OK to finish inserting your row (or column).**

Deleting a column or row is even easier:

1. **Highlight the entire row or column you want to delete.**

2. **Click the row or column selector button.**

3. **Choose Table⇨Delete Rows or Table⇨Delete Columns.**

If you neglect to highlight entire columns or rows in Step 1, Microsoft Publisher 97 usually displays the Delete Rows Or Columns command from the Table menu. Click this command to open the Delete dialog box, indicate whether you want to delete rows or columns, and then click OK.

You can't delete an entire table frame by using the Delete Columns, Delete Rows, or Delete Rows Or Columns commands. Instead, choose Edit⇨Delete Table or press Ctrl+Delete.

Merging and splitting cells

On occasion, you may want to merge multiple cells so that they become one cell. For example, as shown in Figure 6-16, you may want to merge cells so that you can center a heading over multiple columns.

✔ To merge cells, highlight the cells that you want to merge and then choose Table⇨Merge Cells. Your highlighted cells now become one. Any text in the individual cells moves into the one merged cell. You now can work with this merged cell as you would work with any other cell.

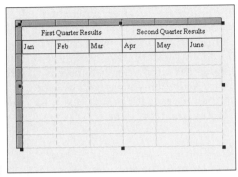

Figure 6-16:
Cells
merged to
create
column
headings.

✔ After you merge a cell, you can split it into individual cells again. Click or highlight the merged cell and select Table⇨Split Cells. (When you're in a merged cell, the Split Cells command replaces the Merge Cells command in the menu.) Your merged cell splits back into the original number of separate cells.

✔ The table's context-sensitive menu contains the commands for inserting and deleting rows and columns and for merging and splitting cells.

Working with table text

As with text frames, you can fill a table frame either by typing the text directly into the frame or by importing existing text from somewhere else. Except for the differences that we point out in the next two sections, typing and importing text into both types of frames is pretty darn similar.

Each cell in a table frame works much like a miniature text frame. For example, when you reach the right edge of a cell, Microsoft Publisher 97 automatically word-wraps your text to a new line within that cell. If the text that you type disappears beyond the right edge of the cell, you have probably locked the table. Choose Table⇨Grow to Fit Text to unlock it. If you want to end a short line within a cell, press Enter. It usually is easiest to fill in your table frame row by row; when you finish one cell, just press Tab to move on to the next one.

If pressing Tab moves you from one cell to the next, how do you insert a tab mark? We don't know why you'd ever need a tab mark in a table frame, but if you do, press Ctrl+Tab.

There is one very important difference between typing in a cell and typing in a text frame: When you run out of vertical room in a cell, Microsoft Publisher 97 automatically heightens that entire row of cells to accommodate additional lines of text. Should you later remove or reduce the size of some of that text, Microsoft Publisher 97 automatically shortens that row. Compare this to typing in a text frame: When you run out of room, the text frame remains the same size, and the program sticks that text into an overflow area or, if available, into a connected text frame.

Importing table frame text

Just as you can with text frames, you can paste or insert a text file into a table frame. Some important differences exist, however. If your text is arranged in a table-like manner, such as in a spreadsheet or a word processing table, Microsoft Publisher 97 senses the arrangement and imports that text across the necessary number of cells in your table frame. If your text isn't arranged in a table-like manner, Microsoft Publisher 97 imports all text into the current cell.

If no table-like feature is available in your other program, you can use tab marks or commas to indicate column separations (called *delimiters*) and paragraph marks to indicate row separations (called end of row markers).

Although you may be able to use the Insert➪Text File command to import text into a table frame (as described earlier in this chapter), the Windows Clipboard is much more reliable. Use it whenever possible.

Do one of the following to paste or insert text into a table:

> ✔ **Cut or copy the text to the Windows Clipboard.** Then click the cell that is to be the upper-left cell of the range and choose Edit➪Paste Cells or press Ctrl+V. If Microsoft Publisher 97 senses that the data isn't tabular, this command appears without the word Cells in it.
>
> ✔ **Choose Insert➪Text File to import text into the table frame.**

When you import text into a table frame, Microsoft Publisher 97 overwrites (replaces) any text that exists in the cells into which you import. To restore accidentally overwritten text, immediately choose Edit➪Undo Paste Cells from the menu.

Here are some other important things to remember about bringing text into your table:

> ✔ If the copied text is arranged in a table-like manner and the current table frame doesn't have enough cells to accommodate all the copied cells, Microsoft Publisher 97 opens a dialog box to ask whether it should insert columns and rows as necessary. Click Yes to make sure that you paste all your text.

✔ If you don't have a table frame selected and if the copied text is arranged in a table-like manner, the Paste Cells command appears as the Paste command. If you choose this command, the program creates a new table frame and places the copied text into that frame.

✔ Although a table frame can look much like a spreadsheet, Microsoft Publisher 97 doesn't have the power to calculate numbers. If you want to calculate the numbers in a table, calculate them in a spreadsheet program before importing. If you don't have a spreadsheet program, get out the hand calculator!

✔ Although you can't put drawn graphics into a Microsoft Publisher 97 table frame, here's a trick that you can use to make it look as if your table frame contains graphics. Layer your graphics on top of the table frame, with each graphic completely within the boundaries of a cell. Then group the table frame and graphics together. No one who sees your printed publication will be the wiser.

Editing table-frame text is much the same as editing text-frame text. You need to know just a few extra things to efficiently highlight, move, and copy table-frame text.

You can use all the same mouse techniques to highlight (select) table-frame text as you can to highlight text-frame text: drag, double-click, and Shift+click. You can also highlight table-frame text by combining the Shift key with any table-frame-movement techniques that we mention earlier in this section.

You also can highlight the contents of an entire cell by pressing Tab or Shift+Tab to move to that cell.

When you highlight any amount of text in more than one cell, you automatically highlight the entire contents of all those cells.

Here are some additional ways to select table-frame text:

✔ To select the entire contents of the current cell, choose Edit⇨Highlight Text or press Ctrl+A (for All).

✔ To select every cell in a column, click the selection bar button above that column.

✔ To select every cell in a row, click the selection bar button to the left of that row.

✔ To select multiple columns or rows, drag across the appropriate selection-bar buttons. Or press the Shift key and click selection bar buttons to extend or diminish a selected range.

✔ To select every cell in a table frame, click the upper-left selection bar button or choose Table⇨Highlight Entire Table.

Moving and copying table text

As with text frames, you can use the Clipboard or drag-and-drop text editing (see Chapter 7) to copy and move text within and between table frames. If you like, you can even copy text between text and table frames.

Working in a table frame has a very important difference, however: Whenever you move or copy the contents of multiple cells into other cells, Microsoft Publisher 97 automatically overwrites any text in those destination cells. To retain the contents of a destination cell, be sure to move or copy the contents of only one cell at a time. If you accidentally overwrite text when moving or copying, immediately select the Undo-whatever command from the Edit menu (Ctrl+Z).

Because of how Microsoft Publisher 97 overwrites destination cells, rearranging entire columns and rows of text requires some extra steps. First, insert an extra column or row where you want to move the contents of an existing column or row. Then, move the contents. Finally, delete the column or row that you just emptied. Repeat these steps for every column and row that you want to move.

Two commands on the Table menu, Fill Down and Fill Right, enable you to copy the entire contents of one cell into any number of adjacent cells either below or to the right.

Do the following to fill a series of cells in a row or column:

1. **Select the cell containing the text you want to copy and the cells to which you want to copy the text.**

   To use the fill commands, you must select cells adjacent to the cell containing the text to be copied.

2. **Choose Table⇨Fill Down to copy the value in the topmost cell to the selected cells in the column below it.**

   Or, choose Table⇨Fill Right to copy the value in the leftmost cell to selected cells in the row to the right.

Formatting table text manually

You can format table-frame text manually to make that information easier to read and understand. You can use all the character- and paragraph-formatting options detailed in the next chapter: fonts, text size, text effects, line spacing, alignment, tab stops, indents, bulleted and numbered lists, and so on. You can even hyphenate table-frame text.

The key difference when applying paragraph formatting in table frames is that Microsoft Publisher 97 treats each cell as a miniature text frame. Thus, when you align text, the text aligns within just that cell rather than across the entire table frame. And when you indent text, that text indents according to that cell's left and right edges.

To improve the look of cells, you can also change cell margins, thus changing the amount of space between a cell's contents and its edges. To change cell margins, choose Format➪Table Cell Properties. The resulting dialog box is shown in Figure 6-17.

Figure 6-17:
The Table
Cell
Properties
dialog box.

Chapter 7

Editors Are Bought, Not Born

. . . .

In This Chapter

▶ Tricks of editing, navigating, and generally messing with text

▶ Tools that search, replace, hyphenate, and check the spelling of your text

▶ How to format each and every character in your document

▶ How to format paragraphs with style — and with styles

▶ Ways to dress your text — frame by frame

. . . .

*I*f you use a word-processing or similar computer program, you know that making changes to text (editing) can be a breeze. Delete a word here, insert a couple words there, rewrite a sentence, add a comma, and the program takes care of the rest. The ease with which you can edit text in a computer program is one of the reasons that typewriters are choking landfills worldwide. (Barrie just bought a new one, completely made of plastic, for $89.)

Editing text in Microsoft Publisher 97 is easy, too. Almost everything you know about editing text in a word processor applies to editing and formatting text in Microsoft Publisher 97. Although Microsoft Publisher 97 doesn't have quite the editing muscle and sophistication of some full-blown word-processing programs, it still does a very respectable job.

Microsoft Publisher 97 is also more than a match for the formatting tools that you find in any word processor. Its many text-formatting features enable you to take control over how your text looks, character by character, paragraph by paragraph, frame by frame. You control the horizontal; you control the vertical.

This chapter focuses on editing and formatting text in Microsoft Publisher 97. It focuses specifically on working with text in text frames, but you can use most of the techniques shown here to work with text in table frames as well.

Tricks of the Editing Meisters

You probably are an editing master already. If you've been banging away at a word processor for a while, chances are that this section is a review for you. If not, we want to mention some of the tricks that you can use to edit text in a text frame.

To edit text, you first must position the insertion point in the text or highlight the text. If you position the insertion point in the text, you can press Delete to remove any characters to the right of the insertion point or press Backspace to remove characters to the left. You can place an insertion point anywhere; when you do, Microsoft Publisher 97 also selects the text frame for you.

If you highlight text, any character that you type replaces that highlighted text. If you don't want Microsoft Publisher 97 to automatically replace your highlighted text, uncheck the Typing Replaces Selection check box on the Editing and User Assistance tab of the Options dialog box. Then, any new text that you type appears to the left of the highlighted text. (To open the Editing and User Assistance tab of the Options dialog box, choose Tools⇨Options; then, click the Editing and User Assistance tab.)

Movin' and groovin'

If you are familiar with keys that move your insertion point in Microsoft Word, you find that they all work inside Microsoft Publisher 97. You can also reposition the insertion point by using your keyboard's movement keys: Home, End, PgUp, PgDn, and the four arrow keys.

Some keyboards offer a separate bank of navigation keys, and some place the keys on the numeric keypad at the right end of the keyboard. To use the keys on the numeric keypad as navigation keys, you must first turn off the Num Lock key on the keyboard. If the Num Lock key is turned on, the keys type numbers rather than move your insertion point. Figure 7-1 shows a classic 101-key computer keyboard.

Table 7-1 lists some of the common movement keys and what they do. Notice that only the numbers on the numeric keypad — and not the ones on the main keyboard — move your insertion point.

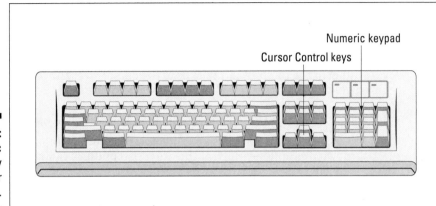

Figure 7-1:
A classic
101-key
computer
keyboard.

Table 7-1	Navigation Keys
Press This	*To Do This*
Home or 7 key	Go to the beginning of current text line
End or 1 key	Go to the end of current text line
Up-arrow or 8 key	Move up one text line
Down-arrow or 2 key	Move down one text line
Right-arrow or 6 key	Move right one character
Left-arrow or 4 key	Move left one character
Ctrl+Home or Ctrl+7	Go to the beginning of current text frame
Ctrl+End or Ctrl+1	Go to the end of current text frame
Ctrl+up arrow or Ctrl+8	Go to the beginning of current paragraph
Ctrl+down arrow or Ctrl+2	Go to the beginning of next paragraph
Ctrl+right arrow or Ctrl+6	Move right one word
Ctrl+left arrow or Ctrl+4	Move left one word

If text is highlighted, pressing the left- or right-arrow key positions the
insertion point at the beginning or end of the text and then removes the
highlighting (deselects the text).

Selection tricks

As mentioned earlier, before you can do any editing or formatting to a piece of text, you must select it. The simplest way to highlight text is to select the Text tool in the toolbox and then drag the cursor over the text that you want to highlight. But here are several other ways to highlight text:

- ✔ Double-click a word to select the word and any blank spaces following it.

- ✔ Click at one end of the text that you want to highlight, press and hold down the Shift key, click at the other end of the text, and then release the Shift key.

- ✔ Combine the Shift key with any of the movement techniques listed in the preceding section. For example, to select an entire line of text, move the insertion point to the beginning of the line and then press Shift+End.

- ✔ Choose Edit➪Highlight Entire Story or press Ctrl+A (for All) to highlight all the text in the current text frame and in any connected frames.

You can also use the Shift key in combination with clicking or any movement technique to extend or reduce an existing highlight.

Drag and drop

Previous chapters in this book illustrate the use of Cut, Copy, and Paste in several different applications. The Cut/Copy/Paste technique is one of the two ways of moving text in text frames. The other is called *drag and drop,* which sounds like a job requirement for airport baggage handlers. By using drag-and-drop text editing, you can move and copy text within and between frames located on any single page or two-page spread without going through all the steps of using the Windows Clipboard. We think of it as a direct form of cut and paste (or copy and paste if you hold down the Ctrl key as you drag and drop).

To remove text from one spot and place it in another by using drag and drop, highlight the text, move your pointer over it, and then click and drag it to a new location. Your pointer turns into a *T* with the word *Drag* next to it as soon as you press the mouse button and move the pointer over the selected text, to indicate that you can drag and drop.

To copy text by using drag and drop, highlight the text that you want to copy, press Ctrl, and then click and drag the selection to a new location. Your pointer turns into a *T* with the word *Copy* next to it to indicate that you can drag and drop the copy.

If your mouse pointer is a plain, left-pointing arrow, the Use Helpful Pointers check box is turned off in the Options dialog box. (See Chapter 3.) Or you may have turned drag-and-drop editing off, although for the life of us we can't think of why you'd want to do that. (We love drag and drop.) The Drag-and-Drop Text Editing check box on the Editing and User Assistance tab of the Options dialog box disables this feature (which is turned on by default) in all your publications.

Drag-and-drop text editing isn't for everyone. If you're mouse challenged, you may want to skip this feature.

Symbols

A big mistake that many new desktop Publishers make is failing to use those special typographic characters that are known in Microsoft Publisher 97 as *symbols.* If you look carefully at this book or almost any well produced publication, you can see symbols all over the place. These special symbols, which include fractions (such as $3/4$); special quotation marks (" "); special hyphens, en dashes (–) and em dashes (—); ligatures (Æ, œ, æ); and so on are a typographer's stock in trade.

Microsoft Publisher 97 provides two ways to put appropriate typographical symbols in your publications: automatically and manually. As you type, Microsoft Publisher 97 automatically replaces inch and foot marks (″ and ′), also known as *straight quotes,* with typographic quotation marks (" ", ', and '), and double hyphens (- -) with em dashes (—). (Typographic quotation marks are often called *smart quotes* or *curly quotes.*) If you import text, punctuation marks in that text remain as they were in your source document.

If Microsoft Publisher 97 doesn't replace these marks for you as you type, you probably turned off the Automatically use smart quotes option on the Editing and User Assistance tab of the Options dialog box. Turn this setting on. It applies to all your Microsoft Publisher 97 sessions.

If you can, try to set up the program that you use to create your text so that it automatically replaces these marks as you type. Microsoft Word offers this feature, for example. Otherwise, you must search and replace the marks manually by using the Edit⇨Replace command on the menu bar.

What if you *want* to type an inch or foot mark? You can turn the Automatically Use Smart Quotes option off for a moment, but an easier way to insert an inch mark is to press Ctrl+Shift+". To insert a foot mark, press Ctrl+ '.

To insert a symbol manually into a publication, choose Insert⇨Symbol and make your selection from the Insert Symbol dialog box, as shown in Figure 7-2.

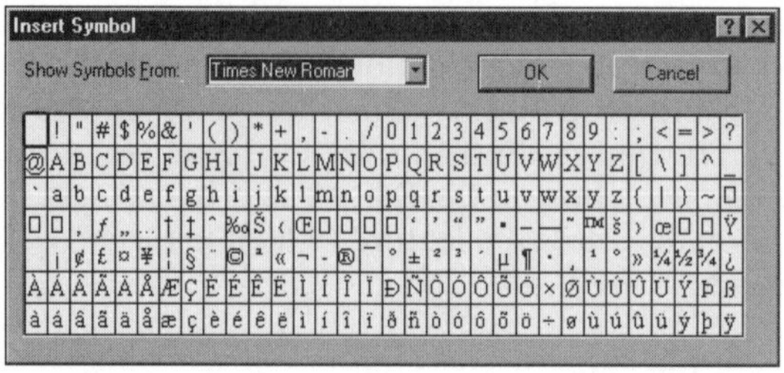

Figure 7-2:
The Insert
Symbol
dialog box.

The Insert Symbol dialog box shows you all the available symbols in your installed system fonts. Your current font appears, but you can switch to other fonts as well — including symbol font. You can find en dashes, fractions, copyright and registration marks, foreign letters and currency symbols, smiley faces, hearts, diamonds, clubs, spades, and even that *é* that you need to type *resumé* correctly. If you are looking for a special symbol, check out the Symbol font by selecting it from the Show Symbols Erom list box. The Wingdings font is also a rich source of symbols such as bullets, buttons, and bows.

Don't bother to insert symbols one at a time to create bulleted lists like the ones you see in this book. Instead, use the bulleted or numbered list feature in Microsoft Publisher 97 to create this special format, as described in the section "Creating bulleted and numbered lists" later in this chapter.

Tools of the Editing Meisters

Any good page layout program comes with a set of basic text management tools. Some of the heavyweight programs come with tools for formatting, text correction, seek and destroy, and other features that any word processor would envy. These tools are important; they increase accuracy and make your text more readable.

Microsoft Publisher 97 offers the following tools:

- Search and replace
- A spell checker
- Automatic hyphenation

Additionally, Microsoft Publisher 97's Tools menu offers some other tools that aren't specific to text management. The Design Checker command looks at your document for common printing problems. And the Design Gallery is a picture browser that enables you to view the Microsoft clip-art collection and add additional images as needed. We discuss these commands in Chapters 11 and 9, respectively. The sections that follow examine the text tools.

Hide and seek: Find and Replace

Any good word processor has a find feature (a command that enables you to hunt down a specific word or phrase in your document). Okay, even *poor* word processors have a find feature. Microsoft Publisher 97 has a find feature and even has a replace feature, which enables you to search and replace one word or phrase with another. If you need to correct text at story length, you just can't get by without these search and replace features.

Here's how to find text:

1. **Select a text frame of the story that you want Microsoft Publisher 97 to search.**

   Before finding and replacing text, press F9 to view your text at a readable size.

2. **Choose Edit⇨Find.**

   The Find dialog box, shown in Figure 7-3, appears.

3. **In the Find What text box, type the text that you want Microsoft Publisher 97 to find, using wildcard symbols, if desired.**

   If you've ever worked in MS-DOS, you probably know about wildcards. One wildcard, the question mark (?), works in the Find dialog box. If you use a question mark in your search criteria, any character can be a match for the character in the question mark position. For example, if you ask Microsoft Publisher 97 to search for the text *no?,* it finds the words *not, now, nod,* and so on. If you need to search for actual question marks, type a caret (^) before the mark, as in ^?. And to find carets, type ^^. Table 7-2 lists codes that you can use to find other special characters.

4. **Click the Match Whole Word Only and/or the Match Case check box if you want those options.**

   The Match Whole World Only option finds any occurrence of your search string that is surrounded by spaces or punctuation marks. It ignores any matches that are part of larger words. With the option on, for example, a search for *publish* ignores the word *publisher.*

The Match Case option searches your document for an exact match of your search string's characters, using upper- and lowercase characters as filtering criteria. With this option on, for example, a search for the word *publish* ignores any occurrence of *Publisher;* a search for the word *Publish*, however, finds *Publisher*.

5. Click the Up or Down radio button to specify the direction of the search.

If you choose the Up radio button, Microsoft Publisher 97 searches from the location of your cursor up to the beginning of the text frame or story. If you choose the Down button, it searches from the cursor location to the end of the frame or story.

6. Click the Find Next button.

Figure 7-3:
The Find
dialog box.

Microsoft Publisher 97 scampers off to look for your text, and one of three things happens:

✔ Your text is found and highlighted.

✔ Microsoft Publisher 97 finds your text, but not the occurrence for which you were looking. Click the Find Next button to continue the search.

✔ Microsoft Publisher 97 gets to the beginning or end of the text without a match and opens a dialog box asking permission to continue looking from the other end. After Microsoft Publisher 97 searches the entire story, it displays a dialog box saying that no matching text was found. Sorry!

Microsoft Publisher 97 can't find text in a WordArt frame.

Sometimes, you may want to search for special characters, such as an end of paragraph mark or a tab space. You can do so by using the codes listed in Table 7-2.

Table 7-2   Find and Replace Codes for Special Characters

To Find This	Use This Code
Two spaces	(type two spaces)
Optional hyphen	^-
Nonbreaking hyphen (a hyphen that doesn't break across a line ending)	^~
Line break	^N
End of paragraph mark	^P
Nonbreaking space (a space that doesn't break across a line ending)	^S
Tab space	^T
White space (a tab character or space between words)	^W

Having Microsoft Publisher 97 help you find text is great, but getting it to replace unwanted text is an even bigger labor-saving device. To both find and replace text, use the Edit⇨Replace command. Here's how:

1. **Select the story containing the text that you want Microsoft Publisher 97 to replace.**

2. **Choose Edit⇨Replace.**

   The Replace dialog box, as shown in Figure 7-4, appears. It looks a lot like the Find dialog box and remembers the last text that you typed in the Find dialog box during your current Microsoft Publisher 97 session.

Figure 7-4:
The
Replace
dialog box.

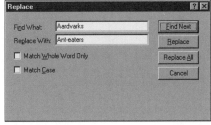

3. **Type the text that you want to find in the Find What text box and the text that you want to replace it with in the Replace With text box.**

   You can also set the same Match options described in the preceding set of steps.

4. **Click Find Next.**

One of three things happens here:

- ✔ A match is found. To replace the found text, click the Replace button. Microsoft Publisher 97 then searches for the next occurrence of the text in the Find What text box.

- ✔ A match is found, but not the match that you want. Click the Find Next button to continue the search.

- ✔ Microsoft Publisher 97 gets to the beginning or end of the text without finding a match, so it opens a dialog box asking permission to continue looking from the other end. Click the Yes button to continue the search or No to end the search. If Microsoft Publisher 97 still can't find your text, it opens a dialog box to say that no matching text was found.

If you choose the Replace All button, Microsoft Publisher 97 replaces all occurrences of the matching text with your replacement text in one fell swoop. Take care when using the Replace All button; unless you are careful, you may replace matches that you didn't intend to change. Mistakes are hard to catch in large stories.

The Replace command is an excellent way to repair text that wasn't prepared the correct typographical way. For example, you can use the command to replace all double spaces with single spaces. Replacing other things, such as double dashes and old-fashioned fractions, with their correct typographic counterparts also is possible. Use the Insert Symbol dialog box (see Figure 7-2) to insert the correct symbol into your text. Cut or copy the symbol to the Clipboard, choose the Edit⇨Replace command, and type the old-fashioned mark that you want to replace in the Find What text box. Then click the Replace With text box and press Ctrl+V to insert the symbol there. The symbol may appear as some bizarre shape totally unrelated to what you copied from the publication, but don't pay any attention to that. The symbol appears correctly again after it's back in the publication. Now you're ready to replace at will — but just to be safe, always test things out by replacing a single match before using the Replace All button to apply the replace universally.

Can you check my spelling?

No doubt about it: Spelling errors make you look bad. To begin checking your spelling, select a text frame and then choose Tools⇨Check Spelling or press F7. Microsoft Publisher 97 immediately searches for the first word that it doesn't recognize; if it finds one, a Check Spelling dialog box similar to the one in Figure 7-5 appears. Microsoft Publisher 97 places that word in the Not in dictionary text box. You can correct the word in the Change To text box, and the spell checker even makes suggestions of close matches in the Suggestions list box.

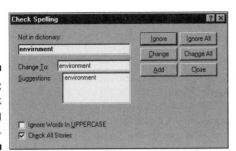

Figure 7-5:
The Check
Spelling
dialog box.

Microsoft Publisher 97 can't check spelling in WordArt frames.

The spell checker is one of those "shared tools" in the Microsoft arsenal. Know one, know them all. Like other Microsoft programs with spell-checking capabilities, Microsoft Publisher 97 doesn't find misspelled words per se. It actually compares every word it comes across against its own 100,000-word electronic dictionary. It considers anything between two spaces or similar delimiting characters to be a word. If a word doesn't match, Microsoft Publisher 97 points it out. That's why the dialog box has a Not in dictionary box rather than a Misspelled word box.

You have several choices for dealing with each word that Microsoft Publisher 97 finds:

✔ If the word is incorrect and you can find the correct word in the Suggestions list box, double-click that correct word.

✔ Alternatively, you can single-click the correct word and then click Change All to have Microsoft Publisher 97 automatically fix every occurrence of the incorrect word as it finds it.

✔ If the word is incorrect and you can't find the correct word in the Suggestions list box, enter the correct word in the Change To text box and then click the Change or Change All button.

✔ If the word is correct but it's not a word that you use very often, click the Ignore button to leave the word as is. Or click Ignore All to leave every occurrence of the word that Microsoft Publisher 97 finds in this spelling check as is.

✔ If the word is correct and it's a word that you do use often (such as your own name), click the Add button to add the word to Microsoft Publisher 97's dictionary. Be careful with this button, though, because if you add an incorrect word to the dictionary, Microsoft Publisher 97 never points out the word again, in this or any other publication!

After you tell Microsoft Publisher 97 what to do with the first word, the spell checker continues on until the end of your highlighted text or to the end of the story. Microsoft Publisher 97 then asks whether you want to continue checking the rest of the current story. If you have more than one story in your publication, Microsoft Publisher 97 checks the current story first and then asks whether you want to check the next story (unless the Check All Stories check box is checked, in which case Microsoft Publisher 97 goes ahead and checks every story without asking). When it comes to checking spelling, Microsoft Publisher 97 is as relentless as our editors. Eventually, though, Microsoft Publisher 97 runs out of words to check and closes the Check Spelling dialog box.

A spell checker is not a substitute for proofreading. Just because all the words are spelled correctly doesn't mean that they're the correct words. We know of one instance when the title of a state document contained the phrase "Department of Pubic Health." This, of course, flew through the spell checker and appeared in several thousand circulated copies, to the amusement of many — but not the author.

Hyphenation

To fit more text in a given space or to make justified text easier to read, you can have Microsoft Publisher 97 hyphenate your text, automatically breaking words in two at line endings. This process is automated, so Microsoft Publisher 97 continually removes and adds hyphens as needed as you type, edit, and rearrange text.

To have Microsoft Publisher 97 hyphenate your text automatically:

1. **Select the text frame or story that you want to hyphenate.**

2. **Choose Tools⇨Hyphenate or press Ctrl+H.**

   The Hyphenate dialog box, as shown in Figure 7-6, appears.

3. **Verify that Automatically Hyphenate This Story is selected and then click the OK button.**

Figure 7-6:
The
Hyphenate
dialog box.

Your text is now hyphenated. Should you later change the text in any way, Microsoft Publisher 97 automatically rehyphenates the text.

So much for automatic hyphenation. If you don't trust Microsoft Publisher 97 to hyphenate your text for you or if you want to manually control where a hyphen in a word occurs, you can click the Suggest Hyphens For This Story radio button. Then, when Microsoft Publisher 97 finds a word appropriate for hyphenating, it shows you that word and how it wants to hyphenate it. You can either approve, modify, or reject this hyphenation. If you use this option, though, Microsoft Publisher 97 doesn't rehyphenate your text for you; you have to issue the Hyphenate command again.

Another control that you have in adjusting hyphenation is the setting in the Hyphenation Zone text box. The smaller the hyphenation zone, the more hyphens Microsoft Publisher 97 uses and the more even the right edge of your text is.

To remove automatic hyphenation, choose the Tools⇨Hyphenate command again. This time, verify that the Turn Off Automatic Hyphenation radio button is selected (it replaces the Automatically Hyphenate This Story radio button) and click the OK button.

You can set up Microsoft Publisher 97 to hyphenate all text by default. To do this, open the More Options dialog box and click the Automatically Hyphenate By Default check box if it's not already selected (it's on by default) and then change the setting in the Hyphenation Zone text box if you want. For any text frame that you now create in any publication, Microsoft Publisher 97 automatically hyphenates the frame's text. Microsoft Publisher 97 doesn't change the hyphenation in any existing frames, however.

Text Formatting

If you've worked in a word processor, you've formatted your share of text. Perhaps you are a text formatting meister. Even so, you may learn a trick or two in the sections that follow. If you don't, reward yourself with three gold asterisks and move on down the line.

Modern word processors and page layout programs divide the formatting that you can apply to text into three levels:

✔ **Character formats:** Formats that you can apply to each character in your text: type styles, fonts, sizes, cases, and so on.

✔ **Paragraph formats:** Default formats that apply to your paragraph. Some of these formats, such as styles, you may be able to change. Others, such as line spacing, may not be changeable, depending on the program that you are using.

✔ **Document formats:** Usually formats that apply to the entire document. (Page margins are an example of a document format.) Because Microsoft Publisher 97 treats stories as if they are documents, document formats apply to text frames and connected text frames with a story in them.

If you understand which formats belong to which category, you can quickly apply the format that you desire to get very professional results — often with dramatic time savings.

The Format toolbar

After you have selected text, a Format toolbar appropriate to text appears under the Standard toolbar. Figure 7-7 shows the Format toolbar for text. Most of the elements of the toolbar should be familiar to you if you have worked in a word processor.

Figure 7-7:
The Text
Format
toolbar.

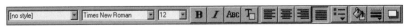

The format options on the toolbar are (from left to right):

✔ **Font Style list box:** A *style* is a set of formats that apply to a paragraph, as explained later in this chapter. This list box enables you to choose a style and apply it to your selection.

✔ **Font list box:** This shows your current font and enables you to select a different font.

✔ **Font Size list box:** This box shows your current font size and enables you to enter a new one.

✔ **Bold, Italic, and Small Capitals buttons:** These buttons set the font style. (Strangely, a button for Underline is missing.)

✔ **Font Color button:** This button opens the color selector pop-up menu, which enables you to choose a font color.

- ✔ **Left, Center, Right, and Justified buttons:** These buttons apply text justification, which is a paragraph-level setting.

- ✔ **Bullet or Numbered List button:** This button accesses a paragraph-level setting that enables you to automatically number your paragraphs or place bullets at the beginning of paragraphs.

- ✔ **Object Color button:** In this instance, the object is the text frame(s) and the color applied is a background.

- ✔ **Border button:** This button enables you to place borders around your text frames.

- ✔ **Add/Remove Shadow:** This button accesses a text frame setting that enables you to add a shadow to the border of the frame.

It's important to realize that the toolbar offers you only highlights of what's possible format-wise. Many of the Format menu commands that the buttons duplicate provide access to dialog boxes containing lots of additional options. Still, the buttons are a convenient, quick way to apply basic formatting.

Character formatting

Character formatting enables you to change the appearance of individual characters. Character formatting is most often used for emphasis, to set text apart from the text surrounding it. For example, words are often italicized to make them stand out in a block of plain text.

One of the really confusing aspects of formatting text is that you can format the text in your paragraphs at the paragraph level and also format individual characters in that paragraph any way that you want. You can think of paragraph formatting as a default format that you can override as needed.

Character formatting can make your text look great, but for even fancier text, try out WordArt, as described in the next chapter.

Choosing a font

Perhaps the most noticeable character format is the *font* (also known as the *typeface*) of your text. The font determines each character's basic shape. Microsoft Windows and Microsoft Publisher 97 together offer you more than 23 fonts. Text always uses some font or another; by default, it's Times New Roman. Two of the fonts, Symbol and Wingdings, are symbol fonts and aren't used for regular text.

As if 23 fonts weren't enough, you may have even more available to you. Other Windows programs may have installed additional fonts on your computer, and your printer may have its own set of built-in fonts. If you become a raving font addict, rest assured that you can buy and install even more fonts.

As Roger C. Parker says in *Desktop Publishing & Design For Dummies* (published by IDG Books Worldwide, Inc.): "He who dies with the most fonts wins."

Do one of the following to change the font for selected text:

- ✔ Select the font name from the Font list box in the toolbar.

- ✔ Select Format⇨Character to open the Character dialog box, shown in Figure 7-8. Enter the font name in the Font list box.

  If no font name appears in the Font box, you've probably highlighted text that is currently formatted with more than one font. You can still use the Font list box to apply the font that you want.

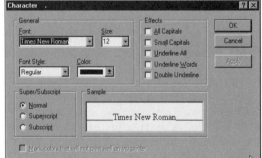

Figure 7-8:
The
Character
dialog box.

Press Ctrl+Shift+F to activate the Font list box and then press the down- or up-arrow keys to move to the font that you want. Press Enter to select the highlighted font.

When you open the Font box's drop-down list, you see an icon next to each font name. The two *T*s icon means that the font is a *TrueType font,* an outline font that any Windows program can use. The little printer icon means that the font is a *printer font,* built into the current publication's target printer. No symbol means that the font is a *system font,* one that Windows itself uses to label windows, dialog boxes, options, and so on.

Which type of font should you use? In general, TrueType is generally the most hassle-free font type, but you may want to go with printer fonts if you're having your publication printed by a service bureau. Many service bureaus use Postscript fonts that require printer descriptions.

Note that if you *do* use printer fonts, those fonts may look bad on-screen. Because Windows has only sketchy information about any given printer font, your on-screen characters may be misshapen and lines of text may appear clipped off in certain views. Everything should look fine when you print your publication, though. Chapter 8 explains fonts and typography in detail.

Changing the font size

There must be something about publishing professionals that makes using standard English terms difficult for them. Even when it comes to measuring the size of text, they can't stick with inches, centimeters, or any other measurement that the rest of the world uses. Instead, they measure the height of text in *points*. A point is approximately $1/72$ of an inch, and you can make text any size from $1/2$ point to $999 1/2$ points, in $1/2$-point increments. In inches, that translates from $1/144$ inches to almost 14 inches high — that's quite a range! Unless you're making banners, though, you probably want to keep your text somewhere between 6 and 72 points.

With typography, nothing is as simple as it seems. Even a standard point size changes depending on the font selected. These and other mysteries of life are explained in the next chapter.

To change the size of selected text:

✔ Select the size from the Font Size list box in the toolbar or enter your own size into the list box.

✔ Alternatively, you can choose Format⇨Character to open the Character dialog box, as shown back in Figure 7-8, and enter the font size there.

If no font size appears in the Size list box, you've probably highlighted text formatted with more than one size. You can still use the Size list box to apply the size you want.

Press Ctrl+> to increase the font size and Ctrl+< to decrease the font size one half of a point size. Press Ctrl+Shift+P to activate the Size list box and enter any size you wish.

With TrueType fonts, you can enter any font size that you want (in the allowed range), even decimal numbers. Some printer fonts support only a limited set of sizes, however. If you plan to use printer fonts, consult the printer's documentation to see whether this limitation applies.

Applying a type style

The last important character format is type style, which Microsoft Publisher 97 refers to as *Effects*. Want to make a word or two stand out? Then apply text effects such as **boldface,** *italics,* or underlining. You can apply the former two effects to selected text by using toolbar buttons; underlining requires either a keystroke or a trip to the Character dialog box.

You can specify whether you want to underline all the selected text or just the individual words and not the spaces between them. You can also create superscripts or subscripts, all caps, small caps, and double-underlined effects in the dialog box.

We think that you will want to know the keyboard shortcuts for these text effects cold: Press Ctrl+B for bold; Ctrl+I for italic; Ctrl+U for underline; Ctrl+= for super-script; Ctrl+Shift+= for subscript; Ctrl+Shift+K for small caps; and, most important, Ctrl+Spacebar for plain text (removes all style formats from selected text).

As with font and font size, you can use either the toolbar buttons or the Character dialog box (more generally) to make your type style selections. If it appears as if the actual letter on an Effect button (B, I, or ABC) is pushed in rather than the button itself, you've probably highlighted some text that uses the effect and some that doesn't. If you click the button once, you apply the effect to all the highlighted text. Click again to remove the effect completely.

Some fonts (not common Windows ones, though) don't support boldface and/or italics. For these fonts, the B (bold) and I (italic) buttons are useless. You can click them all you want, but your text doesn't change.

Getting the yearn to kern

If you're really picky about how your text looks, you can even control the amount of horizontal space between characters, either squishing text together or spreading it apart. Publishing professionals call this *kerning*. (Don't confuse kerning with line spacing. Kerning controls the amount of *horizontal* spacing between characters, whereas line spacing controls the *vertical* spacing between lines of text.)

By default, Microsoft Publisher 97 automatically kerns between relatively large characters — anything 15 points or larger. To get Microsoft Publisher 97 to kern even smaller characters, choose the Tools➪Options command from the menu bar, click the Editing and User Assistance tab, and change the setting in the Kern character pairs above text box. Microsoft Publisher 97 then adjusts the spacing between letters based on a list of letter pairs that are part of a font's definition.

Microsoft Publisher 97 does a good job of automatic kerning, but if you have some specific text that you want to kern manually — for example, a headline that you want to stretch across a page — use the Format➪Spacing Between Characters command. This command opens the Spacing Between Characters dialog box, as shown in Figure 7-9, where you can adjust kerning for the entire paragraph or just the selected characters. Perfect kerning is one of those power features that desktop Publishers die for.

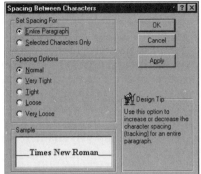

Figure 7-9:
The
Spacing
Between
Characters
dialog box.

If you want to adjust the space between two single characters, put the insertion point between them. Then, press Ctrl+Shift+[to move characters closer together or Ctrl+Shift+] to spread them apart.

Don't bother spending much time kerning small text. Kerning is best done on large text, particularly headline text. Figure 7-10 shows you the difference between tight and loose kerning.

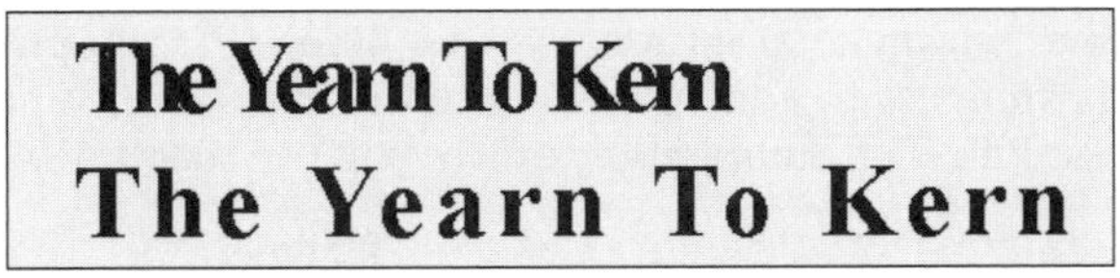

Figure 7-10:
Tight versus
loose
kerning.

The Yearn To Kern

The Yearn To Kern

Paragraph formatting

Whereas character formatting enables you to control text one character at a time, *paragraph formatting* controls entire paragraphs. Paragraph formatting includes line spacing, alignment within a frame, tab stops, indents, and formatting text as bulleted or numbered lists.

You probably discovered in grade school that a paragraph is a group of sentences that form a complete thought. Well, forget it! In Microsoft Publisher 97, regardless of complete thoughts, a paragraph is anything that ends with a *paragraph mark,* one of those special characters that you create every time you press the Enter key. Thus, if you type a three-line address, pressing Enter to begin each new line, that address consists of three separate paragraphs. If you want, you can format each of those paragraphs differently.

With character formatting, you must select all the text that you want to format. But you don't need to bother highlighting entire paragraphs to apply paragraph formatting. To mark a single paragraph for paragraph formatting, just place the insertion point anywhere in the paragraph or highlight text anywhere in the paragraph. To mark multiple paragraphs for formatting, just highlight some text in each of those paragraphs. Keep this in mind during the next few sections whenever we tell you to "mark the paragraph(s)."

Here's a weird one: Microsoft Publisher 97 and word processors store the paragraph format and any variation that you apply to characters in that paragraph in the paragraph mark itself.

Adjusting line spacing

You can control the amount of space that appears above and below each paragraph. This option is important for making headings stand out and for many other purposes.

To change the paragraph(s) line spacing:

✔ Select the paragraph(s) that you want to affect and then choose Format⇨Line Spacing. The Line Spacing dialog box appears, as shown in Figure 7-11.

You can set the Between Lines spinner to control the amount of space between lines within a paragraph. Use the Before Paragraphs and After Paragraphs spinners to add space before the first line of a paragraph or after the last line. The Sample box shows you the result of your settings.

✔ Alternatively, you can press Ctrl+1 for single space text; Ctrl+2 for double space; Ctrl+5 for 1¹/₂ line space; and Ctrl+0 (zero) to remove the space before a paragraph.

Figure 7-11:
The Line
Spacing
dialog box.

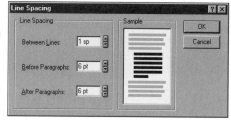

It is considered good typographical practice to set line spacing rather than insert additional paragraph marks to create spacing. Then, if you decide to change the spacing between the paragraph later, you need to work with the attributes of only the paragraphs that contain your content. You don't need to add or delete paragraphs that you use as space holders.

You can specify any and all line spacing settings in terms of inches (in or "), centimeters (cm), points (pt), picas (pi), or Microsoft Publisher 97's special space (sp) measurement. One space in Microsoft Publisher 97 always equals 120 percent of the current text size — an ideal size-to-spacing ratio for single spacing. If you use the sp measurement — 1 sp for single-spacing, 2 sp for double spacing, and so on — your line spacing changes as your text size changes. If you use any other measurement, your line spacing remains the same when you enlarge or reduce your text size, even if the result is wildly squished or spaced out text lines.

Setting paragraph alignment

By default, Microsoft Publisher 97 lines up paragraphs along the left edge of the text frame that holds them. Text aligned in this manner is said to be *ragged right* or *left justified* by typographers. To instead push text to the right edge (ragged left or right justified), center it between the edges (fully ragged), or stretch it from edge to edge (fully justified), you change its *alignment,* also called *justification* in publishing lingo.

Here are some ways to set paragraph alignment for your selected paragraph(s):

- ✔ Click one of the four alignment icons on the Format toolbar. These are, from left to right across the tool bar, Left, Center, Right, and Justified.

- ✔ You can also use the following keystrokes: Ctrl+L for left justified; Ctrl+R for right justified; Ctrl+E for center (think *even!*); or Ctrl+J for fully justified. Press Ctrl+Q to return your paragraph to the default format.

- ✔ You can also align paragraphs using the Indents and Lists command on the Format menu, but using an Alignment tool bar button is much easier.

Justified text can stretch your text out so far that it's difficult to read. To remedy this, try hyphenating the text, as described earlier in this chapter.

The justification that you use, hyphenation, the amount of line spacing, and other paragraph-level formats are important determinants in how your publication looks. They "color" your text and make it either more or less readable. A full explanation of this topic would require more space than we have available. But you should really take the time to visit the style guides that we recommend to you at the end of Chapter 2. See Chapter 11, too, for more information on hyphenating and justifying text.

Setting tab stops

When you press the Tab key in a text frame, Microsoft Publisher 97 inserts a special character called a *tab mark.* How a tab mark affects the text following that mark depends on the *tab stops* set for the paragraph.

By default, left-aligned tab stops are set every half-inch on the horizontal ruler. (When you're working in a text frame, a special subsection of the horizontal ruler measures distances from the frame's left edge.) Thus, each tab mark that you create usually causes the text following that mark to left-align with the next available half-inch mark. For example, if your text is 1¼ inches from the left edge of a frame and you insert a tab mark before that text, the text left-aligns with the 1½-inch ruler mark.

By setting your own custom tab stops, however, you can get tab marks to align a number of other ways. Microsoft Publisher 97 supports four different kinds of tab stops:

- ✔ **Left tab stop:** This setting is the default, and a tab moves text to the right of the tab mark so that it aligns flush left to the tab stop.

- ✔ **Center tab stop:** A tab moves text so that it aligns centered on the tab stop.

- ✔ **Right tab stop:** A tab moves text so that it aligns flush right to the tab stop.

- ✔ **Decimal tab stop:** A tab moves text so that any decimal point aligns to the tab stop. This tab is useful for aligning numeric data in tables.

You can quickly set a tab stop for your selected paragraph(s) by clicking the Move Both Rulers button at the intersection of the two rulers until the type of tab that you want appears. Then, click at the place on the horizontal ruler where you want the tab to go.

But sometimes you may want to use a tab leader. In that case, you need to set tabs by using the Tabs dialog box, as explained in the following steps:

1. **Select the paragraph(s) that you want to affect.**

2. **Choose Format➪Tabs.**

   The Tabs dialog box, as shown in Figure 7-12, appears.

3. **In the Tab Positions list box, specify a position for your tab stop.**

   This position is the distance between the frame's left edge and the tab stop.

4. **Under Alignment, choose how you want text to align to your tab stop.**

5. If desired, set a tab leader.

A *tab leader* is a set of characters that fill any gap created by a tab mark. Dotted tab leaders are commonly used together with right-aligned tab stops in tables of contents (as in the beginning of this book). The dots connect the titles on the left with the page numbers on the right.

6. Click the Set button.

Your tab-stop position now appears in the Tab Positions list box.

7. If desired, set additional tabs by repeating Steps 3–6.

8. Click the OK button.

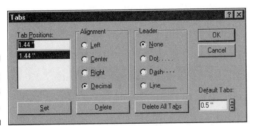

Figure 7-12:
The Tabs
dialog box.

After you set custom tab stops, the horizontal ruler displays those stops, using symbols for the four kinds of tab stops. If you're fairly adept with the mouse, you can fine-tune the position of a tab stop by dragging it back and forth on the ruler. Be careful to point directly to the tab stop that you want to move, however, or you may accidentally create a new stop.

Here are some helpful shortcuts for working with tab stops:

- To delete a tab stop, drag it down off the horizontal ruler. Or use the Tabs dialog box's Delete and Delete All Tabs buttons.

- Notice that the Tabs dialog box provides an option for changing the default tab stops from every half inch to any other increment you like.

- To modify the alignment or leader of an existing tab stop, open the Tabs dialog box and click the stop that you want to change in the Tab Positions list box. Then, set the desired alignment and/or leader, click Set, and click OK.

Remember that tab stops are paragraph specific. If you click or highlight text in another paragraph, the horizontal ruler displays any custom tab stops set in that new paragraph. If the tab stops on the horizontal ruler are gray, you've probably highlighted text in multiple paragraphs that use different tab stops. You can still use these arrows to adjust your tab stops.

Tab stops can be a pain. If you get frustrated working with them, remember that just about anything you can accomplish with tab stops you can often more easily accomplish with indents, table frames, and multiple text frames.

Setting paragraph indents

Indents are like margins that affect only individual paragraphs. By default, all indents are set to 0, which makes paragraphs align with the text frame's margins. By increasing the indent setting, you can move paragraphs in from those margins.

If you want to move every line of text in a text frame, you needn't bother with indents. Instead, just resize or move the frame.

To set indents, follow these steps:

1. **Mark the paragraph(s) that you want to affect.**

2. **Choose Format⇨Indents and Lists from the menu bar.**

   The Indents and Lists dialog box, as shown in Figure 7-13, opens.

3. **Under Indent Settings, verify that Normal is selected.**

4. **From the Preset drop-down list, choose the type of indent that you want.**

5. **If desired, use the Left, First Line, and Right options to fine-tune the preset indent.**

   Left indents the left edge of every paragraph line except the first. First Line indents the left edge of just the first paragraph line, and Right indents the right edge of every paragraph line.

   The Sample box shows the effect of your choices.

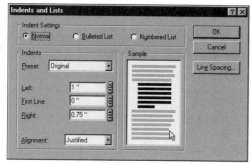

Figure 7-13:
The Indents
and Lists
dialog box
for a normal
paragraph.

6. **Click OK.**

After you set custom indents, *indent markers* — those little black triangles on the horizontal ruler — move to reflect the indenting. If you want, you can change the indents by dragging the indent markers back and forth:

- The top-left indent marker controls the left edge of the first line in the paragraph.

- The bottom-left marker controls the left edge of every line in the paragraph but the first line.

- The right indent marker controls the right edge of every line in the paragraph.

- The rectangle under the bottom-left marker controls both the first line and left indents.

Be careful to point directly to the indent marker that you want to move, however, or you may accidentally create a tab stop. If the indent markers on the horizontal ruler are gray, you've probably highlighted text in multiple paragraphs that use different indents. You can still use the markers to adjust your indents.

It is considered good typographical practice to use a first-line indent rather than tab marks to indent the first lines of paragraphs.

As an example of how indents are used, consider the *hanging indent* shown in Figure 7-14. You create a hanging indent by setting the left indent larger than the first-line indent. Hanging indents are generally used to create bulleted and numbered lists, as described in the next section.

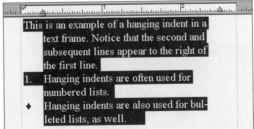

Figure 7-14:
A hanging
indent.

Unlike some word processors, Microsoft Publisher 97 doesn't allow you to set negative indents. That is, your text can't extend beyond a frame's margins. You may, however, be able to get text to move closer to the edge of a frame by reducing the frame's internal margins. To do this, use the Format⇨Text Frame Properties command on the menu bar.

Creating bulleted and numbered lists

Bulleted and numbered lists, which are used frequently throughout this book, are an excellent way to present information. Bulleted lists are often used to emphasize related points, whereas numbered lists often consist of sequential steps. You can set bulleted and numbered lists by creating a hanging indent, manually inserting a bullet or number at the beginning of each list item, and then inserting a tab mark to offset the bullet or number from the item. What a drag! Microsoft Publisher 97 offers you an easier way: automatic bulleting and numbering.

To create a bulleted list:

1. **Select the paragraphs that you want to bullet.**

2. **Choose Format⇨Indents and Lists.**

   The Indents and Lists dialog box appears, as shown in Figure 7-15.

3. **Click the Bulleted List radio button in the Indent Settings section.**

4. **Click the type of bullet that you want, select a bullet size, and set an indent (if desired).**

   By default, bullets themselves are not indented, but the text items that follow the bullets are indented from the bullet by $1/4$ inch. Change the Indent List By setting to increase or decrease the amount of space between bullets and bulleted items. Or, wait and see how your bulleted list looks with a $1/4$-inch indent and then use the horizontal ruler's indent markers to adjust the indents of the bullets and the bulleted items. If you prefer not to indent your bulleted items at all, uncheck the Indent List By check box.

5. **Click the OK button.**

Figure 7-15:
The Indents and Lists dialog box for a bulleted list.

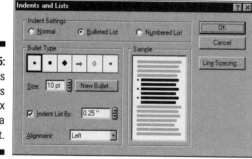

For a wider selection of bullets, click the New Bullet button and select a bullet from the New Bullet dialog box, as shown in Figure 7-16. All other things being equal, your bullets should match the size of your text. (Some fonts have bullet sizes that are too small or too large for the same size text to appear appropriate.)

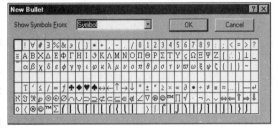

Figure 7-16:
The New
Bullet
dialog box.

To create a numbered list:

1. **Select the paragraphs that you want to number.**

2. **Choose Format⇨Indents and Lists.**

   The Indents and Lists dialog box appears.

3. **Select the Numbered List radio button in the Indents and Lists dialog box.**

   Your dialog box should now look like the one shown in Figure 7-17.

4. **Select the Format for your numbers.**

   You can choose Arabic numerals, lowercase letters, or uppercase letters.

5. **If desired, use the Separator drop-down list box to select some punctuation to follow or surround your numbers.**

6. **If desired, change the setting in the Start At text box.**

   By default, Microsoft Publisher 97 starts numbering at 1, a, or A, but you can start the numbering anywhere you want.

7. **Click the OK button.**

By default, numbers are unindented, whereas numbered items are indented by $1/4$ inch, just as with bulleted lists. Change the Indent List By setting to increase or decrease the amount of space between numbers and numbered items. You can change this in the Indent List By text box when you first create your numbered list. Or you can wait and see how your list looks with

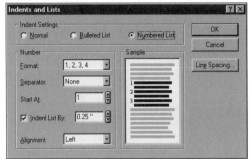

Figure 7-17:
The Indents
and Lists
dialog box
for a
numbered
list.

a ¹/₄-inch indent and then use the horizontal ruler's indent markers to adjust the indents of the numbers and the items. If you prefer not to indent your numbered items at all, uncheck the Indent List By check box.

If the Indents and Lists dialog box overwhelms you with options, it is easier still to use the Bulleted or Numbered List button at the right of the Format toolbar. Click the button to display the menu shown in Figure 7-18 and then click the type of bullet or number that you want. Microsoft Publisher 97 instantly bullets or numbers your paragraphs and gives each paragraph a ¹/₄-inch hanging indent. If you click the More command, the Indents and Lists dialog box opens to the Bulleted List Indent Settings.

Figure 7-18:
The
Bulleted or
Numbered
List button's
menu.

We find that using the Bulleted or Numbered List button is particularly convenient for removing bullets or numbers from a list — all you need to do is click the None option at the top of the menu.

To create a new line within a bulleted or numbered list without having Microsoft Publisher 97 insert a new bullet or number, press Shift+Enter rather than Enter.

Using paragraph styles

You may not want to get into this subject, but many hard-core desktop Publishers prefer to use *text styles* to apply text formatting. (If you've used a modern word-processing program, you may already be familiar with text styles.) A *text style* is a named set of attributes that you can apply to a paragraph.

We use text styles extensively because they are a terrific labor-saving device. For example, if you want all your body text to be double-spaced, 12-point Arial italic text with a $^{1}/_{4}$-inch first-line indent, you can create a text style that contains all those formatting instructions. When you then apply that style to a paragraph, all the text in that paragraph instantly takes on each formatting option specified by the style. Should you later decide to change a text style, all the paragraphs that bear that style change instantly — quite the time-saver! So, most experienced authors, editors, layout artists, and publishers start the text-formatting process by creating a style sheet of all the allowed paragraph types in their document. Then they apply these styles to their work.

To create, change, rename, delete, and even import styles, select Format⇨Text Style. The Text Styles dialog box, as shown in Figure 7-19, appears.

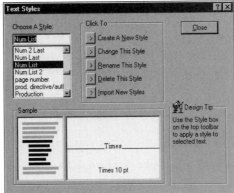

Figure 7-19:
The Text
Styles
dialog box.

Make your selections by clicking one of the Click To buttons in the dialog box. These buttons lead to other dialog boxes that lead you to the various character and paragraph formatting dialog boxes covered earlier in this chapter. You can set the following properties as part of a text style:

- ✔ Character Type and Size
- ✔ Indents and Lists
- ✔ Line Spacing
- ✔ Spacing Between Characters
- ✔ Tabs

The Sample box in the Text Styles dialog box shows you a graphic indicating the effect of your selections.

To apply text styles to selected paragraphs, select a style from the Style list box at the left end of the top toolbar, or change the selection in the Text Styles dialog box.

Press Ctrl+S to activate the Style list box in the Text Style dialog box and then use the down- or up-arrow keys to move to the style that you want.

We think that the import feature of the Text Styles dialog box is particularly helpful. We write a lot of our work in Microsoft Word and import the text into Microsoft Publisher 97. (Remember that you can also do editing-in-place with Microsoft Word, as explained in Chapter 6.) We can import our styles from Word when setting up our document inside Microsoft Publisher 97.

Using the Format Painter

Microsoft Publisher 97 offers a feature called the Format Painter. The Format Painter enables you to copy the format of an object to another object. It is particularly useful when applied to text. *It works generally with any object, however.*

To copy and paste the formatting of selected characters or a paragraph:

1. **Highlight the text with the formatting that you want to copy.**

   Select the characters or any part of a paragraph that contains the paragraph mark.

2. **Click the Format Painter button on the toolbar.**

   Your pointer turns into a paintbrush that looks like the Format Painter button.

3. **Click and drag the pointer over the characters or paragraph mark that you want to change.**

To quickly copy the formatting of one object on a page to another, right-click the object that uses the desired format; then, use the Format⇨Pick Up Formatting command on the menu bar to copy the object's format, select the object that you want to change, and choose the Apply Formatting command. Microsoft Publisher 97 remembers your format until you change it by choosing the Pick Up Formatting command again. (This procedure also works by double-clicking the Format Painter icon; after you're done, click the icon to turn off the effect.)

Frame formatting

Two text formatting features affect entire frames:

- Hyphenating text
- Arranging text in snaking columns

Because these features affect entire frames, it doesn't matter whether you highlight text before you apply them.

The section "Hyphenation," earlier in this chapter, discusses Microsoft Publisher 97's hyphenation feature. (Chapter 11 discusses this feature more fully.) In many programs, hyphenation is done at the paragraph level, but in Microsoft Publisher 97, hyphenation is done an entire frame at a time.

In publications such as newsletters, text is often laid out in *snaking columns,* where text ends at the bottom of one column and continues again at the top of the next. You can create snaking text columns by laying down text frames side by side and then connecting those frames, as described in Chapter 5. But that's the hard way of doing things, and you don't want to do things the hard way, do you?

To set multiple columns within a text frame:

1. **Select the text frame.**

2. **Choose Format⇨Text Frame Properties.**

   The Text Frame Properties dialog box appears, as shown in Figure 7-20.

3. **In the Columns Number spinner, enter the number of columns that you want.**

   You can have up to 63 columns in one frame.

4. **In the Columns Spacing spinner, set how much space you want between your columns.**

   Publishing professionals call this space a *column gutter.* The Sample section shows you an example of the division of your text frame.

5. Click the OK button.

The text in your frame rearranges itself into multiple, snaking columns.

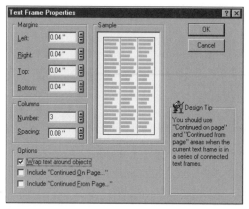

Figure 7-20:
The Text
Frame
Properties
dialog box.

Microsoft Publisher 97 automatically ends one column of text and begins the next after it runs out of room at the bottom of a frame. To lengthen a column, try decreasing the frame's top and bottom margins or resizing the frame.

To force Microsoft Publisher 97 to end a column before it reaches the bottom of a text frame, place the insertion point where you want the column to end, and then press Ctrl+Enter. This keyboard shortcut is the same one that Microsoft Word uses to specify the end of a section, and this keystroke is imported from Word as a column end.

For nonsnaking columns, as in this book's tables, consider using table frames.

Chapter 8

Vintage Type: The Corkscrew, Please

● ●

In This Chapter

▶ Different fonts that you can install in Windows 95

▶ How to install, manage, and print fonts

▶ Styles of typefaces and how to buy them

▶ A short lesson on typography and the use of type in design

▶ How to create special fancy first letters: drop caps and raised caps

● ●

*W*e think that choosing fonts for your publication is like decorating your house. It's great fun, and it is important in giving your publication a personality. Just as some people like art deco whereas others like Bauhaus decor, different designers prefer different fonts. Although you *can* decorate your house with purple velvet wallpaper or alternate orange and black paint on the bedroom walls, chances are that you want to choose more conventional design themes. The same is true in your publications.

In this chapter, we tell you how to buy, install, and use fonts. Some of the chapter deals with the common practices that most desktop publishing experts recommend, and some sections give you the technical details, such as how to work with fonts, what font files are, and how to best use them.

About Type and Fonts

One of us (Barrie) recently went to buy a typewriter for the office. One store offered reconditioned IBM Selectric typewriters that went for $350. Another store had a Brother typewriter made of plastic for $89, a price that we found amazing given what this machine does. Both these typewriters had one thing in common: They could print with only one style of type. You could have any typeface you liked, as long as it was Courier. On the IBM typewriter, the typeface was contained on a print ball; whereas on the Brother, it was on a print wheel.

Now don't get us wrong. We actually like Courier. It is an extremely attractive font and its widespread use is a testament to its durability. We think that Courier's main problem is that it is overused. And certainly, using the same typeface every day gets old fast, no matter how great the typewriter.

The point of this typewriter story is to introduce a basic term of typography: *font*. A font is one typeface, in one style. The print ball and print wheel for those typewriters each contained one font: Courier.

Of course, you can go out and buy other fonts for the typewriters we mentioned. Each manufacturer sells them. When you get to the point in your document at which you need another font, you simply replace the ball or wheel and carry on. Compare that time-consuming process with creating text on your computer: With a computer, you can have as many fonts as you want, and switching to a different font is as simple as making a menu selection. Until you print your document, you can go back and reformat your document to your heart's content — something that you'd need gallons of correction fluid and unending patience to do on a typewriter. It's no wonder that few people buy typewriters anymore.

Font styles

The fonts used today come in four main styles:

- ✔ **Serif fonts:** A *serif* is a small line that hangs off the upper and lower ends of the strokes that make up a text character. Serifs help guide the reader's eye, which is why serif fonts are typically used in body copy. (Body copy, or body text, makes up the majority of the paragraphs in a publication.) Examples of common serif fonts are Benguiat, Bodoni, Bookman, Courier New, Galliard, Garamond, Goudy, Jenson, Palatino, and Times New Roman. Many of these fonts are named after the designers who either created or inspired them.

- ✔ **Sans serif fonts:** Sans serif fonts don't have serifs (*sans* is French for *without*) and are typically square and plainer than serif fonts. In older days, these fonts were described as either *gothic* or *grotesque* faces. They are more commonly used in headlines, in which a limited number of characters need to be read. Examples of sans serif fonts in common use are Arial, Helvetica, Optima, Tekton, and Univers.

- ✔ **Decorative fonts:** Decorative fonts are used to present letters in stylized form. Usually, they are thematic; a set of fonts may be created out of pictures of jugglers and clowns or use cowboy motifs, for example.

- ✔ **Symbol fonts:** This font style presents symbols as a character set. Earlier chapters show examples of the Symbol and Wingdings fonts that are installed in Windows 95. Vendors also sell symbol sets for maps (Adobe's Carta) and for music (Adobe's Sonata).

Figure 8-1 shows you an example of some font styles.

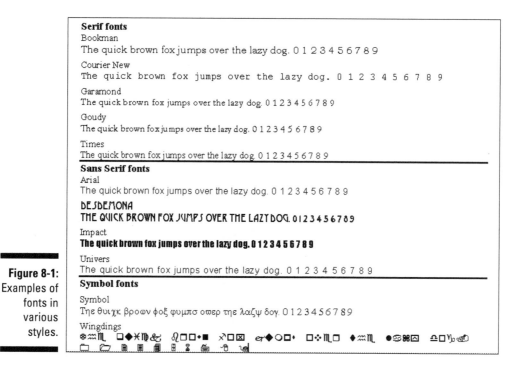

Figure 8-1:
Examples of
fonts in
various
styles.

Fixed fonts

The first computer fonts emulated those found in older typesetting equipment or in typewriters. Each font was a single typeface designed for a specific size. Most of these fonts were designed as bitmapped descriptions (that is, comprised of a collection of dots) and so were called *bitmapped fonts*. You could install Courier 8, 10, and 12 on your computer in plain (roman), italic, bold, and bold italic styles, with one font file each for your screen and for your printer. All together, you would have installed 24 separate files for these three sizes. What a mess!

As time went by, type vendors produced font descriptions that let you create a fixed font in any size from a single description. Today, the use of fixed fonts is extremely limited.

Fixed fonts are usually sold in pairs that contain a *screen font* (used to display the font on your computer screen) and a *printer font* (used to actually print out your text). In Windows 95, an *A* icon in the Fonts folder indicates a fixed font.

When you use a fixed screen font at the size that it was designed to be used, the results look as good as with any font you can use. You also get the added performance advantage of not having to have the font description *rasterized* (that is, converted to a bitmap for display or output), which isn't much of an advantage in these days of very fast computers.

Sizing up your font

You can make a font virtually any size you want. The size of a font is normally measured in *points*. A point is approximately ¹/₇₂ of an inch, but varies somewhat from typeface to typeface. The normal font size used in correspondence is 12 points, but 8, 10, and 11 points are also common.

It's important to remember that the size of a point depends on what font you're using; 12-point type in one font can be substantially different in size from 12-point type in another font, for example. (Figure 8-1 shows you samples in various faces at the same size.)

Not only do the fonts have different vertical dimensions, but their widths are different as well. Font height is usually gauged by the height of the lowercase *x*, whereas the width is usually gauged by the width of the lowercase *m*. For this reason, a font's vertical dimension is referred to as its *x-height*, and its horizontal size is referred to as its *m-width*.

If you use a fixed font at some perfect multiple of the size it was designed for — for example, at ¹/₂ or ¹/₄ size — you also get perfect results. You can even get reasonable results when using a fixed font at two times or four times its intended size. Your screen font looks distorted at other sizes, however, even though your printed material often looks perfect.

Some printers come with their own printer fonts. If Windows isn't familiar with your printer's printer font, it will substitute some other font to display the document on-screen. Although you won't see a realistic display of how your document prints, it prints just fine by using the fonts contained in the printer. Most people have given up on fixed fonts at this point.

TrueType fonts

TrueType is one of two popular font formats (the other is PostScript, discussed in the next section). Unlike fixed fonts and PostScript fonts, TrueType fonts do not require separate screen and printer font description files — Windows can use the same description file to display the font on-screen and to print your publication. Because the font information is contained in one file, you have half the file management chores that you do with fixed fonts and PostScript fonts, which is a major benefit of using TrueType fonts. In addition, Windows 3.1 and Macintosh System 7 and later contain built-in support for TrueType fonts. Without getting into all the technical background, this support results in smaller font file sizes and somewhat faster font display and printing.

PostScript fonts

Adobe PostScript fonts have been available since the middle 1980s. Most service bureaus and professional designers favor PostScript fonts because of their high quality and large library of available font descriptions. We've seen estimates that more than 10,000 typefaces are available in PostScript form.

PostScript fonts come in two types: Type 1 and Type 3. The difference between the two types is that Type 3 doesn't contain special instructions (called *hinting*) that alter the appearance of fonts at small point sizes (11 point and below) to make them more readable both on-screen (if you have the Adobe Type Manager installed) and in your printed matter. Type 1 fonts (as well as TrueType fonts) come with hinting built into their descriptions.

PostScript fonts require a special font rasterizer to convert them to bitmaps that can be displayed on the screen or printed by your printer. For a long time, PostScript fonts required a PostScript printer to print properly. PostScript printers contained a ROM chip that stored the PostScript inter-preter that did the bitmap conversion for output. In 1989, under pressure from other vendors who finally cracked the technology of Adobe hinting, Adobe released Adobe Type Manager and published the specifications of PostScript type encryption and hinting.

Adobe Type Manager (ATM) displays PostScript fonts well and makes printing the fonts to non-PostScript printers possible. Your computer's processor takes the place of the processor in a PostScript printer. Thanks to ATM, you can get great-looking output even from ink jet printers.

Choosing between TrueType and PostScript fonts

In regards to performance and quality, no one has yet been able to show us to our satisfaction that there is much difference — or, in fact, any difference — between TrueType and PostScript fonts. Of course, you get some TrueType fonts free with the installation of Windows and other Microsoft products such as Publisher. You can't beat that.

The best advice that we can give you regarding fonts is the following: If you are an occasional desktop publisher, choose either TrueType or PostScript, but try not to use both. If you do use both, pay particular attention to making sure that you don't use a font with the same name in both styles. In other words, if you set certain body text in TrueType Times Roman, don't set other body text in PostScript Times Roman. Easier said than done.

If you are a professional desktop publisher, you may have no choice but to use both typeface descriptions (TrueType and PostScript). The people who are our gurus of type favor PostScript type. We think that this is largely due to the extremely large library of high-quality fonts available in Postscript, the fact that many service bureaus can't work with TrueType, and the bias of many years of usage. DTP professionals collect type like some people collect wine and toss around the same nonsense about flavor, bouquet, body, and so on.

We remain unconvinced. We like the convenience of TrueType and think that PostScript is worth the additional trouble only when a typeface exists in PostScript that doesn't exist in TrueType.

A primer on buying fonts

You buy fonts in sets. At a minimum, fonts are sold as a single typeface, usually in different sizes and styles. Fixed fonts are sold as individual font files. TrueType and PostScript fonts are sold without regard to font size.

Initially, font vendors sold fonts in a general package meant to serve a variety of needs. The first LaserWriter collection of 35 fonts in 7 typefaces was this kind of package. We've seen a movement afoot for the last few years to sell fonts in related families for a related purpose. Now you can buy packages meant for newsletters, faxes, correspondence, and decorative purposes, to name but a few. Typically, these packages offer three or four typefaces in several styles. If you are font-minded (and who isn't these days!), you can buy many vendors' entire font libraries on CD-ROM. The fonts on the CD-ROM are usually encrypted, and you need to obtain a serial number from the vendor in order to "unlock" the fonts so that you can install them. The vendor gives you the serial number for a particular font when you buy that font.

The Bézier versus the Spline

TrueType fonts are outline fonts based on the mathematical B-Quadratic Spline curve. These curves are similar to the Bézier curves upon which Adobe PostScript fonts are based. Unlike PostScript fonts, TrueType fonts do not require separate screen and printer fonts. The rasterizing software in Windows contains the necessary interpreter to output the same file description to your printer as it does to your monitor — with excellent results to both. This is TrueType's major advantage; you have less file management to worry about with TrueType fonts.

TrueType fonts are rasterized — converted to a bitmap for display or output using software built into Windows 3.1 and later. Macintosh System 7 and later also contains a TrueType rasterizer. The advantage of using a built-in rasterizer may be seen in reduced font file sizes for TrueType fonts, and somewhat faster display and print times.

Buying fonts in families is a great way to add to a collection. Most designers recommend that you be conservative in your use of fonts, so a collection of fonts in the same family makes sense. It's better to collect one typeface in many styles — even to collect special character sets such as Small Caps for a font such as Times — than it is to have an incomplete collection of several faces.

Without a doubt, font technology has undergone an explosion since the introduction of the personal computer. More and better fonts have been created in the last ten years than in all of the previous five centuries of type design. We won't say that the best type designers are alive today, as that would be presumptuous of us. (But we wouldn't be surprised if that were true.) And certainly the most prolific designers are out there working in their studios today.

We'd like to mention some recent developments in font technology because they are important and valuable. First, several typefaces have been created that contain both sans serif and serif members. Our favorite of this ilk is the Adobe Stone family, designed by noted type designer Sumner Stone.

Another development is the introduction of "intelligent font technology." Adobe has introduced a family of typefaces called *Multiple Masters*. These fonts can be varied infinitely over a range through three or four axes, so that you can have a single font description yielding plain, condensed, expanded, italic, bold, or different sized characters. These fonts require version 2.6 or later of the Adobe Type Manager.

Most computer stores and computer direct-marketing catalogs sell fonts in packages from one vendor or another. What you can find in these mass market outlets are the most well-known and commercial font packages. These sources are adequate for the occasional desktop publisher.

For more complete collections of fonts, you should contact the font vendors themselves. Each of the vendors in the following list publish very attractive magazines with samples of all their fonts. Adobe's *Font and Function* appears quarterly, for example. The magazines also highlight new fonts that appear. Addresses are as follows:

Adobe Systems, Inc. (or the company's outlet, ImageClub), 1585 Charleston Road, P.O. Box 7900, Mountain View, CA 94309-7900; phone 415-961-4400; Internet: http://www.adobe.com

Agfa Division, Bayer Corp., 100 Challenger Rd., Ridgefield Park, NJ 07660-2199; phone 201-440-0111

Bitstream, Inc., 215 First Street, Cambridge, MA 02142; phone 617-497-6222, 800-522-3668; Internet: http://www.bitstream.com

Casady & Greene, Inc., 22734 Portola Drive, Salinas, CA 93908-1119; phone 408-484-9228, 800-359-4920; Internet: http:// sales@casadyg.com

FontBank, Inc., 2620 Central St., Evanston, IL 60201; phone 708-328-7370; Internet: jerry@jworld.com

The Font Bureau, Inc., 175 Newbury St., Boston, MA 02116; phone 617-423-8770; America OnLine: fontbureau

FontHaus, Inc., 1375 Kings Highway E., Fairfield, CT 06430; phone 203-367-1993, 800-942-9110; America OnLine: fonthaus

ITC Fonts, 866 Second Avenue, New York, NY 10017; phone 212-371-0699, 800-425-3882; Internet: hgrey@interport.net

Letraset USA, 40 Eisenhower Drive, Paramus, NJ 07653; phone 201-845-6100, 800-343-8973

Linotype Hell Company, 425 Oser Avenue, Hauppauge, NY 11788; phone 800-633-1900

Monotype Typography, Inc., 150 S. Wacker Drive, Suite 2630, Chicago, IL 60606; phone 312-855-1440, 800-666-6897; Internet: sales@monotypeusa.com

URW America, 4 Manchester Street, Nashua, NH 03060; phone 603-882-7445

Our apologies to the many other fine typographers whose firms we couldn't list here. Picking up a book of typestyles, such as *Typestyle,* by Daniel Will-Harris (Peachpit Press) and *The Electronic Type Catalog,* by Steve Byers (Random House) also wouldn't be a bad idea.

How to Work with Fonts

When you install Windows 95, it installs some basic fonts that it needs to use for system menus and dialog box displays. It also installs a few additional fonts for your use. Other programs that you install, such as Microsoft Publisher 97, often install additional fonts. You can also buy fonts on disk. Fonts that you buy on disk are called *soft fonts.*

Most printers, especially laser printers, come with fonts built into their ROM (read-only memory). You can purchase different models of some printers that have more or fewer fonts, called hard fonts. Also, you can purchase these fonts on cartridges that you insert into a slot in your printer. That way, you can vary the number and types of fonts that your printer knows about. Typically, hard fonts require installing screen fonts from disk as well as inserting the font cartridge.

Most people buy and use soft fonts these days. We can't think of a reason to use hard fonts instead.

Tracking down TrueType fonts

In Windows 95, TrueType Windows fonts reside in the Fonts folder, found inside the Windows folder on My Computer. The best way to open and see your Fonts folder is to select it by using the Control Panels command on the Settings submenu of the Start menu. The Control Panel folder contains a shortcut (shown here in the margin) to your Fonts folder. Just double-click the icon to open your Fonts folder. An example of a Fonts folder is shown in icon view in Figure 8-2.

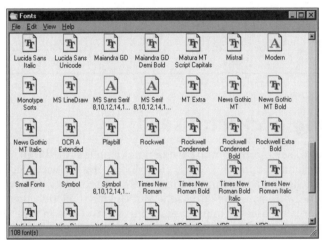

Figure 8-2:
A Fonts
folder.

Actually, the Fonts folder in Figure 8-2 contains a couple of different font types: TrueType fonts, such as Rockwell and Times New Roman, which are marked by the double *T* icon; and fixed screen fonts, which include the MS Serif, Modern, and Small Fonts families and are marked with the *A* icon. TrueType fonts take the TTF file extension, fixed fonts use the FON extension, and PostScript fonts take either the PFB (screen font) or PFM (printer font) extension.

If you are on a network, you can store your fonts in a folder on a remote computer. Typically, that computer is a server because you always want to make sure that the fonts are available to everyone on the network. But you can store the fonts on a client if you prefer.

Don't move the TrueType fonts that your system needs to display menus and other interface elements. Keeping the basic fonts that came installed with Windows 95 in the local Fonts folder (the one on your computer) is a good idea as well. Table 8-1 lists the minimum fonts that you should keep and the names of the font files.

Keep a copy of any font with the prefix MS or the word *System* in it in your Windows\Fonts folder.

Table 8-1   Minimum Fonts in Your Local Windows\Fonts Folder

Font Name	Normal	Italic	Bold	Bold Italic
Arial	ARIAL.TTF	ARIALI.TTF	ARIALBD.TTF	ARIALBI.TTF
Courier New	COUR.TTF	COURI.TTF	COURBD.TTF	COURBI.TTF
Symbol	SYMBOL.TTF			
Times New Roman	TIMES.TTF	TIMESI.TTF	TIMESBD.TTF	TIMESBI.TTF
Wingdings	WINGDING.TTF			

Viewing character sets

If you want to see a representative example of an installed font, double-click the font file icon to open the Quick View dialog box shown in Figure 8-3. This dialog box tells you a few things: the name of the font, its size, what kind of font it is, and who owns the copyright. But the most useful things that the Quick View dialog box contains are examples of the font in various sizes (12, 18, 24, 36, 48, 60, and 72 points). The text sample, "The quick brown fox jumps over the lazy dog," was selected because it shows you every letter in the alphabet. We are amused.

You can also print the contents of the Quick View dialog box, which may be useful to you if you want to create a printed collection of font samples.

Although the Quick View dialog box is useful, it doesn't show you each and every character that is part of a font's character set. The Insert Symbol dialog box, shown in Chapter 7, does show you all the characters. When we really want to explore our installed fonts, however, we open the Windows 95 Character Map program and check out its display. This program lets you select characters and copy them to the Clipboard. It's a small program and can be minimized to the Taskbar so that it's always easily available.

To use the Character Map, choose Start⇨Programs⇨Accessories⇨Character Map. The Character Map dialog box appears, as shown in Figure 8-4.

Figure 8-3:
The Quick
View
dialog box.

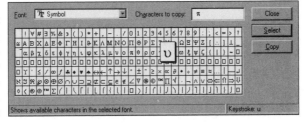

Figure 8-4:
The
Character
Map
dialog box.

If you want to see a character in expanded form, such as the υ symbol in
Figure 8-4, click and hold the mouse button. Double-click a character or click
the <u>S</u>elect button to add the character to the Cha<u>r</u>acters to copy text box.
Use the <u>C</u>opy button to place your selection on the Clipboard.

Installing PostScript fonts

To use PostScript Type 1 fonts, you need a copy of the Adobe Type Manager
(ATM) on every PC that uses those fonts. Adobe Type Manager is the
PostScript font rasterizer. Typically, you purchase ATM with a basic collection of 35 LaserWriter fonts or get the program with any collection of Adobe
fonts that you purchase. ATM comes on a disk called the ATM Control
Panel Program Disk. If you need a copy of ATM, you can call Adobe at
800-833-6687.

If you have ATM Version 3.0 or later, you can install all types of PostScript fonts in your system. You can determine whether you have ATM by using the Windows 95 Find command (on the Start menu) to search for the ATMCNTRL file or by looking for that file in the Main folder of the Programs submenu of the Start menu. Only one copy of ATM is required. If you need to install ATM, use the INSTALL.EXE program on the installation disk.

Follow these steps to install PostScript font(s):

1. **Open the ATM Control Panel by double-clicking its icon in the Control Panel window.**

   Figure 8-5 offers a look at the Control Panel.

2. **Verify that the O<u>n</u> radio button is selected.**

3. **Click the <u>A</u>dd button.**

   The Add ATM Fonts dialog box appears, as shown in Figure 8-6.

4. **Using the <u>D</u>irectories list box, locate the font file(s) that you want to install.**

   Check the target directories near the bottom of the Add ATM Fonts dialog box. PostScript fonts are normally placed in a folder called PSFONTS. This folder contains Type 1 fonts. A subfolder named PFM contains the PostScriptMetric fonts.

5. **Select the font(s) of interest from the Available <u>F</u>onts list box.**

   Use the Shift key to extend or reduce your range of selection and the Ctrl key to select fonts from a discontinuous range.

6. **Click the <u>A</u>dd button.**

   Windows checks the Registry to see whether any of the fonts are already registered. If so, it posts a dialog box asking you for instructions.

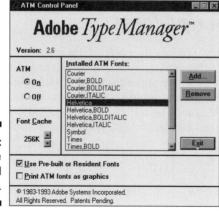

Figure 8-5:
The Adobe
Control
Panel.

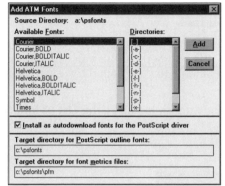

Figure 8-6:
The Add
ATM Fonts
dialog box.

Because Windows doesn't list PostScript fonts in the Fonts folder, the best way to figure out whether the fonts were successfully installed is to open the Microsoft Publisher 97 Character dialog box and see whether the fonts are listed.

Installing and removing TrueType fonts

We suppose that you could figure out how to install and remove fonts if you had the time, but we don't find this topic to be particularly discoverable. The command that lets you install a font is hidden away in the File menu of the Fonts folder. That command is appropriately named Install New Font. The process is straightforward after you get that far.

Always check the licensing agreement for your fonts before you install them. Some font vendors give you a "printer license" that entitles you to print to a single printer only, but install the font on any connected computer. Other vendors give you a single CPU license, which sometimes limits installation on a laptop. Still other vendors license their fonts by the registered owner. What a mess.

Follow these steps to add fonts to your computer:

1. **Click the Windows 95 Start button and then choose Settings⇨Control Panel from the menu.**

2. **Double-click the Fonts folder icon in the Control Panel folder.**

3. **From the Fonts folder, select File⇨Install New Font.**

   The Add Fonts dialog box, shown in Figure 8-7, appears.

4. **Use the Fol_ders and Dri_ves list boxes to find the folder containing the fonts that you want to install.**

   Typically, you install fonts from a disk supplied by the program, printer, or other output device that you bought. But you can also install fonts from any drive that is available to your computer, even one on a network.

5. **Select the fonts that you want to install in the List of _fonts list box.**

6. **Click OK.**

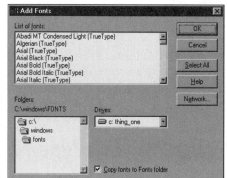

Figure 8-7:
The Add
Fonts dialog
box.

Unless you are a masochist, make sure that the Copy fonts to Fonts folder check box is selected. Otherwise, you waste time trying to find and manage your new fonts later on.

Using the Installer to copy fonts into your computer is most important. The Installer makes the fonts known to the Windows Registry. Do not simply copy the font files to the Fonts folder and expect that to work.

Fun as it is to have lots of fonts installed and at your fingertips, it can also eat up your computer's memory and hard drive storage space before you know it. Even we run out of disk space from time to time! In our never-ending quest to collect more fonts than Roger Parker, we really collect a bunch of font junk. So, every so often we set about to purge our system of truly ugly fonts or fonts that we're just tired of seeing. As an added benefit, it improves our system performance.

Luckily, removing fonts is even easier than installing them. You can do it in either of the following ways:

- ✔ Highlight the font(s) in the Fonts folder and select _File⇨Delete.
- ✔ Just drag the font(s) to the Recycle Bin.

If you change your mind about deleting a font file, don't forget that you can highlight the file in the Recycle Bin and select the Restore command from the File menu. That command returns the file to the Fonts folder from whence it came.

You can also use the Rename command to change the name of a font file, but don't do that. It you rename a font, any document that uses it won't be able to find it again. Font substitution will occur.

Selecting fonts in your publication

In Chapter 7, we explain that you set the attributes for your selected characters and paragraphs from either the Font list box in the Format toolbar or the Character dialog box (Format⇨Character). Figure 8-8 shows you the Character dialog box again with the Font list box open. Notice that the list has two different types of fonts — TrueType fonts and printer fonts — with icons appearing for each.

Figure 8-8:
The
Character
dialog box.

Another thing to notice about the Character dialog box is that when you have a TrueType font selected, it offers you four different Font Styles:

- ✔ Regular
- ✔ *Italic*
- ✔ **Bold**
- ✔ ***Bold Italic***

You also have access to five different effects:

- ✔ <u>A</u>LL CAPITALS
- ✔ SMA<u>L</u>L CAPITALS
- ✔ <u>Underline All</u>
- ✔ <u>Underline</u> <u>Words</u>
- ✔ <u>Double Underline</u>

And you have three different Super/Subscript options:

- ✔ <u>N</u>ormal
- ✔ <u>Super</u>^{script}
- ✔ <u>Sub</u>_{script}

You can mix and match styles, effects, and line placement options. As you may have figured out by now, the TrueType font rasterizer synthesizes these various options from the single TrueType font description.

Printing with fonts

When you print a publication that contains fonts found in the printer's ROM (permanent memory), the printer uses those hard fonts. Many printers allow you to attach a hard drive or CD-ROM drive that you can use as secondary storage for font descriptions. Then that printer knows about a lot more fonts. When you print a document with fonts that aren't in a printer's ROM, a couple of different things can happen.

First, your computer can rasterize the font descriptions (convert them to a bitmap that the printer requires) and send the converted font information to the printer's RAM (temporary memory). This process is known as *downloading*. The font descriptions are stored in the printer's RAM until the print engine needs them — which makes it obvious why having a lot of RAM in a printer is valuable. Alternatively, the printer may be able to do the bitmap conversion on its own, freeing up your computer for other work. PostScript printers have this capability.

If your document contains more fonts than can be contained in the printer memory, your computer may store them in a *font cache*. You can change the size of the font cache in the Adobe Type Manager and thus improve printing performance. After a font is rasterized and stored in the cache, it doesn't have to be rasterized again.

Typography 101

We don't have room here to tell you everything about typography that you should probably know. Typography is a big topic and one with a fascinating history. That history has generated more jargon than you could shake a stick at, so to speak. If you want an in-depth background in typography, we refer you to the references mentioned previously, or to *Desktop Publishing For Dummies* by Roger C. Parker (published by IDG Books Worldwide, Inc.). For now, though, a rundown of some basic terminology is in order. Figure 8-9 shows you a sample font with some of its features called out.

Figure 8-9:
Typographic
terms.

Most designers recommend that you choose a serif font for your body copy. You can add some variety and visual interest to your pages by using sans serif fonts for headlines and subheads. A classic combination is to use the sans serif font Helvetica (also called Arial) for heads and the serif font Times Roman for body copy. This pairing (like Courier), however, has been overused. For that reason, you may want to try other combinations.

The font that you use for the body copy of a long piece is of particular importance. It colors your work and affects readability. Serif fonts have letters that are different sizes, which makes it easier for the eye to recognize words. For this reason, italics, scripts, and sans serif fonts are typically reserved for headlines or captions. Try taking a look at a page of body copy in several fonts to see which one works best with your piece.

The typographical size of a font varies according to its design. If you need to fit a lot of copy onto a single page, select a compact font. Many of the leading fonts were designed for these special purposes. For example, the omnipresent Times New Roman font was created in the 1920s as part of a redesign of the *London Times*. The intent was to make copy readable but very compact — the better to sell advertising space, my dear. Other fonts, such as Bookman, were created with a more open typestyle to make novels and other books easier to read. Most font catalogs offer suggestions as to how particular fonts are best used and recommend fonts that go well with them as body or display fonts.

The one overriding piece of advice that most designers give is to avoid using too many fonts on your page. Too many fonts make your publications seem cheap, poorly designed, confusing, and hard to read. We've all seen those "ransom note" designs where each letter is in a different font. Most people's sensibilities are better than that — especially because we've been bombarded with well-designed printed material for our entire lifetimes.

The best way to impose good type practice in a publication is to create and manage your publication with style sheets, as described in Chapter 6.

You have a lot of control over the way the type looks on your page. You can adjust the following characteristics to open up your text:

- ✔ Use bigger font sizes
- ✔ Adjust letter spacing or kerning
- ✔ Add additional line spacing
- ✔ Add spacing between paragraphs
- ✔ Use paragraph indents
- ✔ Shorten the length of your lines by adjusting your frame width
- ✔ Change the justification of your text frame

In regard to the last point, left-justified text is generally considered the most readable text and is most often seen. Right-justified and center-justified text is much less common and is generally used for special purposes such as headlines, captions, or pull quotes. Fully justified text works reasonably well for line lengths of about 10 to 12 words and is commonly used in dense newspaper or newsletter pages.

Using display text for headlines is a great way to pull a reader's eye to a section of a page. Often, headlines use larger and bolder fonts, display fonts, or some other special font treatment. Because the headline is the thing that most people see first on a page, it pays to be particularly attentive to the selection of font and font size. Also, proper kerning of a headline is well worth the additional effort. See Chapter 7 for details on kerning. It's also worthwhile to adjust the line spacing of a headline so that the words seem to clearly belong together. We like to use mixed casing in our headlines unless the headline is very short. In that event, we sometimes use all caps or small caps. When we use scripts in headlines (infrequently), we tend to use them in mixed case only.

WordArt frames often give you an effective way of creating attractive headlines. (See the next section for more information.)

Another way to set off headlines and sections of your documents is to use *rules*. Rules are lines, either horizontal (for headlines) or vertical (for columns). Rules are very effective and they don't have to be thick, either. A single-point rule will suffice in most cases except for separating the headline of your page.

No matter how much time you take designing your publications, you can always learn something from other people's work. When you are doing a project, take a look at the best examples that you can find of similar pieces and see which fonts were used, and how.

WordArt

Microsoft WordArt enables you to create especially fancy text objects, called WordArt objects. Microsoft Publisher 97 provides WordArt frames for the very purpose of creating and holding WordArt objects. When you draw a WordArt frame, Microsoft Publisher 97 automatically loads the Microsoft WordArt program, which is an OLE server program. When you create a WordArt object, you insert a special OLE object into your publication. (See the Chapter 1 sidebar, "Shout OLE and watch the bull fly!", for a discussion of using OLE objects.) To make this particularly easy, the toolbox contains an icon for a WordArt frame.

Figure 8-10 shows you a WordArt frame in the editing-in-place mode typical of some OLE objects in Microsoft Publisher 97. In Figure 8-10, the WordArt tool is labeled in the toolbox as a reminder.

Your WordArt text appears in the fuzzy box on your screen, and you enter and edit the actual text in the Enter Your Text Here window that appears below it. Notice the completely new menus and toolbars. Even though it sort of looks like you're in Microsoft Publisher 97, you're actually in the Microsoft WordArt program, ready to create a WordArt object.

You will want to explore the use of the tools in the Format toolbar when WordArt is open. Figure 8-11 shows you a labeled WordArt toolbar. Table 8-2 describes these tools and what they do. You should note that WordArt comes with its own online Help system. To get more information about using WordArt, select the WordArt Help Topics command from the Help menu.

Follow these steps to create a WordArt object in a WordArt frame:

1. **In the Enter Your Text Here dialog box, type the text that you want to be your WordArt object.**

WordArt tool

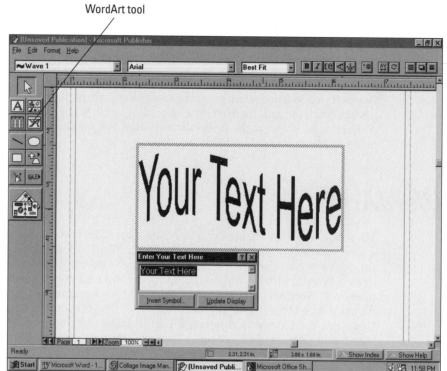

Figure 8-10:
A sample
WordArt
object.

Rotation

Shape   Size   Italic Flip Align   Shadow

Figure 8-11:
The labeled
WordArt
toolbar.

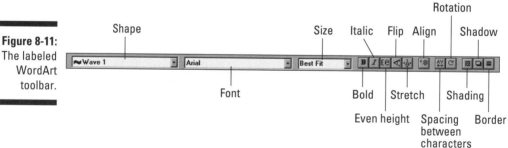

Font   Bold   Stretch   Shading

Even height   Spacing   Border
between
characters

If you want multiple-line text, press Enter to create new lines.

2. **In the Enter Your Text Here dialog box, click the Update Display button.**

The WordArt object on your publication page now displays the text that you typed.

3. **Use any or all of the Microsoft WordArt tools to fancify your WordArt object.**

   As you use each tool, the WordArt object automatically changes to show the effect you set.

4. **When your WordArt object looks the way you want, press Esc.**

   This step exits Microsoft WordArt and returns you to Microsoft Publisher 97.

Table 8-2	Microsoft WordArt's Toolbar Tools
Tool	*Purpose*
Shape	Opens a list that enables you to fit your text to a specific path or shape
Font	Opens a list of installed fonts
Size	Opens a list of text sizes (when in doubt, leave this set to Best Fit)
Bold	Boldfaces the text, making each character thicker
Italic	Italicizes the text, slanting each character to the right
Even Height	Makes all characters the same height
Flip	Changes a line of text from horizontal to vertical alignment
Stretch	Stretches text in all directions to make it completely fill the WordArt frame
Align	A pop-up menu with three flavors of justify plus center, left, and right
Spacing Between Characters	Opens a dialog box that enables you to adjust the amount of spacing between characters
Rotation	Opens a dialog box that enables you to rotate and skew your text
Shading	Opens a dialog box that enables you to set a pattern or color for your text
Shadow	Opens a list of shadow effects that you can place around your text
Border	Opens a dialog box that enables you to change each character's outline

The Enter Your Text Here dialog box disappears, Microsoft Publisher 97 takes back control of the menu bar and the top toolbar, and the WordArt frame loses its fuzzy edge and gains regular selection handles.

Creating an electronic watermark

If you hold expensive typing paper or foreign currency up to a light, you sometimes can see a *watermark,* an almost transparent image of a company logo, some dead king's portrait, or whatever. A very cool effect!

You can use Microsoft WordArt to create a similar effect electronically. Draw a full-page WordArt frame, use Microsoft WordArt to create an attention-getting message such as *Confidential* or *Important Notice,* and then format the message as you'd like. Now, use Microsoft WordArt's Shading tool to make the object a very light color or shade of gray. Press Esc to return to Publisher, and layer your WordArt object behind all other page objects or place the object on a background so that it appears on every publication page.

If you did everything just right, you now should be able to see your electronic watermark behind your other objects. Way cool!

If you inadvertently click in the publication window when you're working in Microsoft WordArt, you may end up back in Microsoft Publisher 97 with little warning. (You can tell you're back when your WordArt frame loses its fuzzy border.) To return to Microsoft WordArt, just double-click the WordArt frame.

Some WordArt effects can cancel out other effects. For example, if you have Best Fit set in the Size box, the Align options have no effect. Just experiment a while. And have fun!

To modify an internal component of a WordArt object after you return to Microsoft Publisher 97 — for example, if you want to change a character or fit the text to a different path — you must first reload Microsoft WordArt. To do this, double-click on the WordArt object. The WordArt frame regains its fuzzy border, Microsoft WordArt once again takes over the menu bar and top toolbar, and the Enter Your Text Here dialog box reopens. You are in the edit-in-place mode for an OLE server.

Microsoft Publisher 97 treats the WordArt object as a picture. You can move, resize, and crop it just as you can any picture (see Chapter 9).

Be careful of your typing in Microsoft WordArt. The WordArt program doesn't have a spell checker, and because Microsoft Publisher 97 treats a WordArt object as a picture rather than as text, it won't check the object's spelling, either.

Other Special Text Effects

Many publications use special large letters to start off a text block. When this letter extends below the top line of the text, it is called a *drop cap*. A large letter that appears above a line of text is a *raised cap*. Figure 8-12 shows you an example of each: The top *L* is an example of a drop cap, whereas the bottom *L* is an example of a raised cap. The shaded box between them is a *pull quote*.

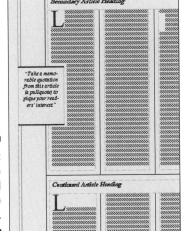

Figure 8-12:
A drop cap (top) and raised cap (bottom).

The CD-ROM version of Microsoft Publisher 97 includes a collection of what it calls "fancy first letters" that you can use as drop caps and raised caps. If you have the floppy disk version of the product, you can download the files from the Microsoft Publisher 97 Web site.

Many people use fancy first letters in place of smaller headlines. It's a good idea to spread these effects about your page and not to put them on the same line as the actual headline. Typically, we try to use only one of these caps on a page at a time.

To add a fancy first letter:

1. **Click the paragraph that is to contain the fancy first letter.**

2. **Choose Format⇨Fancy First Letter.**

   The Fancy First Letter dialog box, shown in Figure 8-13, appears.

3. **If you want to create your own fancy first letter, click the Custom First Letter tab of the Fancy First Letter dialog box.**

    The Custom First Letter tab of the Fancy First Letter dialog box, shown in Figure 8-14, appears. On this tab, you can select the number of special characters, their position with reference to the first line, the font, and font size.

4. **Click a Choose Letter Position button to set a drop cap or a raised cap; choose a font; and/or select the number of letters that you want to stylize.**

5. **Click the OK button.**

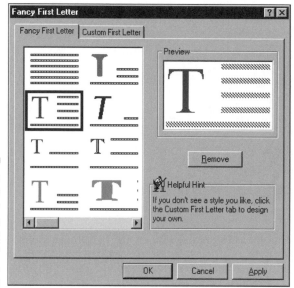

Figure 8-13:
The Fancy
First Letter
tab of the
Fancy First
Letter
dialog box.

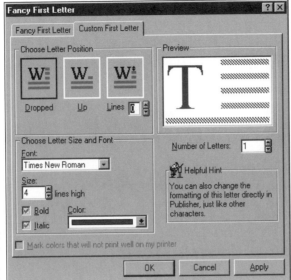

Figure 8-14:
The Custom
First Letter
tab of the
Fancy First
Letter
dialog box.

Part IV
Picture That

The 5th Wave   By Rich Tennant

BrainSoft

"Our new program has been on the market for over 6 months, and not one intellectual property lawsuit brought against us. I'm worried."

In this part . . .

Reading a publication without graphics or pictures in it is like listening to a ballet without seeing it. You know something's missing. Microsoft Publisher 97 lets you incorporate graphics into your pages to make them more interesting to look at and to convey information in a compact form. In the two chapters that comprise this part, you'll see the various ways of incorporating graphics as a design element in your publication. Microsoft Publisher 97 helps you import photographs, drawings, paintings, and other images directly into your work with ease. You can also use a library of clip art or work with a library of design elements (that Microsoft Publisher 97 supplies) to create snappy, sophisticated layouts. Microsoft Publisher 97 makes it easy, and you'll find it a lot of fun to work with this aspect of the program.

Face it, color sells. Color can highlight a section, set a mood, or perform any number of design functions. Microsoft Publisher 97 lets you work with spot colors one at a time, or create colors from the whole universe of colors in a full-color page. The second chapter in this part is a primer on working with color. You'll see what colors are, how they are represented, how to match colors, and how to get the best and most accurate output of the colors that you want.

Chapter 9

You Ought to Be in Pictures

*A*t the risk of repeating an old cliché, singing an old song, seeing an old saw, a picture really can be worth a thousand words. Why use dozens of paragraphs explaining what an Aurora X-100 looks like when you can just show your readers a picture of one?

Although Microsoft Publisher 97 really isn't the place to draw complex pictures, it's mighty flexible when it comes to importing pictures created elsewhere. Some desktop publishers rely heavily on collections of electronic clip art and libraries of photographs, whereas others are daring enough to create their own pictures using specialized graphics programs. Whether you're working from a clip art collection or creating your own pictures, this chapter shows you how to get pictures into and out of your publications and how to work with pictures after they're in Microsoft Publisher 97.

This chapter also shows you how to use some related tools that come with Microsoft Publisher 97. You find out how to use Microsoft Draw to create your own drawings, use the Design Gallery to obtain publication elements, apply border art, and even use your own scanner from within Microsoft Publisher 97 to bring images directly into the program.

Understanding More about Picture Frames

Microsoft Publisher 97 uses picture frames to display graphics on a layout. A picture frame can contain either drawings or images. The differences between drawings and images are described later in this chapter.

You don't create graphics inside a picture frame; they must be created elsewhere. The graphic contained in a picture frame can either be a data file or an OLE object that is managed by another program.

You can create picture frames in two ways. You can draw them yourself or have the program create them for you when you insert or import a graphic of some kind. Which method is best depends upon your purpose:

- ✔ When you need to place a picture frame of a specific size at a specific position in your layout, draw the frame with the Picture tool (in the toolbox) and fill the frame with a picture manually.

- ✔ When the content and size of the graphic determine the size of the frame, have Microsoft Publisher 97 create the frame for you as you bring in the picture. You can always adjust the frame's size and position later on.

Getting Yours

Microsoft Publisher 97 provides four ways to insert or import pictures:

- ✔ Copy a graphic from another Windows program onto the Windows Clipboard and then paste it into a picture frame.

- ✔ Choose Insert➪ClipArt to open the Microsoft ClipArt Gallery, which provides easy access to the dozens of pieces of clip art that you install with Microsoft Publisher 97.

- ✔ Choose Insert➪Picture File to import any picture that is saved in a format that Microsoft Publisher 97 can recognize.

- ✔ Use the Insert➪Object command to fill a picture frame with any OLE object.

If you don't want to make a trip to the Insert menu to choose the last three commands, you can also get to them by right-clicking on a picture frame, which displays the context-sensitive menu shown in Figure 9-1. The context-sensitive menu also offers the Windows Clipboard commands: Cut, Copy, and Paste.

We assume that you know how to use the Windows Clipboard at this point, although you may want to know more about what kinds of graphic formats the Clipboard supports. The three other methods for bringing pictures into a picture frame are discussed in the sections that follow.

No matter how you put a graphic into a picture frame, you can use any of the methods to replace that picture.

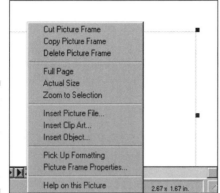

Using the Microsoft ClipArt Gallery

Microsoft ClipArt Gallery is a visual showcase of hundreds of pieces of clip art that install along with Microsoft Publisher 97. The Gallery itself is actually a piece of software — an image browser — that lets you view your clip art collection. Rather than use the Insert➪Picture File command to insert a clip art file — which requires you to remember the name and location of the picture file (files are stored in the ClipArt folder) — you simply click a miniature version of the picture in the Gallery.

The clip art contained in the collection that Microsoft gives you is saved in the Computer Graphic Metafile (CGM) format, which can be edited in Microsoft Draw. A metafile format lets you save both drawn and painted images in the same file; however, CGM is almost always used for drawings. The files that have the extension PCS contain the thumbnail versions of the clip art pictures; don't try to open or edit these files.

To insert a picture using Microsoft ClipArt Gallery:

1. **If you want to import the picture into a specific picture frame, select that frame.**

   Otherwise, make sure that no frame is selected — Microsoft Publisher 97 creates a frame for you in this case.

2. **Choose Insert➪ClipArt.**

   The Microsoft Clip Gallery dialog box, shown in Figure 9-2, appears. The Gallery is actually a self-contained program and not a dialog box.

3. **Click a specific category in the list box located to the left of the pictures, if you want.**

   If you select All Categories, the Gallery shows you every piece of clip art, regardless of category.

4. **Scroll as necessary and then double-click the picture that you want.**

5. **Double-click the picture or click the OK button.**

If you selected a picture frame in step 1, the picture completely fills that frame. Otherwise, Microsoft Publisher 97 creates a big picture frame for you in the center of the current view and places the picture in that new frame.

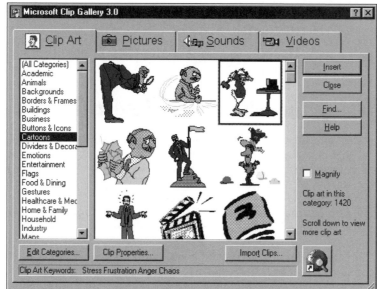

Figure 9-2:
The
Microsoft
Clip Gallery
dialog box.

The first time that you issue the ClipArt command, a dialog box opens to ask you whether you want to add clip from Microsoft Publisher 97. Click Yes and then wait a few moments as Microsoft ClipArt Gallery has a protracted conversation with your computer. (It's building the thumbnails that it needs to display the images and storing the references to the original file's locations.) If you installed Microsoft Publisher 97 from a CD-ROM rather than a floppy disk, you may have to insert the CD-ROM before Microsoft ClipArt Gallery can access its pictures.

If you draw a picture frame before you import a picture from Microsoft ClipArt Gallery, Microsoft Publisher 97 will display a dialog box asking whether you want to change the frame to fit the picture, or change the picture to fit the frame. If you decide to change the picture to fit the frame, Microsoft Publisher 97 may distort the picture as it squishes it into your frame. To restore the picture to its proper proportions, use one of the Scale commands, as described later in this chapter.

It's very easy to replace the picture from the clip art collection with another picture. Just double-click the existing picture to reopen the Microsoft Clip Gallery dialog box. Click a different picture and then click the Insert button. You also find a Microsoft ClipArt Gallery Object command on the picture frame's context-sensitive menu. Using that command displays a submenu with a Replace command that lets you reopen the Gallery also.

If you have other Microsoft programs on your computer (such as PowerPoint or other Microsoft Office components), they also share the Microsoft ClipArt Gallery. (In fact, you can access the Microsoft ClipArt Gallery from almost any modern Windows program, if you know how.) So, you may find more than just Microsoft Publisher 97 pictures there; you may also find pictures installed by Word, Excel, and so on.

You can do a couple of cool things with Microsoft ClipArt Gallery that many people never check out. One is to search for pictures by description, filename, or file format. Click the Microsoft ClipArt Gallery's Find button to access these options. The other is to run a search for pictures throughout your entire computer — and office network, if you're attached to one — and then add them to the Microsoft ClipArt Gallery.

Here's how to add pictures to the Microsoft ClipArt Gallery:

1. **Click the Import Clips button in the Clip Gallery dialog box.**

   The Add clip art to Clip Gallery dialog box, shown in Figure 9-3, appears.

2. **Find and select the picture of interest and click the Open button.**

   (You are not limited to CGM files; you can select files in TIF, BMP, and other formats that Microsoft Publisher 97 understands.) The Gallery adds your picture and opens the Clip Properties dialog box, shown in Figure 9-4.

3. **Fill out the Clip Properties dialog box.**

   Enter one or more keywords for the picture in the Keywords text box and choose one or more categories in the Categories list box.

4. **Click the OK button to add the image to the Gallery.**

   If the picture that you add is not in metafile format, it does not appear on the Clip Art in the Clip Gallery dialog box. Click the Pictures tab to find your new addition.

It may seem like whimsy or technobabble to walk you through the process of adding pictures to the Gallery. If you manage large numbers of images, however, you find this process a valuable one.

One other aspect of all this deserves mentioning: If you have the floppy disk version of Microsoft Publisher 97 (with 150 images), you don't have all the available clip art that the CD-ROM version offers (more than 5,000 images). You may want to add the extra art or art that you find elsewhere to your collection. You can find the missing clip art on the Microsoft Publisher 97 Web site. Its address is as follows: `http://www.microsoft.com/ publisher`. There you find additional clip art images, sounds, videos, photos, and the latest information on Microsoft Publisher 97. By default, Microsoft ClipArt Gallery offers only those pictures that install with Microsoft Publisher 97 and other Microsoft programs. Thus, if you create a picture yourself or get it from some non-Microsoft source, you won't find the picture in Microsoft ClipArt Gallery. (That is, unless you *add* your picture to Microsoft ClipArt Gallery.)

Inserting picture files

The Insert⇨Picture File command imports a picture stored on disk into your publication. When you find a picture of interest and highlight it in the Insert Picture File dialog box shown in Figure 9-5, Microsoft Publisher 97 builds a preview of the picture for you in the dialog box.

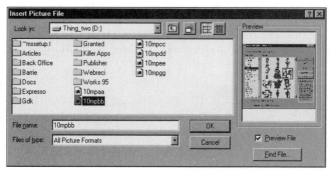

Figure 9-5:
The Insert
Picture File
dialog box.

One downside of using the Insert⇨Picture File command is that you must concern yourself somewhat with picture file formats. Microsoft Publisher 97 understands 12 of the most commonly used graphics file formats and is a very capable program for importing a wide variety of graphics.

To insert a picture using the Insert⇨Picture File command, follow these steps:

1. **If you want to import the picture into a specific picture frame, select that frame.**

   Otherwise, make sure that no frame is selected — Microsoft Publisher 97 creates the frame as needed.

2. **Select Insert⇨Picture File.**

   The Insert Picture File dialog box appears, as shown in Figure 9-5.

3. **Find the file that you want to insert and click OK.**

What happens next depends upon the type of file that you selected:

   ✔ If you selected a drawn image (such as a CGM file), Microsoft Publisher 97 automatically resizes the image to fill your frame.

✔ If you selected an image type for which the image has a specific size and resolution (such as a TIF image), Microsoft Publisher 97 opens the Import Picture dialog box (see Figure 9-6), asking you how you want the image handled if the frame is not of the appropriate proportions.

You can adjust the picture to the frame or adjust the frame to the picture by clicking the corresponding radio button in that dialog box. If you resize the picture to fit the frame, you distort your picture, which may or may not be an effect that you desire. If you don't know what you want to do, the Change The Frame To Fit The Picture option is the safer choice. You can always resize the frame later manually or by using the Scale Picture command described in the next section.

Figure 9-6:
The Import
Picture
dialog box.

If you import a picture and later decide that you want a different picture, just double-click the existing picture. The Insert Picture File dialog box reopens. Click a different file name and then click OK.

If Microsoft Publisher 97 doesn't understand the format of the picture that you're trying to import, it whines: `Cannot convert this picture`. If you have access to the program that created that picture, try saving the picture in a different format. Or, if you can open the picture in any other Windows program, try copying the picture to the Windows Clipboard and pasting it into your picture frame.

If you import a picture using the Clipboard and later want to change internal components of that picture, try double-clicking it in your publication. Depending on how your computer is set up, your double-click may load the program that created the picture. Make your changes in that program and then exit the program. Your changes display in Microsoft Publisher 97.

Modifying pictures

After you import a picture, you can adjust it in Microsoft Publisher 97 in several ways: You can resize it, chop off parts of it (called *cropping*), and add some space between the picture and its frame to create a border. These changes apply to the format of the frame and not to the picture itself. A picture frame can only display graphics, not change them.

If you want to edit the internal components of a picture — for example, to change a zebra's black-and-white stripes to purple and green or to add extra hair to a digital photograph of yourself (the poor man's hair-replacement system!) — forget Microsoft Publisher 97. You need to use a specialized graphics program. If you used the Clipboard to import the picture, you may be able to load the appropriate program just by double-clicking the picture. If that doesn't work, try using the Clipboard to export the picture to the graphics program, make your changes there, and then reimport the picture.

Try using Microsoft Paint or Microsoft Draw to edit your image. One of these two programs should enable you to open and modify most images. If you know the picture's file type, consult the last section in this chapter to find out what kind of image it is. Use Microsoft Paint for bitmap or image files and Microsoft Draw for vector or drawn graphics.

Resizing a picture

To resize a picture, you resize its frame. By default, both the picture and its frame are the same size and proportions. You can resize a picture frame much as you would resize any other frame: by dragging any of its selection handles.

To maintain the proportions of a picture and its frame, hold down the Shift key as you drag a corner selection handle.

If Microsoft Publisher 97 distorted your picture when you imported it, holding down the Shift key as you drag a corner selection handle simply maintains that distortion. To undistort a picture, try using one of the Scale commands described next. (*Scaling* in Microsoft Publisher 97 is just another term for *resizing*. Scaling in snakes and pipes is another thing entirely.) The Format➪Scale Picture command is also a way to resize a picture without using the mouse.

Here's how to resize a picture using the menu command:

1. **Select the picture that you want to resize and/or restore.**

2. **Select the Scale Picture command from the Format menu or from the picture's context-sensitive menu.**

   The Scale Picture dialog box, shown in Figure 9-7, appears.

   You may notice that when you resize your picture, the title of the Scale Picture dialog box reads Scale Object instead. What this is telling you is that the picture is a registered file type of an OLE server. In all other regards, these two dialog boxes work equivalently.

3. **Enter numbers in the Scale Height and Scale Width text boxes to set the percentages to which you want to resize your picture.**

   These percentages vary according to the picture's original file size. Use the same percentages to retain the figure's proportions.

   To see the picture at its original file size, click the Original Size check box.

4. **Click OK.**

   Both the picture and its frame resize accordingly.

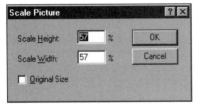

Figure 9-7: The Scale Picture dialog box.

If you use the Clipboard to import a picture into an existing picture frame and that picture becomes distorted, a value of 100% in the Scale Picture or Scale Object dialog box may *not* equal the original size. In this case, you have to play with the percentages until the proportions look correct. Or, save yourself some grief by reimporting the picture *without* using an existing picture frame.

Don't forget that resizing a bitmap graphic will lower the quality of the image. You can, however, resize vector graphics (drawings) to your heart's content without doing any damage.

Cropping a picture

Publishing professionals who still assemble publications *without* a computer often remove unwanted edges of a picture by lopping off those edges with a pair of scissors. In the publishing world, editing a picture in this way is called *cropping*. Why bother with scissors, though? As shown in Figure 9-8, you can use Microsoft Publisher 97 to crop a picture *electronically*.

To crop a selected picture:

1. **Click the Crop Picture button on the Format toolbar.**

2. **Point to one of the picture frame's selection handles.**

   Your mouse pointer changes to a *cropper pointer* — two scissors with the word *Crop*.

3. **Drag inward until you exclude the part of the picture that you don't want and then release the mouse.**

Figure 9-8:
The left
picture is
the original;
the right
picture was
cropped to
remove the
house's
second
story.

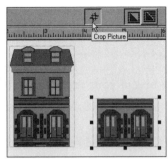

Cropping a picture doesn't permanently remove any picture parts; it only hides them from view. To restore a picture part that you've cropped, repeat the preceding steps, but drag outward. Regardless of whether you've cropped or not, you can drag outward on any picture to *reverse crop*, thus adding space between the picture and its frame. (You also can add space between a picture and its frame by increasing the picture frame's margins in the Object Frame Properties dialog box.)

Here are a few more cropping tips to keep in mind:

- ✔ To crop or reverse crop the same amount at each edge — thus keeping the picture in the center of its frame — hold down the Ctrl key as you drag a corner selection handle.

- ✔ By default, Microsoft Publisher 97 enables you to crop only in a rectangular fashion. For more customizable, irregular cropping, apply the Wrap Text to Picture option and then click the Edit Irregular Wrap button to create and/or modify the adjust handles. See Chapter 5 for details.

- ✔ If you want to resize a picture immediately after cropping, click again on the Cropping tool to turn off the cropping option. You can also turn off the cropping option by deselecting and then reselecting the picture.

- ✔ To remove all cropping and reverse cropping from a selected picture with the least amount of effort, select the Scale Picture or Scale Object command from the Format menu, check the Original Size check box, and click OK.

Working with captions

Sometimes, pictures are not enough. They require an explanation. You can create captions for your pictures and have them move with their respective pictures in travels across your layout. Unlike the high-priced layout programs,

Microsoft Publisher 97 doesn't automate the process of creating and renumbering captions for you. But you already possess the skills required to create a caption and attach it to a picture.

To create a caption, follow these steps:

1. **Draw a text frame and enter the text of your caption into it.**

2. **Move the text frame next to the picture and select both the picture and the frame.**

3. **Click the Group Objects button to lock it and create a group.**

   Figure 9-9 shows you an example of a figure with a caption.

Figure 9-9:
A figure
with a
caption.

Hey, that's it! What do you think this is, rocket science? Well, there is one trick that you can apply to make a caption even better. Select your text frame and then select the Text Frame Properties command from either the Format menu or the text frame's context-sensitive menu. In the Text Frame Properties dialog box, set all of the margins to 0. Then your captions can get up close and personal with your graphics.

Applying borders and BorderArt

You can give your picture frame a border by using the Border command's dialog box or the pop-up menu of the Border button on the Format toolbar. If the picture frame is a regular rectangle, you can also apply BorderArt to it. (You can't apply this feature to irregular picture frames.) You can also apply BorderArt to text frames, table frames, and even WordArt frames.

Here's how to apply BorderArt to a selected frame(s):

1. **Select Format⇨Border.**

   The BorderArt dialog box appears, as shown in Figure 9-10.

2. **Click the BorderArt tab of the BorderArt dialog box.**

   The BorderArt tab of the BorderArt dialog box appears, as shown in Figure 9-11.

3. **Make your selection from the Available Borders list box, set a Border Size and Color (if desired), and click the OK button.**

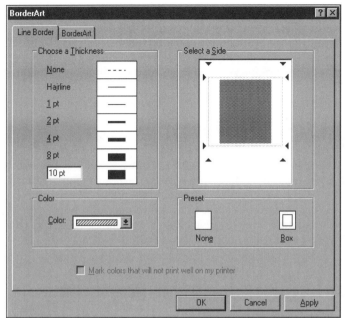

Figure 9-10:
The Line
Border tab
of the
BorderArt
dialog box.

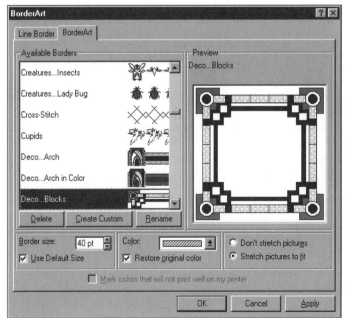

Figure 9-11:
The
BorderArt
tab of the
BorderArt
dialog box.

The BorderArt dialog box is one of those simple features that's so well implemented that using it is a breeze. Simply use the arrow keys to move through the list of borders in the dialog box. As you scroll through the list, the Preview section displays the different borders. This dialog box offers tons of fun borders for you to try, and you'll definitely enjoy playing with it.

Working with Different Picture Types

Computers use two types of graphics: drawn graphics and painted graphics. The type of graphic that you are using determines many features about how a graphic displays on your screen and the quality of the printed output. The two types use different file formats and require different types of programs for creating and editing graphics. But Microsoft Publisher 97 can work with both types of graphics, even in the same publication.

Painted versus drawn graphics

Painted graphics are also referred to as *images* or *bitmapped* or *raster* graphics. In painted graphics, the image is composed of a set of tiny dots, called *pixels* or *pels,* that forms a mosaic. The image is two-dimensional, although the manner in which the image is painted can give the effect of three dimensions.

A painted image is akin to a mosaic of tiles that you might see in a Roman temple. The smaller the tiles, the more realistic the image looks. The size of the tile — or in the case of a computer image, the size of the pixel — is called the *resolution* of the image. This value is often given in *dots per inch* or *dpi.* Because a bitmap is designed for a specific resolution, it looks great at that resolution. It can also look great at larger or coarser resolutions (smaller dpi) because you have more data than you need. Painted graphics do not scale up well, however. For example, a 72-dpi image that displays perfectly on a screen would not print well on your laser printer at 300 dpi.

Programs that create painted images are either paint programs such as Microsoft Paint or image-editing programs such as Adobe Photoshop. We take a look at Microsoft Paint in a moment — because it comes bundled with Windows, it's there for you to use gratis.

At the very highest end of the spectrum, images can be photorealistic and can be rendered to show textures, reflections, and shadings. The file size of a bitmap image is directly related to the size of the image, the number of colors stored, and the resolution.

Drawn graphics are referred to as *vector* or *object-oriented* art. With a drawing, the lines, arcs, and other elements that make up a graphic are stored as mathematical equations. Because drawings are created in this way, they are resolution independent. They are calculated to display or print at the best capability of the output device — which is why they are referred to as *device independent*. This feature makes using drawings generally (but not always) preferable to using paintings in desktop publishing applications.

Here's an important point, though: Regardless of how a drawing is stored, it must be converted to a bitmap when it is printed or displayed on-screen. This process is referred to as *raster image processing (RIP)* and it is done to display graphics to any output device. When you RIP a bitmap image, the only conversion required is the resampling of the bitmap to either throw away or interpolate data from the bitmap.

When you RIP a drawing, the processing can be simple (for lines and simple drawing primitives) to very complex (for sophisticated descriptions of fill patterns). Thus, a complex PostScript drawing with many, many features and complex fills and strokes may take a really long time to calculate and process. These types of drawings may also require large file sizes — thus defeating their advantage over painted images. The crossover point is reached when you attempt to create a natural image as a drawing. Such graphics are better stored as a bitmap.

Paint with Microsoft Paint

You can buy very expensive paint and image-editing programs as a supplement to Microsoft Publisher 97. Still, if your needs are reasonable, you can create nice bitmapped images (or edit the ones you have) in Microsoft Paint. Microsoft Paint is one of the "accessories" that is installed with Windows 95.

To create a Microsoft Paint OLE object in Microsoft Publisher 97, do the following:

1. **Click the OLE button in the toolbar and select the Bitmap Image command from its pop-up menu, as shown in Figure 9-12.**

   Your cursor turns into a crosshair.

2. **Drag a frame that you want to use as your paint canvas.**

   The Microsoft Paint OLE engine opens on your screen, as shown in Figure 9-13.

3. **Create your painting by using the paint tools in the toolbox at the left and the color palette at the bottom of your screen.**

4. **When you are done, click outside the frame to return to Microsoft Publisher 97.**

Figure 9-12:
The OLE
button's
menu.

Figure 9-13:
A Microsoft
Paint OLE
object
being
edited in
place.

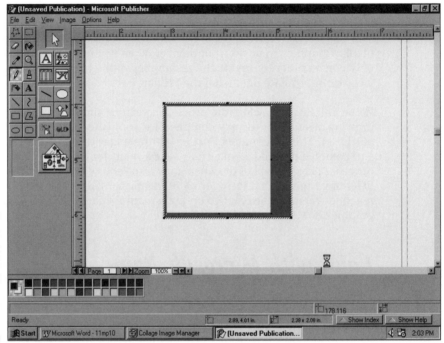

The connection of your painted object to Microsoft Paint is an intimate one. To edit the image in place again, simply double-click it. The image is actually part of the Microsoft Publisher 97 file, however, and does not have an outside or independent existence. That is, you can't open the image as a file from within Microsoft Paint.

You often can use Microsoft Paint to edit images from other sources. To do this, create a Microsoft Paint frame on your layout. Then switch to the picture frame that contains your bitmapped image. Copy that image and paste it into your Microsoft Paint frame. When you double-click the Microsoft Paint frame now, it opens with your image in it.

Microsoft Paint has many features and tools that we don't have room to tell you about here. It's also useful for adjusting image colors. You may want to consult its online Help system for instructions.

Microsoft Paint is based on one of the earlier versions of ZSoft's Paintbrush, which was one of our favorite paint programs a number of years ago. If you open the Paint OLE engine inside Microsoft Publisher 97, you need never worry about file formats. If you travel from the Start menu to the Programs folder and into the Accessories folder to find and launch Microsoft Paint, however, you can open and work with several important bitmapped file formats. Microsoft Paint can open the three most common bitmapped image file formats around: PCX files (the ZSoft format), Window's native BMP format, and the ever-popular TIF. That makes Microsoft Paint a very good program to use to edit and print these kinds of images.

Draw with Microsoft Draw

We have almost no drawing talent whatsoever, so we avoid drawing programs like the plague. We are, therefore, fond of clip art and opt for collections such as the one that comes with Microsoft Publisher 97. If you, however, are able to draw a horse that looks more like a horse than a cat, you may want to create your own pictures from scratch. Although you certainly can go out and buy a full-blown professional graphics program, a very nice graphics program — Microsoft Draw — installs (free!) along with Microsoft Publisher 97.

Anytime that you want to create a picture, you can load Microsoft Draw from within Microsoft Publisher 97, use Microsoft Draw's specialized tools to create that picture, and then exit Microsoft Draw. Your picture automatically becomes part of your current publication. The process is exactly the same as described in the preceding section for Microsoft Paint.

To create a Microsoft Draw OLE object in Microsoft Publisher 97, do the following:

1. **Click the OLE button in the toolbar and select the Microsoft Drawing command from its pop-up menu (refer to Figure 9-12).**

   Your cursor turns into a crosshair.

2. **Drag a frame that you want to use as your paint canvas.**

   The Microsoft Draw OLE engine opens on your screen, as shown in Figure 9-14.

3. **Create your drawing using the draw tools in the toolbox at the left and the color palette at the bottom of your screen.**

4. **When you are done, click outside the frame to return to Microsoft Publisher 97.**

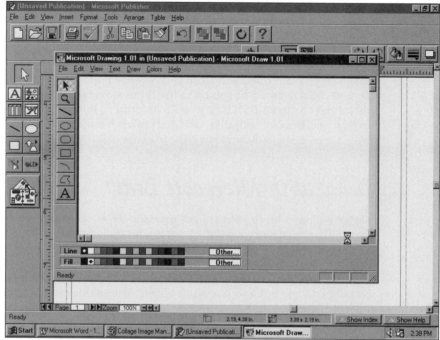

Figure 9-14:
A Microsoft
Draw OLE
object
being
edited in
place.

To modify an internal component of a Microsoft Draw object, reload Microsoft Draw. To do this, double-click the Microsoft Draw object. After you complete your editing and return to Microsoft Publisher 97, the program treats the object just like any other picture. You can move, resize, and crop it at will.

Don't use Microsoft Draw to draw very simple graphics such as lines and boxes. Instead, use Microsoft Publisher 97's own limited drawing tools. These tools create graphics that have smaller file sizes and are more compactly described than a Microsoft Draw frame with objects in it.

You often can use Microsoft Draw to edit the internal components of a drawing created by another program. If you've already imported a drawing into Microsoft Publisher 97, select that picture and copy it to the Clipboard. Then open a Microsoft Draw window and paste the drawing into it. You can then double-click the drawing to edit it in Microsoft Draw.

Avoid using Microsoft Draw to edit image files whose filenames end with BMP, JPG, PCD, PCX, or TIF. Instead, try to edit the picture with a paint-type program such as Microsoft Paint. Similarly, avoid using Microsoft Paint to work with files that use the EPS, WMF, CDR, DRW, or WMF formats. Use Microsoft Draw for those file types. Mixing the wrong format and program results in garbage being displayed on your screen, if anything displays at all.

The next section in this chapter explains how to load other Windows programs from within Microsoft Publisher 97.

Say OLE!

You've now seen four examples of using OLE servers in Microsoft Publisher 97: WordArt (in the previous chapter), ClipArt Gallery (earlier in this chapter), Paint, and Draw. You should be an OLE meister at this point in the book. But you've just started to scratch the surface of the programs that are out there at your service. Many more OLE server programs get installed when you install Windows or other programs.

Before you know it, you'll have sound servers, video servers, coffee servers, and more. (*More* is the operative word here.) To see what you've got installed in your system at the moment, select the More command from the OLE button's menu in the toolbox. The Insert Object dialog box shown in Figure 9-15 appears. The servers are listed in the Object Type list box. You have the option of creating a new data object that is part of your Microsoft Publisher 97 publication or inserting an object contained in a data file. If you want other programs to access the data object, use the Create from File radio button. If you want the object managed inside your publication, click the Create New radio button. The Display As Icon option lets you suppress the display, which is valuable in improving screen performance.

We think that Microsoft Chart is one of the OLE servers that you may find most useful. It can take Excel or Works spreadsheet data and create charts and graphs from it.

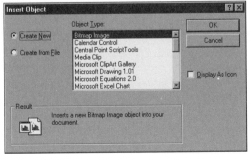

Figure 9-15:
The Insert
Object
dialog box.

Did you notice that Microsoft Draw and ClipArt Gallery load very differently from Microsoft WordArt? Whereas Microsoft Draw and ClipArt Gallery open in their own, separate windows, Microsoft WordArt takes over part of the Microsoft Publisher 97 window and fuzzies up your WordArt frame. The term *open editing* describes how Microsoft Draw and ClipArt Gallery load: Each program displays in its own window. The term *editing-in-place* describes how Microsoft WordArt loads: The fuzzy-bordered object remains in place while the original program's window adjusts accordingly. In-place editing is one of OLE's newer features, so you'll see it more and more as you begin to use newer programs on your computer.

We are at the beginning of the era of compound documents or rich data type documents. Here, small programs manage your data within a file. Our publications will be all singing, all dancing wonders.

Using the Design Gallery

One feature that you should definitely visit in your page layout work is the Design Gallery. The Design Gallery is not a graphics creator per se, although it does rely on graphics in many instances. The Design Gallery is a browser that displays a collection of page layout parts that you can use inside your document to create even more compelling publications. The original set of parts that you can use includes headlines, ornaments, pull quotes, tables of contents, sidebars, and titles. The Design Gallery offers you several styles including classic, jazzy, modern, and plain designs. Just as you can with the ClipArt Gallery, you can add selections to the Design Gallery and use them in other publications.

Follow these steps to insert a Design Gallery object into your layout:

1. **Create a picture frame to contain your design element.**

   If you choose not to create a frame, the Design Gallery will create one for you.

2. **Click the Design Gallery button in the toolbar, shown in Figure 9-16.**

   The Design Gallery dialog box appears, as shown in Figure 9-17.

Figure 9-16: The Design Gallery button.

3. **Click a selection in the Choose a Category list box and an item in the Choose a style for your publication list box.**

4. **If you don't see an object that's to your liking, click the More Designs button and select another style by name.**

5. **With your object selected, click the Insert Object button to have the object appear on your layout in a new frame.**

Or, click the Replace Selection button to replace your selection with the object.

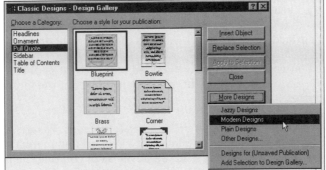

Figure 9-17:
The Design Gallery dialog box.

Figure 9-18 shows you a sample pull quote from the Design Gallery placed on a layout, with its text selected for editing.

Figure 9-18:
An inserted pull quote.

If you create something in your work or see something that someone else created that you want to save in the Design Gallery and reuse, that's easy to do. Just select the object and then open the Design Gallery dialog box. At the bottom of the More Designs pop-up menu, select the Add Selection to Design Gallery command. The program displays a dialog box asking whether you want to create a design set. You can then add this object to a named collection. Between the ClipArt Gallery and the Design Gallery, Microsoft Publisher 97 gives you two very powerful methods for managing a collection of graphics and page layout parts to speed your work.

Tracking Down Other Picture Sources

With Microsoft Publisher 97, you have just scratched the surface of available picture sources for your work. If you go online, either on the Internet or commercial online services, you discover an almost unlimited number of images that you can use. Many of these images are freely distributed and of high quality. Even most user group bulletin boards have graphics sections with images that you can download. Many images that aren't free are very reasonably priced — or are free if you use them for noncommercial work.

Make sure that you check any downloaded files with virus detection software. Most services do a good job of checking files, but the Internet is wide open to viruses.

You can also find many commercial sources for images. We are inundated with brochures from companies that want to sell us commercial clip art. Chances are that if a company is in the business of creating the images, the images that they sell are of high quality. If a company is in the business of harvesting images from other sources, as you often find in low-priced CD-ROMs, you can be less sure of quality. One good place to look for image sources is *Canned Art: Clip Art for the Macintosh,* by Fenton and Morrissett (Peachpit Press). Most of the collections referenced in the book are available for the PC, as well as for the Mac — or are easily converted.

To the companies 3-D Graphics and Image Club for drawn graphics, we would add the names of Adobe (Mountain View, CA, 800-344-8335) and Artbeats (San Bernadino, CA, 714-881-1200) for excellent collections of patterns and fills; Multi-Ad Services (Peoria, IL, 309-692-1530) for business graphics; and T/Maker (Mountain View, CA, 415-962-0195) for general images. The Dover Publications image books (Mineola, NY, 516-294-7000) are also great sources of images that you can scan into your publication.

Try to buy your drawn graphics in either the CGM or WMF formats, as they are the easiest to work with. If you need very high-quality drawn images, then use EPS graphics.

For image collections, PhotoDisk (Seattle, WA, 800-528-3472) is excellent. We are also impressed with the selections from Image Club, which was recently bought by Adobe. You can see selections of photos from the latter catalog in the Adobe Web site at `http://www.adobe.com`. Kodak also offers a service that can be used to preview and download (for a fee) images from an image server. The software is called Kodak's Picture Exchange, and it's really practical for people who use and need high-quality images frequently — such as advertising agencies. You may want to visit the Kodak Web site to see what's available there: `http://www.kodak.com/digitalImages/samples/samples.shtml`.

Image ethics

You need to pay particular attention to the source of any image that you intend to use in your work. Someone created the image, and someone owns it. The two "someones" aren't always the same person. Whoever the owner is controls the use of the image and can let you freely use it, let you use it for noncommercial use, or charge you a fee.

Don't be fooled into thinking that just because an image is a picture of something well known in the public domain — for example, a picture of the Statue of Liberty — it doesn't belong to the person who took the picture. It does.

Microsoft Publisher 97's license allows you to freely use its clip art in your publications. You cannot sell the clip art electronically as software, either individually or in a collection. This is a generous license. Other companies let you use low-resolution images freely, but charge for the use of high-resolution images.

You must check out the license that comes with the image. The problem is, though, that many images don't come with a license. In that case, it is better to err on the side of caution and use an image whose source and conditions of use are known.

Just to muddy up the waters, an aspect of copyright law allows for the "fair use" of text and images in some instances. If you are using a piece of a document or an image for journalistic criticism, you are free to use the work of others. The restriction is that the piece you use must be a small part of the work and not something central to the use of the work. For example, you could use a still frame from a movie or a short video clip, but not a long one. The fair use doctrine has not yet undergone long scrutiny of the law (something that could be said of much of our current copyright law). Each country also has its own copyright laws.

Scanning the Picture

If you can see it on paper, you can get it into Microsoft Publisher 97. The ultimate way to bring images into Microsoft Publisher 97 is by using a scanner. A *scanner* is a machine that digitizes images into bitmapped files. You can buy scanners that can read film or slides; you can also find related equipment for video digitization.

The most popular devices for desktop publishers probably are flatbed desktop scanners. You can get a medium-quality, full-color desktop scanner such as a ScanJet IIc or Epson Color Scanner 300 for $1,000 to $1,200. These scanners create files in 24-bit (full) color at 600 x 600 dpi. Images of this type are adequate for medium-quality magazine work.

You can also rent scanners at service bureaus or have service bureaus scan your images for you. In the latter case, the equipment used can be high quality, but the charges are greater.

Scanners can create digital images in the following modes:

✔ **Black-and-white scans:** This mode creates images with only black or white pixels. It is suitable for images that are predominantly white or black and don't have much detail, but not for art with patterns or textures that you want to preserve. This mode creates very small file sizes.

✔ **Line art scans:** This mode is used for finely detailed artwork done in black and white. Turn the brightness up when you scan line art.

✔ **Grayscale scans:** This mode preserves any shades of gray in a black-and-white photograph or converts color values in a color image to shades of gray. It gives photographic results and preserves patterns and textures. The eye can see about 80 shades of gray, but it is typical for most people to scan at up to 256 shades of gray for higher-quality work, because that is what computer monitors can display. File sizes can be large but are still only a third of the file sizes of color scans.

✔ **Color scans:** This mode is used to create images with pictures in full color. File sizes can be extremely large. Pay particular attention to minimizing the file size when creating these images and to making sure that the color fidelity is correct.

Many printed materials are printed as *halftone images.* In a halftone image, black-and-white images are created with spots, dots, lines, or other repeating patterns. These images don't offer true black and white and, therefore, scan poorly. Scanner software often has special facilities to handle halftones in order to get adequate scans. Chances are that scanned halftones will result in images called *moiré patterns,* which are very unattractive. Often, you can avoid moiré patterns by reducing image size, positioning the picture in your scanner at an angle, and applying filtering in an image-editing program to the image. Then, if you're lucky, moiré patterns don't print. But your best bet is to avoid scanning halftone images if you can.

Large scanned images can take a really long time to display on your layout. They can make scrolling about painful to do. Microsoft Publisher 97 has a feature that helps you by reducing the detail of your pictures or hiding pictures on a layout from view. You can also display your pictures in a reduced form, which results in a slight improvement in performance.

To hide pictures on a layout, select View➪Picture Display. The Picture Display dialog box (shown in Figure 9-19) opens, where you can click the Hide Pictures radio button.

When you have the Hide Pictures option turned on, your picture frames have an X through them to indicate that they contain a picture. Frames without content appear without an X.

Scanners can be used to import not only pictures but also digitized images of any object: paper, marble, cloth, and so on. You can get great and creative graphics by using scanned images in your work.

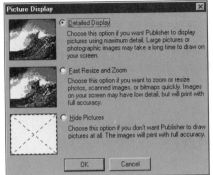

Figure 9-19:
The Picture
Display
dialog box.

Scanning is a complex topic and one that requires specialized knowledge to get just so. We would like to recommend one outstanding book on the topic of scanners and digital imaging technology: *Real World Scanning and Half-tones* by David Bladner and Steve Roth (Peachpit Press). This book is both technically excellent and well written with a sense of humor.

The most important thing that you can remember about the process is that you should scan your images with the purpose of the image in mind. If you are scanning an image for screen display, a resolution of 72 dpi is sufficient. For a laser printer, you don't want to scan at more than 300 dpi; anything more is wasted and can't be used. Similarly, although you can scan any image size to great color depth and your image can be reduced, it is a waste of resources to do so. Use a color and image size appropriate to your work. For example, an 8 1/2 x 11-inch, 24-bit color image at 300 dpi (150 lines per inch or medium-quality magazine printing at full color) consumes about 25MB of disk space! So it pays to save.

For example, if you are printing only in black and white, then scan in black and white — or better still, in shades of gray. You can get great results from 256 shades of gray, and very good results from 64 shades of gray, with enormous file size reductions. You just have to know the intended use of the graphics.

Microsoft Publisher 97 lets you directly incorporate scans using software that supports the TWAIN standard. This standard is scanner driver software that installs into Microsoft Publisher 97's Insert menu as a set of menu commands. If your scanner supports this standard, you find the Acquire Scanned Image command on the menu. When you select the command, the driver runs and a program appears that lets you scan your image in the scanner. When you close the program, your scanned image appears in your selected picture frame or in a frame that the driver creates for you. In this regard, TWAIN works similarly to any other OLE server that you would use.

If you don't see these commands on the Insert menu, then all is not lost. Many scanner manufacturers upgrade their software, and you may want to check with your manufacturer to see whether an upgrade exists. Also, third-party software that supports your scanner may be available. For example, the highly regarded Ofoto software supports many common scanners and offers advanced features.

Reviewing File Formats

Graphic image file formats are a rat's nest of acronyms — a veritable alphabet soup. Unfortunately, you have to know something about each format in order to decide which format you want to import a file from. File formats come in three basic types: paint or bitmapped image files, drawing or vector image files, and metafiles, which let you store either type of picture. A file's extension tells you the format of the file. This section describes in brief the file formats that Microsoft Publisher 97 is capable of importing.

You can't save a picture from Microsoft Publisher 97 directly. You can copy and paste a picture from Microsoft Publisher 97 into another program and save it there, however.

The following formats are bitmapped or painted image file formats supported by Microsoft Publisher 97:

✔ **JPEG Filter:** Files in the JPEG format take the JPG file extension. These files are very high-quality color files that offer advanced file compression techniques for reducing their image files. JPEG is one of the best choices for full-color images. Most image-editing programs save to JPEG. You will also find JPEG images in scientific work and as a standard file format on the Internet because the format is cross-platform.

✔ **PC Paintbrush:** ZSoft's PC Paintbrush was a popular early paint program. The program saves its files using the PCX file extension. Originally, this file format was strictly for black-and-white images, but it was extended to include full-color images as well. PCX has been very widely adopted on the PC and is one of the favored bitmapped file formats. Most paint and image-editing programs support this format, and many screen captures are done in PCX.

✔ **Tagged Image File Format 5.0:** This format, also known as TIFF, is an industry standard file format that creates files that use the TIF extension. The format was created by Microsoft and Aldus and is openly published and supported. TIFF creates files with very high-quality images. The specification is up to level 6, but level 5 was the first that supported file compression. All paint and image-editing programs open and save to TIFF. TIFF is probably the favorite bitmapped file format for desktop publishing applications.

Several variations of TIFF exist, so you can have problems opening TIFF files.

Many programs, such as Photoshop, read one flavor of TIFF and save out to another. So if you are having trouble with a TIFF file, try converting it through a program such as Photoshop or a file-conversion program.

✔ **Kodak PhotoCD:** The PhotoCD standard produces files with the PCD file extension. This is a very high-quality photographic image storage file format. You can go to a processing center and have your pictures converted to the PCD standard and placed on a CD-ROM disk. Most modern CD-ROM drives read this format. The standard saves images in several sizes and resolutions so that you can use the images for a variety of purposes. PCD is a favored format for use in high-quality image work. It is a cross-platform standard.

✔ **Windows Bitmaps:** These files are painted images in the Microsoft Paint format and can be either black and white or color. They take the BMP file extension. You can open and edit these files in Microsoft Paint. BMP files are simple ones. They work well for lower-quality paint images, but are not commonly used for images.

TIFF, JPEG, and PCD files are the favored high-quality image file formats.

You can import the following formats for drawn or vector images:

✔ **Encapsulated PostScript:** Files in this format end with the EPS file extension. EPS files are written in the PostScript language using plain text to indicate graphics and text with formatting. EPS files can be displayed, but require the creator application to alter. You need a Postscript printer to print EPS files correctly.

EPS files often import incorrectly and appear as a black or gray box in a picture frame, but print correctly.

EPS is a very high-quality format that many service bureaus favor. You often find high-quality clip art stored in this file format. When you send an EPS file to a service bureau, it is complete. That is, it contains all the font information it needs and doesn't require the service bureau to set up their computer to print your EPS file.

✔ **WordPerfect Graphic:** This is a proprietary format used for drawings inside the WordPerfect word processor and related products from WordPerfect (now owned by Corel). Otherwise, this file format is infrequently used.

✔ **Corel Draw Picture:** This is the proprietary drawing format for the very popular CorelDRAW! illustration program. Its files take the CDR file extension. CDR files are of good quality, but EPS is favored for high-quality draw output.

✔ **Micrografx Designer/Draw:** This format is another popular software vendor's proprietary drawing format. Files take the DRW file extension. The preceding comments about CDR files apply to DRW files, too.

Microsoft Publisher 97 can import the following metafiles:

✔ **Computer Graphics Metafile:** This standard produces images with the CGM file extension. CGM is widely used for drawn images and almost never contains bitmaps. CGM is used by many IBM PC clip art collections. This format is never used on a Macintosh.

✔ **Windows Metafile:** This is the native file format for the Windows Clipboard. It creates files with the WMF file extension. Because WMF is specified by a single vendor (Microsoft), you encounter few difficulties with it. WMF files are nearly always drawings; it is rare to find a file of this type with a bitmap in it. Many PC clip art collections now use the WMF format, as it produces good results.

✔ **Macintosh PICT:** The PICT format is the native file format of the Macintosh Clipboard. In earlier days, the Macintosh was the source of many illustrations used on the PC. These days, this is much less true. PICT files often contain either bitmaps or drawn images, or both. Images are of moderate quality, and PICT is not a favored high-quality format. The files take the PCT file extension.

Phew! We told you that the world of file formats was a rat's nest. Still, Microsoft Publisher 97 is blessed with a large and varied collection of file format import filters. All the popular ones are included, so you should have little trouble working with images from outside sources.

Chapter 10

Color by the Numbers

Color sells. What once appeared to be dull, listless text looks like supertext when you add color. Microsoft Publisher 97 makes incorporating color into your publications easy. Some of its features are close to those found in the high-priced spreads.

In this chapter, we tell you how to use color in your publications. We also give you theories on color usage and enough information about color modeling to get you started. We help you get more color in your publications for less money by explaining how to apply color in a cost-effective way.

How Color Improves Your Page

Which would you rather look at: a black-and-white photograph or a color photograph? A black-and-white movie or a color movie? Most people prefer color, even though black and white has its artistic merit.

Color creates highlights, blocks sections of your page, and draws the eye to important sections. Studies show that when color is used correctly, the average reader spends more time on a page and has a higher comprehension of its contents. When color is used badly — an easy thing to do — the average reader finds something better to look at. Studies show that, too.

Following are the keys to using color well:

- ✔ Don't go overboard when using color.
- ✔ Choose complementary colors. (More about this later.)
- ✔ Be consistent in your use of color in a publication; use the same color for the same page elements.
- ✔ Create a color scheme and then stick to it.

By following these suggestions, you help your reader stay focused on the content of your page without being distracted by the color that you put there. (If you think that these suggestions about not overdoing it with color sound a lot like the suggestions we made to not overdo it with type in Chapter 8, you're right.)

What Is Color?

In technical terms, color is a reaction of the receptors in the eye, the optic nerve, and the human brain to different wavelengths of light. Color also has a certain strength, measured by the amplitude of its wavelength. If a color has no amplitude, it is black and you can't see it. Any color with a strong enough amplitude appears white.

If you mix a color with black, that color darkens and the resulting color is called a *shade*. If you mix a color with white, the color lightens and the resulting color is called a *tint* of your original color.

So far, so good. The color that an object appears to be is affected by whether the object is a source of light and transmits light (such as a colored piece of glass), or whether the light is reflected from its surface (such as printed paper). This feature affects not only the *range* of color but also the intensity of the color. Transmitted light has a greater range and is usually more intense than reflected light. That's why you can get better scans from slide scanners than from desktop scanners that are scanning colored paper. It's also the major reason why output on your computer monitor looks great but printed output sometimes doesn't. Even great-looking printed output doesn't hold a candle to your computer monitor.

Color Models

If your computer has a color monitor, open the Display Properties dialog box by choosing Start⇨Settings⇨Control Panel and double-clicking the Display icon. Select the Appearance tab and then click the Color sample box (as indicated by the pointer in Figure 10-1). From the resulting pop-up menu, click the Other button. The Windows 95 Color dialog box appears. Now we can talk a little about color theory and the various models of color.

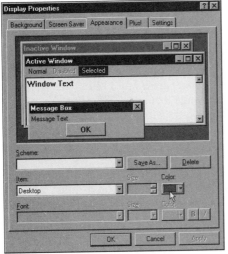

Figure 10-1:
The Appearance tab of the Display Properties dialog box and its Color sample box.

Anytime that you select color in a Windows 95 program, this Color dialog box (shown in Figure 10-2) may open. Microsoft Publisher tries very hard to shield you from this monstrosity, but if you keep clicking "More Colors!" — as in "I must have MORE colors!" — eventually you open something that looks similar to the Windows 95 Color dialog box, or selector. Oh, well.

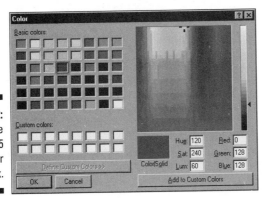

Figure 10-2:
The Windows 95 Color dialog box.

To select a color in the selector, click it or drag the crosshair. When you do, you see the values change for a color's hue (Hu<u>e</u>) and saturation (<u>S</u>at), as well as all three values for red, green, and blue. *Hue* is the name of the color; *saturation* is the intensity of the color. The third value, which doesn't change, is the *luminosity,* or lightness. To change the luminosity value, you move the color in the bar to the right of the Color selector box.

In one model, the HSL color model, these three values — hue, saturation, and luminosity — uniquely identify a particular color. In the second model, the RGB model, represented in the Color selector, any color is seen as a combination of three values of red, green, and blue (the *primary* colors). Values in the RGB model can range from 0 to 255, thus describing 256 colors per primary color or 16.7 million possible colors in the spectrum. That 16.7 million is a number that computer programs and manufacturers often toss about.

Remember the color wheel? It's a representation of all the colors. (No, it doesn't actually show all 16.7 million.) Using the primary colors, the sequence around the wheel is red-orange-yellow-green-blue-violet.

You can describe four basic color schemes based on the position of the colors on the color wheel, as shown in Figure 10-3:

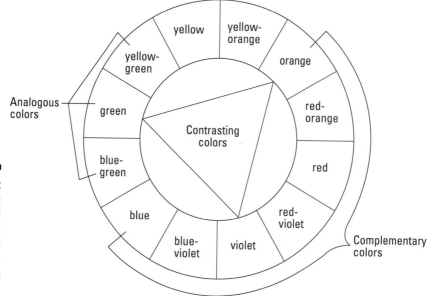

Figure 10-3:
Using the color wheel to describe color schemes.

- **Monochromatic:** A single color on the color wheel. Monochromatic schemes appear uniform.

- **Analogous:** Colors that are close to each other on the color wheel. Analogous colors create color schemes that are soothing and harmonious.

- **Complementary:** Colors that are directly opposite each other on the color wheel. Complementary colors attract the most attention of all color schemes.

- **Contrasting:** Color combinations that consist of at least three colors that are an equal distance from each other on the color wheel. Contrasting colors are balanced.

We want to pass along some good recommendations for establishing color schemes. When using one color, create a monochromatic scheme by using that color's shades or tints. When using complementary colors, use one dominant color and shades or tints of its complement. When using contrasting colors, use the brightest color as a highlight and the palest color as the background.

Here's a piece of trivia about complementary colors. People who are color impaired are most often color impaired in pairs of complementary colors: Some people are red-green color impaired; others are yellow-blue color impaired.

The RGB color model represented by the values in the Windows 95 Color selector is called a *computer color model.* That is, it represents color as if the human eye were a perfect measurement device — but it is not.

Perhaps the most widely accepted perceptual model of color was developed by the Commission Internationale de l'Eclairage (CIE) in the 1920s based on populations of people matching a color to mixtures of three primary colors. The results of this model are probably the most accurate indication of true perceived color that we now have. In the *CIE space model,* similar colors appear near each other, and the CIE space looks like a set of hyperbolas with white at the center. Any paint or ink vendor worth its salt calibrates colors to one CIE space or another. Most advanced computer color matching schemes are based on CIE space as well.

Printing in Color

Printers can print color in one of two ways: by using a specific colored ink or by creating a color using a mixture of other colors. To assign color in a computer program, you specify a color either as a specific ink *(spot color)* or as a process mixture *(process color)*. You can use either, neither, or both in your work.

To print color correctly, you have to tell Microsoft Publisher 97 which print process you are going to use — spot color or process color — as well as the printer that you are going to use. Microsoft Publisher 97 lets you print to a desktop color printer using a local print driver at low to medium resolution (up to 600 dpi).

If you are going to create a print-to-disk file for your local copy shop or commercial printer, you need to find out whether the shop has any special requirements. Ask your commercial printer to loan you a copy of its printer driver to work with, if you don't already have it. (Windows 95 ships with many types of printer drivers.) Printer drivers affect not only color fidelity, but margins and other features. See Chapter 12 for more about printer drivers.

Microsoft Publisher 97 also has an outside printer option. Using this option, you can specify process color or spot color. Spot color can print at high resolution, which can be 1200 dpi or greater. (High-resolution imagesetters go as high as 2800 dpi, with 2400 dpi being common.) Process color prints at medium resolution. We have more to say on this topic in Chapter 12.

Process color (full-color) printing

Microsoft Publisher 97 refers to process color printing as *full-color printing,* and supports output to color printers with up to 600 dpi resolution. With process color selected, you see 35 colors in the color palette of the Text Color and Object Color toolbar buttons. If that is not enough, you can click the More Colors button. The Colors dialog box then appears with the Basic colors option selected. In that mode, you see 12 shades of 7 colors (purple, blue, green, yellow, orange, red, and black).

Figure 10-4 shows the Basic color selections. If you click the All colors radio button, you see the Colors dialog box that Windows 95 makes possible in Microsoft Publisher 97, as shown in Figure 10-5.

You can create colors with gradient patterns (that vary from light to dark or from one color to another in steps) by making selections from the Patterns dialog box. Doing so creates striking results.

Because of imperfections in the properties of CMY (cyan, magenta, and yellow) inks, they do not blend to form black. Instead, you get a dark brown. For this reason, and because process black requires more ink than most papers can absorb, black ink is used as a fourth color.

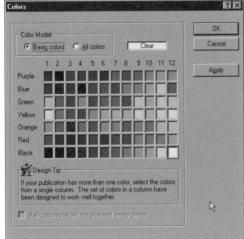

Figure 10-4:
The Basic colors selector radio button.

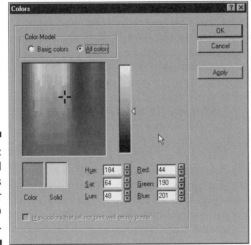

Figure 10-5:
The All colors selector radio button.

Process color may be applied in two ways. In the first, the inks are applied one on top of another and blended into a *contone,* or continuous tone, image. In the other scheme, color spots are placed side-by-side to create a halftone pattern. With well-crafted halftone patterns, the viewer's mind blends the colored spots to create the color.

Spot color printing

With the spot color option selected for an outside printer, you can see only black, shades of gray, and your selected spot colors in the color palette (see Figure 10-6). You can't see the colors here, but the top two rows are black and grays; the middle two rows are shades (actually tints) of blue; and the bottom two rows are shades of red. Note that the same palette appears under the Font Color button on the toolbar. In either case, your selection of colors is always the same.

Figure 10-6:
The Color
Object
palette with
two spot
colors
selected.

A spot color adds an additional color to the black ink that is normally used in printing. Adding a single spot color to black is referred to as *two-color printing,* because black ink is also a color. Some commercial print equipment can print two, three, or four colors, including black, in a print run. You can specify any number of spot colors, but because each color must be set up by your service bureau or commercial printer, it may be more cost-effective at some point to switch to full-color (or process color) printing. (Microsoft Publisher recommends that you consider process color at the two-color stage, which is probably too conservative.) The number of copies being printed is also a factor in whether to use spot color or process color. Discuss color options with your commercial printer for the best deal.

When you use spot colors, you have the opportunity to mix your color with blacks (shades) or whites (tints) and thus extend the range of colors. You can also replace black ink with another color and use colored paper rather than white to further introduce color into your work. Be careful, though, because the color of the paper affects the appearance of the color of the ink.

Microsoft Publisher 97 has an option that lets you print color separations as proof pages that you can hand to your printer when you use spot color. Proofs serve as a check to see that color is being applied to your document in the right places for each colored ink; the term *separations* refers to the fact that each proof is a separate color. Each spot color prints as a separate sheet in black, as does the color black itself. To enable this option, click the Print Color Separations check box in the Print Proof dialog box before a print run.

You must have a color printer selected or use the Outside Printing option with spot color selected to see the Print Proof command on the File menu in place of the Print command.

Because of the high cost of full-color printing, we nearly always prefer spot color to process color. You can get good results by printing spot colors at high resolution and making good use of shades and tints. We often substitute another color for black ink and use colored paper for an additional color.

Color Matching

Every device that can display color also has a range of colors that it can create. That range is called its *color gamut.* Computer monitors have a color gamut, as do desktop scanners and printers. Because color monitors emit light, their color gamut is larger than the color gamut of printers. That's why the color that prints on your color printer often does not match the color that you see on your color monitor. *Color matching* is a process that attempts to match the colors on one device to the nearest color available on another. The results are often less than satisfying.

Matching process color

It's likely that your computer monitor displays fewer than 16.7 million colors, and therefore, a number of colors are unavailable on your screen. Windows shows an unavailable color as a dithered pattern of two colors in the Color sample box of the All colors mode of the Color selector dialog box. The nearest pure color displays in the Solid color sample box. Dithered color happens quite a lot if your system (like ours) has 256 on-screen colors.

When the object can be displayed in the dithered or "true" color that you have selected, Microsoft Publisher 97 does so. Colored text and objects with fill patterns cannot use dithered color (the text and fill patterns would drop out); for those objects, Microsoft Publisher 97 uses the closest matching color.

In some printing processes, different color inks are applied one on top of the other to produce a color of any kind. Three inks are used to create process colors: cyan, magenta, and yellow (CMY). These are complementary colors that should theoretically result in a process black (but don't, as we noted earlier).

Microsoft Publisher 97 can mark colors that fall outside a particular printing device's color gamut. It refers to this process as *marking colors that print poorly.*

To mark all colors that print poorly, do the following:

1. **Click the object to which you want to apply a color.**

2. **Click the Object Color button to display the color selection menu; then select the More Colors button from that menu.**

3. **Click the check box labeled Mark colors that will not print well on my printer.**

   All colors that will not print well are marked with an X.

For a monitor or printer to use this system, it must ship with a display driver or print driver that uses the Image Color Matching (ICM) standard. If this option is not available to you, get an updated driver from the manufacturer. The ICM system was first included in Windows 95. (Of course, black-and-white printers such as laser printers cannot use this system.) You do not see this option enabled if you run Outside Print Setup and then choose Print Proof. Chapter 12 describes outside printing in detail.

If you want to match the colors that you see on your monitor with the colors that you can print, Microsoft Publisher 97 has a setting in the Options dialog box (selected from the Tools menu) called Improve Screen and Printer Color Matching. The match, although not perfect, is at least close.

Even when the color values on a monitor exactly match what a printer is capable of, most printed color output looks pale and washed out in comparison. Most times, special paper made for a particular printer dramatically improves print quality. (We are impressed with the results from the low-cost Epson Color Stylus printers, which rely on special paper stock, even though the printers are very slow.)

Most print shops will correct a piece for poor color, provided that you have made it clear that color matching is important. You should have reasonable expectations, though.

Matching spot color

If you print a spot color, you get a color that is uniform but perhaps not exactly the color you intended. If you need to match a particular spot color exactly, you must specify it by using a color matching system, available with many computer programs.

Several color paint matching systems are in use today; the best known is Pantone. The Pantone company produces about 900 standard color swatches that printers can match their printing to. Many ink manufacturing companies match their inks to Pantone colors. Microsoft Publisher 97 does not offer Pantone matching (or any other kind) in its current version.

You can buy a swatch book of Pantone inks at design retail stores and through most desktop publishing catalogs. With swatch book in hand, you can select the Pantone color that you want and mark that color on each separation. Give those marked pages to your printer and that should do the trick.

When you specify that a color in a publication should be a Pantone match, it is up to the printing service to match that color as part of its contract with you. The results vary, but not nearly as much as when you specify process color printing. Expect to pay more for Pantone inks due to the extra care necessary in their preparation.

We prefer Pantone colors to custom colors that your printer can blend. Custom colors are cheaper, however, and may be worthwhile if you don't mind some variance from print run to print run. Custom colors work best when you do a single print run and don't have to do any matching.

Pantone has created a computer matching system that breaks apart standard colors into component inks so that they can be created with process inks. Some programs, such as Adobe Illustrator, can specify Pantone inks in terms of their color values. Pantone uses a mixture of up to seven ink color components to do its color matching. Pantone is not the only matching system, just the most commonly used.

Color Resources

Color is such a complex topic that we want to recommend some other books on the subject:

- ✔ *Using Computer Color Effectively*, by L.G. Thorell and W.J. Smith, 1990, Prentice-Hall, Englewood, NJ

  This book tells you more than you would ever want to know about the subject and is chock-a-block with great illustrations. It's the best book we've seen on the subject of color and computers.

- ✔ *The Color Resource Complete Color Glossary,* by Miles Southworth, Thad McIlroy, and Donna Southworth, 1992, The Color Resource, San Francisco, CA

- ✔ *Pocket Guide to Color Reproduction,* 2nd Edition, by Miles Southworth, 1987, Graphic Arts Publishing Co., Livonia, NY

- ✔ *The Desktop Color Book,* by Michael Gosney and Linnea Dayton, 1995, MIS Press, New York, NY

- ✔ *The Gray Book,* by Michael Gosney, 1990, Ventana Press, Chapel Hill, NC

- ✔ *Understanding Desktop Color,* by Michael Kiernan, 1994, Peachpit Press, Berkeley, CA

You can also get lots of tips on color and other design issues in *Desktop Publishing & Design For Dummies,* by Roger Parker, from IDG Books Worldwide, Inc.

Part V
Just So Output

The 5th Wave   By Rich Tennant

"Shoot, that's nothing! Watch me spin him!"

In this part . . .

After your layout is complete, most of your hard work is done. Many gotchas can crop up when you go to print your publication, however. Some are the tiny little errors that seem to bedevil everyone, and some errors are of the thorny, hairy devil type. In the chapters in this part, we discuss the most common problems that appear in a publication in its final stages of production and how to get rid of them. If you're like most of us, you've spent tons of time massaging your work to get it right. It's a shame not to go the extra mile and make sure that the printed work is as good as it can be. Printing is expensive, and mistakes are costly when you make them. The first chapter in this section can save you a lot of money and frustration.

Microsoft Publisher 97 has a number of special features that help you guide an outside print shop to print your work. The second chapter in this part shows you how to set up your publication for a commercial printer. You find out about output quality, printer types, and the many factors that influence the quality of your printed work. A short treatise on paper and ink is included in this chapter. You also see how to work with an outside printer, how to get quotes, and how to save time and money.

Chapter 11

Final Checks

· ·

In This Chapter

▶ Giving your pages the once-over

▶ Using the Design Checker

▶ Discovering techniques for copyfitting text

▶ Adjusting text spacing and line endings

▶ Improving page design with special page elements

▶ Adding drawn objects, borders, shaded areas, and special symbols

· ·

*Q*uality desktop publishing means sweating the details. We're not talking about jumping up and down in your sweatsuit with Richard Simmons' video "Sweating to the Oldies," but we are talking about getting absorbed in the details of your publication before you send it to the printer — where real money changes hands. In this chapter, we look at things that you can do to make sure that your publication reflects the care you took in its design.

The Eyes Have It

The single best piece of advice that we can give you about checking your publication is this: Look it over in printed form. Microsoft Publisher 97 lets you create proof prints; avail yourself of this opportunity. You should also create a proof for an outside printer. The proof is your "contract," telling the printer "This is what I want."

You can't — or at least you shouldn't — expect to catch all the errors in your publication the first time you look at it. The more people who look at your work, the better chance you have of finding things that should be changed. (Spotting your own errors can be difficult.) When possible, try to live with the final design for a while before you commit to spending money for printing.

Make yourself a nice checklist of items that you want to check in your publication after you complete the design. We highly recommend this activity to you.

The Design Checker

The Design Checker is an automated tool in Microsoft Publisher 97 for finding things that are wrong with your publication. It catches many errors that you wouldn't be likely to catch until after the publication was printed. The Design Checker checks for the following:

- ✓ Objects that will not print
- ✓ Text in the overflow mode
- ✓ Empty frames
- ✓ Covered objects

Use these steps to check your design with the Design Checker:

1. **Choose Tools⊅Design Checker.**

   The Design Checker dialog box appears, as shown in Figure 11-1.

2. **Select the range and type of pages that you want to check.**

   - Under Check which pages, click All or Pages. If you click Pages, enter from and to page numbers in the corresponding text boxes.

   - To check only the foreground pages, deselect the Check background page(s) check box by clicking it to remove the check mark.

3. **Click the Options button to open the Design Checker Options dialog box and select your options.**

   The Options dialog box is shown in Figure 11-2. Select the checking options that you want to perform by clicking the check box next to the option.

4. **Click OK or press Enter to return to the Design Checker dialog box.**

   You can click Cancel if you want to ignore the selections you've made.

5. **Click OK or press Enter to start checking your publication (or certain pages in it) for the problems that you've selected.**

   The Design Checker goes to the first problem and posts an explanation. For example, Figure 11-3 shows a dialog box noting a hidden-object problem. Notice that the Design Checker dialog box offers suggestions for correcting the problem.

6. **For all design problems noted by a Design Checker dialog box, you can correct the error or click the Ignore, Ignore All, or Continue button to continue checking your publication's design.**

   The Explain button opens up the Help system with directions for correcting the error. Ignore moves you to the next error. Ignore All ignores all errors of that type.

7. **After the last error, Microsoft Publisher 97 posts a dialog box asking whether you want to check the design again from the beginning.**

As one of your final checks, you just can't beat running the Design Checker.

Figure 11-1:
The Design
Checker
dialog box.

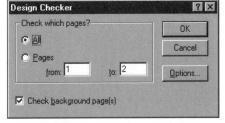

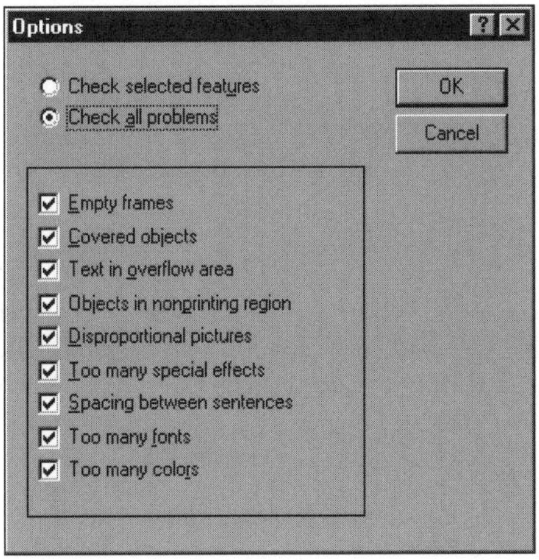

Figure 11-2:
The Design
Checker
Options
dialog box.

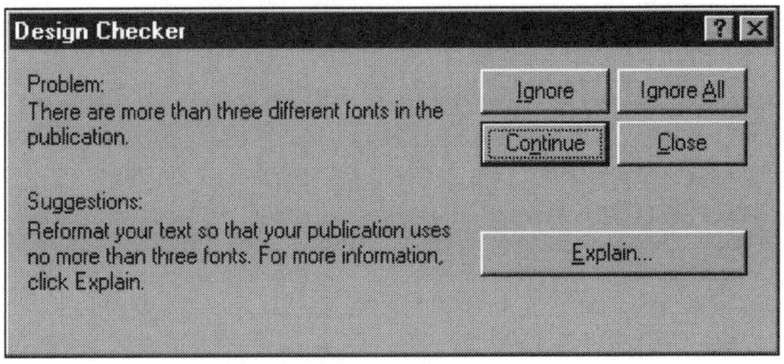

Figure 11-3:
A layout
error
caught by
the Design
Checker.

Word Fitting Techniques

When working with a layout to get it exactly the way you want, one of the hardest tasks is fitting the text into text frames. If your layout is *frozen*, the amount of text that you can have is set. Also, you may find that the formatted text simply looks ugly.

A common problem in fully justified text is large interword spacing throughout a frame. The text looks as if it has rivers running through it. You probably can't change the justification of your text frames, but you can work with the hyphenation feature (see Chapter 7) to break words and improve the look of your text. But even the automated hyphenation tool isn't perfect. So, you may want to manually hyphenate justified text. We describe this technique and others for making your words fit in the following sections.

Copyfitting

You can rephrase nearly every paragraph to reduce or add words without changing the meaning. In general, people doing page layout don't have the luxury of editing text. That job belongs to the author or the editor. If you are both layout artist and author, however, you can copyfit your text by adding and removing words.

Editing text written in short sentences or phrases is more difficult because you have fewer words to work with. In those cases, a thesaurus can be your best friend. *Roget's Thesaurus* is a classic. Microsoft Bookshelf (sold alone or with Microsoft Works or Microsoft Office) includes an online version of *Roget's Thesaurus.*

The Microsoft Publisher 97 spell checker (see Chapter 7 for information on how to use it) contains more than 100,000 words. The spell checker's dictionary is large, but it won't help you if you use a valid word incorrectly — such as *two* rather than *to.*

Always proofread your text for errors caused by properly spelled but incorrectly used words.

If you are working with Microsoft Word, you can use its grammar checker on your text. You can use the Edit Story in Microsoft Word command from the context-sensitive menu of a text frame to check the grammar in your story. You open the grammar checker in Word 97 with the Spelling and Grammar command on the Tools menu. If that command isn't on your Word 97 menu, you need to install the grammar checker (which isn't installed as a default choice in the Microsoft Office installation).

Wrong word usage is particularly difficult for authors to spot. We think the best way to proofread is to get as many people as possible to read your publication before you commit to printing it. If your publication is important, you may want to spring for a professional proofreader.

Adjusting spacing

Microsoft Publisher 97 gives you many ways to adjust the spacing in and between your text frames. Use the ideas in this section as a reminder and check list.

Working with headlines

A common error in headlines is too much spacing between letters and between lines. Headlines nearly always benefit from proper kerning and from reducing the default line spacing that Microsoft Publisher 97 gives to large letters. Kerning is particularly important in headlines with serif fonts.

Figure 11-4 is an example of a headline that dominates the page. In Figure 11-5, the headline's Spacing Between Characters (kerning) was changed from loose to tight, and the Line Spacing was adjusted to 0.75 sp. In addition, the headline frame can now be reduced to make the headline less prominent.

You may find that substituting a WordArt frame for a text frame in headlines works well. WordArt has a best-fit option that adjusts text automatically.

If you have a headline that belongs with a block of text, leaving more space above the headline than below it is a very good idea so that your reader has a visual clue that the headline applies to the text that follows.

Another problem to watch for is a headline that breaks across lines in a way that makes the meaning unclear to the casual reader. If you can improve the readability of your headline by grouping phrases, do so. For example, in the headline "Colts Win Super Bowl," put the line break before *Win* instead of after it. Then go see your psychiatrist.

Make sure that the placement of your headlines agrees with the page numbers in the table of contents (if your publication has one). Many page layout programs automatically renumber the table of contents, but Microsoft Publisher 97 does not. Also, if you used headlines as headers and footers and placed these elements in the background, make sure that they are correct when you go to proofread your pages.

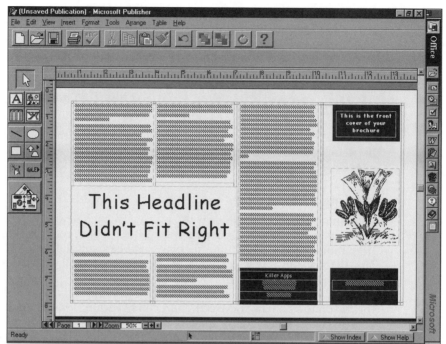

Figure 11-4:
A large
headline
before
adjustment.

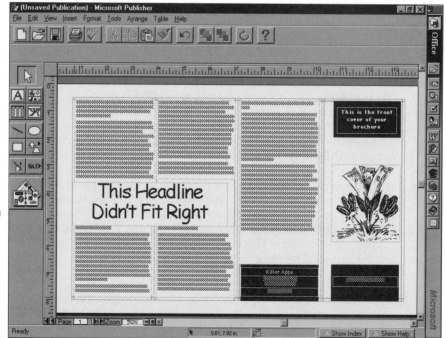

Figure 11-5:
The same
headline
after
kerning and
line space
adjustment.

Working with text frames

One way to make text fit your text frame is to simply adjust the size of the frame. This is straightforward if you have a single text frame on a page. With several text frames in a multicolumn page layout, however, resizing frames can affect all columns simultaneously. One subtle way to work around adjusted text frames is to play with the lines and spacing in your headlines. If you made your frames smaller and now have extra space on the page, you can add a line to a headline or put in a secondary headline to take up that space. If you made your frames larger, you can remove extra headlines to give yourself more room.

The amount of line spacing dramatically affects the amount of text that you can fit into a text frame. You can adjust line spacing from a single frame, from all the frames on a page, or from all the frames on a two-page spread. You also can change the spacing before, after, and between paragraphs. If you do adjust line spacing, you do so for the entire text frame and, ideally, for all text frames on a page or on a two-page spread.

You don't have to make large changes in line spacing to get results. Check your adjustments on a printed page to see whether the results are acceptable; don't rely on how your page looks on the screen. Figure 11-6 shows the result of changing line spacing in a set of paragraphs. Notice how different the three paragraphs look.

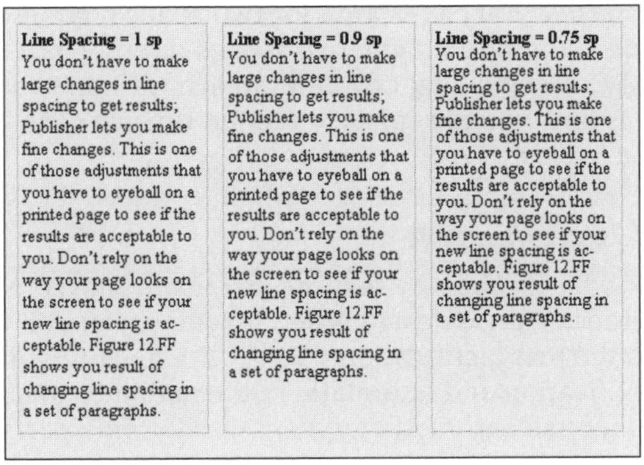

Figure 11-6:
Three frames with different line spacing.

Line Spacing = 1 sp	Line Spacing = 0.9 sp	Line Spacing = 0.75 sp
You don't have to make large changes in line spacing to get results; Publisher lets you make fine changes. This is one of those adjustments that you have to eyeball on a printed page to see if the results are acceptable to you. Don't rely on the way your page looks on the screen to see if your new line spacing is acceptable. Figure 12.FF shows you result of changing line spacing in a set of paragraphs.	You don't have to make large changes in line spacing to get results; Publisher lets you make fine changes. This is one of those adjustments that you have to eyeball on a printed page to see if the results are acceptable to you. Don't rely on the way your page looks on the screen to see if your new line spacing is acceptable. Figure 12.FF shows you result of changing line spacing in a set of paragraphs.	You don't have to make large changes in line spacing to get results; Publisher lets you make fine changes. This is one of those adjustments that you have to eyeball on a printed page to see if the results are acceptable to you. Don't rely on the way your page looks on the screen to see if your new line spacing is acceptable. Figure 12.FF shows you result of changing line spacing in a set of paragraphs.

We also like kerning as a way to slightly alter text to make it fit correctly in a text frame. (When you use kerning in this way, the change isn't obvious to a casual observer.) To see how kerning affects text size, consider the three text frames in Figure 11-7. In these examples, we applied Normal, Loose, and Tight kerning to the entire text (except for the first line). Chapter 7 tells you about various techniques for adjusting the spacing between letters in your text.

Kerning = Normal
You don't have to make large changes in line spacing to get results; Publisher lets you make fine changes. This is one of those adjustments that you have to eyeball on a printed page to see if the results are acceptable to you. Don't rely on the way your page looks on the screen to see if your new line spacing is acceptable. Figure 12.FF shows you result of changing line spacing in a set of paragraphs.

Kerning = Loose
You don't have to make large changes in line spacing to get results; Publisher lets you make fine changes. This is one of those adjustments that you have to eyeball on a printed page to see if the results are acceptable to you. Don't rely on the way your page looks on the screen to see if your new line spacing is acceptable. Figure 12.FF shows you result of changing line spacing in a set of paragraphs.

Kerning = Tight
You don't have to make large changes in line spacing to get results; Publisher lets you make fine changes. This is one of those adjustments that you have to eyeball on a printed page to see if the results are acceptable to you. Don't rely on the way your page looks on the screen to see if your new line spacing is acceptable. Figure 12.FF shows you result of changing line spacing in a set of paragraphs.

Figure 11-7: Three frames with different kerning settings.

When adjusting text frames, pay particular attention to preventing widows. A *widow* is a short line at the top of a page or column, or a word or portion of a word on a line by itself at the end of a paragraph.

One common mistake to watch for is two spaces between sentences. This practice is a holdover from the days when people used typewriters — the extra space made sentences more obvious.

To check for extra spaces, you can search for two space characters and replace them with one. To do this, type two spaces directly into the Find What text box in the Replace dialog box and replace with one space. It's not a bad idea to run this search and replace a second time, in case three spaces were typed together.

Hyphenating and justifying text

Another method for altering the way text fits in a text frame is to change the justification. (Sometimes after a design is set, however, you don't have the flexibility to change the text justification.) To get the most text into a text frame, apply full justification and automatic hyphenation to the frame. Remember, you cannot use automatic hyphenation for only part of a text frame.

Note that when you use automatic hyphenation, you can no longer control the location of line breaks. To regain control, turn off hyphenation; then, turn it back on and request to confirm each hyphenation as it occurs.

When you use right- or left-justified text (also called *ragged* text) as opposed to full justification, you often make the text more readable but you won't fit as much text in a column. To gain more space, hyphenate.

In ragged text, you can force a line ending by using a soft carriage return (Shift+Enter). When you force a line ending, however, you change the line endings of every line that comes after that point. This won't be a problem if automatic hyphenation is on, but it can cause grief if you hyphenated your text manually. Therefore, forced line endings should be the last resort.

You can also force a line ending at the position where the automatic hyphenation tool places a hyphen. To do so, move your cursor to that position and press Ctrl+- (hyphen). An optional hyphen shows up only when the entire word won't fit on the line. Therefore, optional hyphens aren't affected by soft carriage returns. If you want to make sure that a word is never hyphenated (at the position where Microsoft Publisher 97 would hyphenate it), go to that position and press Ctrl+Alt+- (hyphen). We recommend this safeguard for a compound word that already contains a hyphen: for example, *double-barreled* rather than *double-barrel-ed*. Common practice is to never end a column or text frame with a hyphen.

Always use optional hyphens rather than regular hyphens to hyphenate text.

When you hyphenate text in a paragraph, try to have no more than two consecutive hyphenated lines. Hyphenated text is harder to read and understand. For this reason, some page layout professionals avoid hyphenation, although it greatly increases the amount of work necessary to fine-tune the layout. Whatever you do, don't hyphenate headlines; they must be readable at a glance.

You can control the amount of hyphenation that Microsoft Publisher 97 uses by changing an option on the Editing and User Assistance tab of the Options dialog box. Enter a smaller number in the Hyphenation zone text box to smooth out your ragged edge and to reduce the amount of white space between words. To have fewer hyphens or to have fewer short syllables before and after the hyphen, make the Hyphenation zone larger.

Improving the Page

People tend to read a page from the top-left corner to the bottom-right corner. If you have a two-page spread, that principle applies to the top-left corner of the left page down to the lower-right corner of the right page. Putting your most important page elements along this diagonal is good design practice.

One nice feature of page layout programs is that they impose a design structure to your pages. You want your readers to instinctively find common elements, such as page numbers, on a page. We recommend setting common page elements (in the background of your pages) in one place for all left pages and in another for all right pages. With these common elements in place, you can move on to break up the tedium of your pages by having some elements stand out. The longer the publication, the more important it is to have elements that draw the eye to one section or another.

Adding special page elements

You've already seen some techniques for breaking up a page and drawing attention to various sections. The following are useful techniques for making your pages more interesting:

- **Pictures:** Pictures instantly attract attention. When you put a picture on a page, it becomes a focus of attention. Putting pictures off the reader's diagonal path — in the lower-left or upper-right corner of a page or two-page spread — creates a good effect. If you use too many pictures, however, you greatly reduce their effectiveness.

- **Drop caps or raised caps:** Microsoft Publisher 97 calls these design elements *fancy first letters.* They are an excellent way of starting a chapter or a section, and they draw the reader's attention regardless of where they appear on the page.

- **Ornaments:** Ornaments are pictures such as temple columns, notepads, theater tickets, or any other small pictures that stand out.

- **Rules and shaded boxes:** We like rules and shaded boxes a lot. They are particularly valuable for making headlines stand out. If you think that a section of text is important, put it in a shaded box.

- **Pull quotes or sidebars:** A *pull quote* is a short section that highlights the important point you are making on a page. To make a pull quote stand out, place it outside your text frame.

  Sidebars are longer sections that you want to make stand out. You can reserve sidebars for optional reading or make them central to your text treatment.

Don't forget that the Design Gallery comes with a selection of specially formatted headlines, ornaments, pull quotes, sidebars, table of contents, and titles. If you create any design elements that you want to use elsewhere, create your own category in the Design Gallery and save those elements under it. We talk about the Microsoft Publisher 97 Design Gallery in Chapter 9, and we like it so much that we wish it were greatly expanded. Figure 11-8 shows you the Design Gallery with Ornaments from the Plain Designs style.

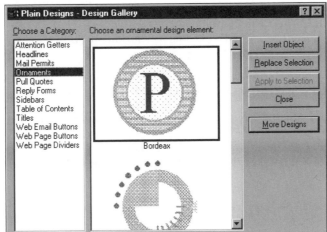

Figure 11-8:
Ornaments
in the
Design
Gallery.

Inserting an object from the Design Gallery is just the beginning. You are free to resize the object and to ungroup it so that you can work with its components. You can also change the text in a Design Gallery object, and adjust colors and shading.

One nice effect that you can make with shaded areas is called a bleed. A *bleed* is a section of color that extends past the normal margins and all the way to the edge of your page. You can use bleeds with single pages and to span the inside margins of a two-page spread. If you use bleeds in your work, consult with your printer shop to make sure that its presses are capable of printing bleeds. Bleeds often require special treatment and cost more money, but the effect can be worth it.

Adding drawn objects

Although most tools in the toolbox can't draw objects for you, you can use them to create nice effects. You can also find special shapes in the Custom Shape tool menu. Drawn objects don't have to be small; they can be major page elements as well. For example, if you are creating a publication that includes a topic for discussion or the dialogue of a play, you could use a cartoon balloon shape (which is ordinarily used to hold captions) as your entire page frame. Be creative and have fun!

Also, you needn't be constrained by the shapes that appear in the toolbox. You can combine shapes to create other shapes, such as combining triangles, circles, and lines to create a mountain landscape with the moon rising in the background. When you combine shapes with colors, patterns, gradients, and shadings, you have a wealth of tools at your disposal.

Borders and shading

Borders and shading are nice ways of separating a section of your page. You can place borders around your pictures by using rectangles and circles, or create a matted-photograph look by putting colored frames in back of your pictures. If you try this, we suggest using bold colors to emphasize the picture.

When you use borders and shading with text, try to understate their presence. If a shaded block is colored gray, keep the gray level at 10 to 15 percent. You can overuse color on a page very easily. Similarly, if you use shading in back of text, make sure that the shading makes your text more readable, not less. As the shading gets darker, it is more difficult to see black text but easier to see white text. Note that white text (called *reversed text*) is generally less readable than black text. It works well only in front of black backgrounds and in short phrases such as headlines.

Borders and shading are valuable when you create tables. The Microsoft Publisher 97 table frame automatically creates shades and borders for you. If you create an array of information without a table frame, consider adding these features to your work.

In *Desktop Publishing & Design For Dummies* (IDG Books Worldwide, Inc.), Roger Parker recommends that you avoid *boxing* an entire page unless you want to create a classical look. We concur and prefer to see pages designed with simple rules that separate headers and footers from the body of the page.

Do you want to know the most readable color combination for text? Take a look at the cover of this book. Surprise! It's black type over a yellow background. To change the color of text, use the Font Color tool, which appears on the Format toolbar when you have text selected.

Special symbols

If you use capitalization in a paragraph, you may find that using SMALL CAPS looks better, particularly for a whole sentence of capitals. Also, changing a line of capitals to small caps can shorten your paragraph measurably and help you with copyfitting. If you have a paragraph that must be lengthened to fit the text frame, consider making the first sentence all caps — especially if the first sentence *makes the point* for the paragraph or section.

Keyboards have feet (') and inch (") marks for single and double quotation marks. Typographers prefer the use of stylized *smart quotes* instead: ' and ' for single quotation marks and " and " for double quotation marks. To automatically insert these symbols into your text when you type single and double quotation marks, turn on the Automatically Use Smart Quotes check box in the More Options dialog box. (This option is set by default.) If you have text that needs straight single or double quotation marks, press the Ctrl key while you type an apostrophe or a quotation mark. You can also use the Insert Symbol dialog box to insert any of these characters.

You may want to try a typographical technique called a *hanging* quotation mark. Suppose that you want to align the first character of a headline or a pull quote with the text frame that appears below or above it. Having a regular quotation mark could disrupt that visual alignment and be distracting. Therefore, you may want to put an opening quotation mark to the left of the headline or pull quote. Some page layout programs let you format a paragraph so that it has a hanging quotation mark. In Microsoft Publisher 97, use the following steps to create this feature manually:

1. **Type your paragraph or pull quote with smart quotes at the beginning and end of the text.**

2. **Create a small text frame that is large enough to hold the quotation mark.**

3. **Position the small frame to the left of the paragraph or pull quote for an opening quotation mark or to the right for a closing quotation mark.**

   Zooming in to see your text is helpful when placing the small text frame.

4. **Select (highlight) the quotation mark in your paragraph or pull quote and then Cut it to the Clipboard.**

5. **Click an insertion point in your small hanging text frame; then, Paste the cut quotation mark into the frame.**

Unfortunately, because you have separate frames, your hanging quotation doesn't automatically follow your headline as it moves about on your page. Therefore, group the hanging quotation mark frame with the headline or pull quote frame. Figure 11-9 shows you an example of a beginning hanging quotation mark.

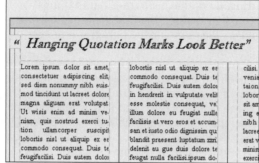

Figure 11-9:
A beginning
hanging
quotation
mark.

Other symbols that typographers use (that may be new to you) are en dash
(–) and em dash (—) in place of two hyphens (- -) and three hyphens (- - -),
respectively. They're called an en dash and an em dash because they are the
width of a capital *N* and *M* in the font being used. Many desktop publishing
programs automatically substitute these symbols whenever you type two or
three hyphens. Microsoft Publisher 97 automatically substitutes the em
dash when you type two hyphens together.

Good typographical practice recommends using en dashes when you are
indicating a range of numbers (where you would normally put the word *to*)
or when you have a compound word, as in Barrington Smythe–Jones. Use an
em dash to set off a parenthetical remark — as we do in this sentence —
before you end your thought and use up your brain cells.

If you need an en dash in Microsoft Publisher 97, you must enter it as an
ANSI character. You commonly enter an ANSI character by first pressing
Alt and then typing the code for the character on the numeric keypad. In
the case of the en dash, the key combination is Alt+0150. Frankly, we can
never remember ANSI characters, and we can't be bothered with looking
them up. So, we use the Insert Symbol dialog box instead. Both the en and
the em dash characters are to the right of the period character, as shown
in Figure 11-10.

En dash

Figure 11-10:
The en dash
character
selected in
the Insert
Symbol
dialog box.

If you look closely, you find that most fonts contain typographer's fractions. The $^{1}/_{2}$ and $^{1}/_{4}$ symbols appear to the right in the Insert Symbols dialog box, one line down from where the en and em dashes appear. Also, most fonts have characters for copyright (©), trademark (™), and registration (®) symbols. These special characters are best used as superscripts in the same font size. You also find various currency symbols ($, £, ¢, ¥), accented characters (Á, ç, é, ô), ligatures (Æ, æ), and so on.

It pays to study the Insert Symbols dialog box to see which special characters your current font offers.

You may require a special fraction beyond what's offered in a standard character set. Here's how you create those:

1. **In standard text, type the fraction that you want, such as** 3/8.

2. **Format the numbers to the left and right of the division sign at about 60 to 70 percent of the text size.**

    For example, if you have 12-point text, use 8-point numbers.

3. **Format the left number as a superscript and the right number as a subscript by choosing Format⇨Character and clicking the corresponding radio buttons in the Character dialog box.**

Don't forget that you can use noninteger point sizes (such as 11.5) if you are using TrueType fonts or Postscript fonts and the Adobe Type Manager.

What if you need a superscript number such as 2^8 or a subscript number such as H_2O? You can apply these formats to selected text from the Character dialog box or by pressing the Ctrl+ + (plus) or Ctrl+Shift+ + (plus) key combinations. Press these combinations again to toggle the super- or subscript back to normal text.

Chapter 12

Printing, Print Shops, and Paper

● ●

In This Chapter

▶ Specifying which printer you want to use

▶ Printing page proofs on your own printer

▶ Setting up an outside printer

▶ Investigating the quality offerings of common printing devices

▶ Selecting and working with an outside printing service

▶ Deciding how and when to use your various paper options

● ●

A desktop publisher's best friend is her mother. A desktop publisher's next best friend is the person responsible for printing her publication. You should call your mother at least once every week and send her flowers on Mother's Day. And you should talk to your printing professional before and during the development of any desktop publishing project that you won't be printing yourself.

In this chapter, we wrap up our exposition of Microsoft Publisher 97 by considering how to work with professional print shops and other outside printing resources. Specifically, we show you how to set up your publication for whatever printer you're using, how to select paper, and how to take advantage of the special paper (from PaperDirect) that Microsoft Publisher 97 lets you use. We also go over common problems and concerns about using an outside printer. Our experience shows us that people find working with a professional printer for the first time to be something of a mystery.

Printers and Output Quality

Print quality is determined by the printer *engine* (the mechanism that makes the printer print). Typically, print quality is measured in the number of dots per inch (*dpi*) that a printer can deliver to a printed page. That measurement isn't the whole story, however. The shape of the dots, their placement in relationship to a letterform, and the density of the dots can dramatically change the perceived quality of a printed page.

For example, many printers (such as the Hewlett-Packard LaserJet series) use a *resolution enhancement technology* to improve print quality. HP calls its technology *RET;* other vendors call theirs something else — Intellispot, Varidot, Omnishade, or whatever their lawyers can trademark. When placing spots (or dots) at the edge of a printed character, an HP laser printer varies the size and intensity of the spot to better conform to the character's border. The net effect is that the printed text appears to be at a higher resolution, and *halftones* that print with shades of gray (created by black spots) appear to have more grays in them.

Following is a brief description of printer types and common uses:

- **Impact printers:** Impact printers include dot matrix and print wheel printers. They print by striking ribbons (like a typewriter) and transferring the ink from the ribbon to the page. Some are capable of printing graphics, but as a group, these printers are not used in desktop publishing applications.

- **Ink jet printers:** Ink jet printers print by spitting ink droplets under pressure. Their output quality varies widely. Desktop ink jet printers at the low end print up to 600 dpi in either color or black and white. Print quality is moderate, but print speeds are low. Special paper improves ink jet output. More expensive ink jet printers can deliver very impressive color output at medium resolutions.

- **Laser printers:** Laser printers produce black-and-white output and grayscale (shades of gray) output. Color laser printers are just now coming to market at prices from $5,000 to $10,000. Common desktop laser printers print at the 600-dpi range, although you can buy enhanced laser printers (or add special controller boards) to improve print quality to 1200 dpi — considered to be near imageset quality.

- **Xerographic printers:** Many copy shops and service bureaus have printers that are essentially fancy copy machines. These xerographic printers offer high speed and moderate resolution (600 dpi). In this category, the Xerox DocuTech Publisher is a 50-page-per-minute *(ppm)* production scanner/printer.

  Other xerographic printers offer higher resolution and color printing, such as the Canon Color Laser Copier (CLC), a laser printer/copier that can input digital files in a number of formats. You can get good full-color, continuous tone (contone) output from these printers. They not only scan a printed piece of output but also take electronic files in standard output formats such as EPS (Encapsulated Postscript).

✔ **Dye sublimation printers:** These printers work like ink jet printers but use heads to sublime (vaporize and deposit) special dyes onto paper. Some use crayons and waxes; others use low-melting dyes or liquids. They are used almost exclusively for color work. In most cases, ink jet printers produce a halftone image, but dye sublimation printers can produce contone (continuous tone) images.

✔ **Imagesetters:** These printers are high-resolution laser printers (2000 – 3000 dpi). The output that they create is printed paper or (more often) film that, in turn, is used to create printing plates. You find imagesetters in service bureaus and commercial printers. They are used in very low-volume printing to create original print masters.

You may find any or all of these printers — except for impact printers — at a copy shop or service bureau.

Selecting the Target Printer

Each printer that you use (whether in-house or in a professional print shop), offers you different page sizes, minimum margin widths, color options, and so on. When you print to your desktop printer, you set those options in the Page Setup dialog box. If you are using a printer that's at a professional print shop, you can install and use the *printer driver* (the interpreter that lets your computer talk to the printer) for the print shop's printer as the *target printer* on your desktop computer. *Target printer* is just a spiffy term for the machine on which you intend to print a given publication. Your target-printer selection and setup are *publication-level settings;* that is, they are a part of your current publication but do not affect any other publications.

Note that the target printer doesn't have to be *your* printer. That is, although you probably have your own printer attached to your computer, you may not want to use that old banger. You may have access to an even better printer that offers color, faster speed, the capability to print on bigger sheets of paper, a slot that dispenses hot beverages while you wait, or whatever. If this other printer is the one that you intend to use to print the final version of your publication, that's what you should select as your target printer.

Windows 95 contains many printer drivers; some belong to expensive color printers or imagesetters. If you can't find the target printer that you intend to print to on this list, you can always ask your service bureau, copy shop, or commercial printer to supply you with the driver. Most will "loan" you their printer drivers without charge.

Follow these steps to select and set up a target printer:

1. **Select File⇨Print Setup.**

   A Print Setup dialog box, like the one in Figure 12-1, opens with your default printer listed. Your printer may offer you different options from the ones shown in the figure.

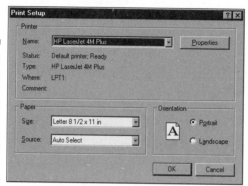

Figure 12-1: The Print Setup dialog box for the HP LaserJet 4M Plus printer.

2. **If you don't want to use the default printer, select a different printer from the Name drop-down list box.**

   The default printer is determined by Windows. To change the default printer, choose Start⇨Settings⇨Printers, right-click the printer of choice, and select the Set as Default command from the resulting pop-up menu.

3. **In the Orientation section, click the desired paper orientation if it isn't already selected.**

   Your choices are Portrait (lengthwise) and Landscape (sideways).

4. **In the Paper section, use the Size drop-down list box to choose the size of paper on which you plan to print, if it isn't already selected.**

   The selected printer determines the available sizes.

5. **Also in the Paper section, use the Source drop-down list box to choose the appropriate paper source for your publication, if it isn't already selected.**

   The selected printer determines the available sources. Some printers have different trays, feeders, tractors, and other methods for getting paper into themselves.

6. **Click OK.**

If you can't find the target printer in the Name drop-down list box, you need to use the Windows Control Panel to install a driver for that printer.

Printing your pages

The operations described in these sections are controlled by Windows 95; Microsoft Publisher 97 uses the services of the operating system to print. You can print to a local or network printer, or you can set up to print to an outside service bureau. Often, you do both, printing draft or sample copies on your local printer for proofing, and receiving final output from a service bureau.

Printing problems are legion with computers. If you are having difficulties printing, try getting help by selecting the Troubleshooting topic in the Windows Help system. Use the Help command on the Start menu to access the Windows Help system when you are inside Microsoft Works. Also check out the Print Troubleshooter on the Help menu of Microsoft Publisher 97. This command opens the Help system and shows you topics of interest in solving printer problems.

To print to a local or network printer, called *inside printing,* you can use various methods:

✔ Click the Print button (shown in the margin) in the Shortcut Bar. Microsoft Publisher 97 immediately begins printing your entire publication using the current print settings.

✔ Select File⊅Print or press Ctrl+P. The Print dialog box, shown in Figure 12-2, appears with your default printer selected. Make your selections from that dialog box and then click OK.

✔ Drag and drop a publication file onto a printer icon or shortcut on the Windows Desktop or in the Windows Explorer.

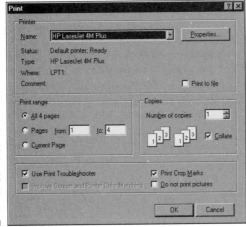

Figure 12-2: The Print dialog box for the HP LaserJet 4M Plus printer.

The Print dialog box

The Print dialog box contains the following important features:

- ✓ **The Name drop-down list box:** This box lets you select the printer that you want to use from your currently installed list of printers. Your default printer appears first in the dialog box. To send a print job to another printer, select that printer by name from the Name drop-down list box.

- ✓ **The Properties button:** Use this button to change aspects of your printer: page size, type, orientation, and handling; graphics; fonts; and other properties specific to your printer.

- ✓ **The Print range section:** Select All to print all pages, select Pages and enter the number of the first and last page that you want to print in the from and to text boxes, or select Current Page to print just the page in which you're working.

- ✓ **The Copies section:** Specify the number of copies that you want to print and whether you want these pages to be collated.

- ✓ **Other options:** Depending upon your printer, you may be able to specify the print quality, what to print, printing order (for labels), and other features.

The capabilities that you see in the Print dialog box are determined to some extent by which printer you have selected. Nearly all printers, however, allow you to select a range of pages to print, as well as to print multiple copies or copy a file to disk and have the file printed on another printer. Many other capabilities — such as collating, color capabilities, two-sided printing, and other options — are specific to each printer. Check out the Properties dialog box by clicking the Properties button in the Print dialog box to find out more about your printer's capabilities. Also, your printer's manual is a good place to learn more about your specific printer.

When you accept the Print dialog box settings, Microsoft Publisher 97 creates a print job and sends (or *spools*) it to your printer. To see the set of documents (called the *print queue*) sent to the printer, double-click that printer's icon in the Printer folder. A window opens, showing you the current print jobs and offering you commands necessary to modify your print jobs. You can delete print jobs, suspend them, and move them about in the queue.

The Print Setup dialog box

If you are printing to a desktop printer, you owe it to yourself to choose File⇨Print Setup and explore your printer's Print Setup dialog box. The Print Setup dialog box is somewhat deceptive because it hides the most interesting settings in the Properties sheet. To access these settings, click the Properties button. With these settings, you control such things as paper size, graphic resolution (number of dots per inch), font quality, and other options.

The Print Troubleshooter

Microsoft Publisher 97 has a feature called the Print Troubleshooter that is turned on by default in the Options dialog box (on the Tools menu). The Print Troubleshooter is a set of online topics that helps you with the following problems:

- Text that doesn't print correctly
- A picture, gradient fill, or pattern that doesn't print correctly
- A book-fold publication that doesn't print correctly
- Any general printing problems, such as slow printing, printout cut-off, memory overflow, and so on

Choose the Print Troubleshooter from the Help menu to view these topics in the online Help system.

Planning for outside printing

You can have two printers specified in Microsoft Publisher 97: your *inside printer,* which appears in your Print dialog box (useful for page proofs); and your *outside printer,* which lets you set up for a printing service (for your final publication). The Outside Print Setup command lets Microsoft Publisher 97 select a printer driver that is best for the outside printing that you are likely to do: black-and-white, full-color, or spot-color printing. When you set up to print to an outside printer, your inside printer becomes a proofing device for the outside printer. The Print Proof command replaces the Print command on the File menu and uses the same Ctrl+P keystroke combination.

Using Outside Printing Services

Microsoft Publisher 97 lets you print to any common desktop printer that you can attach to an IBM PC. For low-volume output, a desktop printer is sufficient. You may have times when you need to print in large quantities, however, or with capabilities beyond those of most desktop printers (such as printing in color, reproducing photographs on glossy stock, or printing in high resolution). In these cases, you need to visit a service bureau, copy shop, or commercial printer. Each of these establishments offers different capabilities, and each requires different degrees of hand-holding.

The following ideas may help you in your quest to select an outside printing service:

- ✔ **If you have friends who use printing services, get a recommendation.** If you don't, let your fingers do the walking through the Yellow Pages and try out a few services. Ask to see samples of their work and get the names of other clients with whom they've worked. Good printers deliver quality work on time and on budget. You're paying good money for the work, and you should get good results.

- ✔ **Know what you expect from your service.** Click the Print Outside Printing Checklist button at the end of the Outside Print Setup wizard to have Microsoft Publisher 97 print a sheet of questions for you to use when screening printing services.

- ✔ **Evaluate the printing quotes.** If you need to print several thousand copies of a piece, a commercial printer is the best choice — and will likely save you money. Copy shops and service bureaus offer lower pricing at volume levels, but commercial printers can go even lower on the cost per page.

- ✔ **Ask about their policy on** *overage.* Most printers print a set amount above your print order to be on the safe side. Some charge for the overage. Make sure that you know when they do. An overage charge of more than 15 percent of the print price is excessive.

- ✔ **Our rule of thumb is, "Don't pick a printer that offers the cheapest price."** You usually pay for the money that you save with longer print turnaround times and less attention to your work. Printing is a very competitive industry. After you cost out the paper and inks, labor is the only variable.

Working with an outside service

Be sure to understand what your outside service requires of you in order to print your publication. At the minimum, an outside printing service is likely to ask that you provide the following materials before it can do your print job:

- ✔ Page proofs of each page, with each spot color or process color separation printed as a proof
- ✔ A listing of your fonts, files, and printing directions

  Use the Infosheet and Checklist for this purpose.
- ✔ The files themselves in Microsoft Publisher 97 or Postscript format, with any needed font files and graphics files included
- ✔ Any original drawings or photographs that need to be scanned

The Microsoft Publisher 97 Infosheet contains the basic information that you need to provide your outside printer. The following are among the Infosheet items:

- ✔ Filenames
- ✔ Creator applications
- ✔ Page size, sheet size, and number of sheets in the publication
- ✔ Colors used: black and white, grayscale, spot, or process colors
- ✔ Printer marks

  If crop marks and registration marks were printed on the proof, they tell your printer where to trim the page and where to align different color separations.
- ✔ Printer format, the definition of the printer driver
- ✔ Horizontal/Vertical resolution (in general, as defined by the output device)
- ✔ Device used to print the page proofs

Go ahead and take the Infosheet and Part B of the checklist to your printing service, and even attach them to your job orders.

Avoiding problems

Using special fonts can be the most troublesome aspect of working with an outside copy shop or service bureau. The following are some of the troubles you can encounter:

- ✔ Many shops keep only a limited collection of fonts. In some cases, busy shops may simply hand you the output of your file with whatever font they substituted for the fonts they didn't have.

- ✔ If you overload your document with fonts, you can overload an imagesetter's memory and get Postscript overflow errors that add to your costs.

- ✔ Using gradient fills can also quickly overload an imagesetter's memory, as can special WordArt effects.

Another troublesome aspect of working with outside printers is forgetting to include all the graphics files that your publication needs.

- ✔ If you submit scanned graphics, make sure that the resolution of the scan is appropriate to the kind of printing that you are doing.

- ✔ Try to use scanned graphics that are simply placed in your publication. If you crop, rotate, or otherwise modify your scanned images, you create large, complicated files.

Check to see that your copy shop or service bureau has the fonts that you used in your publication. Also, if you submit EPS (encapsulated Postscript) files, make sure that the printing service has the same creator application for your publication and its components.

If you are printing a very costly print job, you may want to request a *press check*. That is, you ask your printer to set up the printing press and run off sample copies of the publication for you to check. Your printer is more likely to be willing to do this if you are on hand at the time that the shop runs your job.

Sit down and evaluate any print job that you get back from a printer. If you find a problem, let your printer know about it. And don't forget to let your printer know if you are especially happy with the work. Our favorite way of letting our service providers know that their work was good is to recommend them to other people.

Setting Up for Outside Printing

The Outside Print Setup command lets Microsoft Publisher 97 select a printer driver that is best for the outside printing that you are likely to do: black-and-white, full color, or spot-color printing. When you set up to print to an outside printer, your inside printer becomes a proofing device for the outside printer. The Print Proof command replaces the Print command on the File menu and uses the same Ctrl+P keystroke combination.

Unfortunately, after you select and set up a target printer for a publication, you may not be able to use your own printer to print any drafts of that publication. This happens because printers use all sorts of differing technologies, and few printers are compatible with each other. It's like trying to plug in your small appliances in a foreign country — except that the chance of fire is slightly smaller.

Outside printer setup

You can specify an outside printer driver of your choice or use one of Microsoft Publisher 97's generic printer drivers: the MS Publisher Color Printer and the MS Publisher Imagesetter. Using the actual specific printer driver has the advantage that what you see on your screen accurately represents how the document will be printed. If you don't have the right driver or don't know which printer you intend to use, however, Microsoft Publisher 97's generic printer drivers should get you by.

Follow these steps to print to an outside printer:

1. **Choose File⇨Outside Print Setup from the menu.**

   You see the first step of the Outside Print Setup wizard — Step 1: What type of printing do you want from your printing service?

2. **Select one of the four radio buttons in Step 1:**

   I've decided not to use a commercial printing service, thanks. Selecting this option resets your publication so that your desktop printer is your default printer. Use the *I've decided not to use a commercial printing service, thanks* radio button to turn off the outside printer option.

   Black, white, and shades of gray, on any printer. Use this selection for black-ink printing at any resolution, from low-resolution ink jet printing all the way up to high-resolution printing on an imagesetter. This choice offers no additional options.

Full color, on a color printer at less than 1200 dpi resolution. This option is self-explanatory; it offers no additional choices.

Spot color(s) at greater than 1200 dpi resolution. This option is used for black, white, and gray, plus tints of up to two additional colors. Making this selection gives you the dialog box that you see in Figure 12-3.

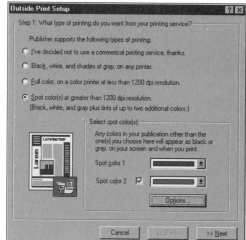

Figure 12-3: Step 1 of the Outside Print Setup wizard for spot color output.

3. **For spot color work, select the color(s) that you want from the pop-up color palette, click Options to set your overprint options, and then click OK to return to wizard Step 1.**

   The Spot Color Options dialog box is shown in Figure 12-4. If you remove the check marks and don't overprint black objects, then any color beneath a black object or type will have its color *knocked out* (not printed).

Figure 12-4: Setting overprint options in the Spot Color Options dialog box.

4. **Click Next in to respond to** Step 2: What printer will you use?

5. **Click Use Publisher's outside printer driver or Select a specific printer.**

   Figure 12-5 shows you the Step 2 dialog box with the Select a specific printer radio button selected.

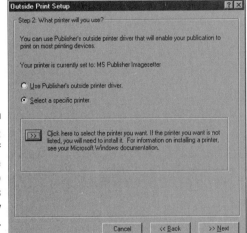

Figure 12-5:
Step 2 of the Outside Print Setup wizard lets you specify the printer.

6. **To change outside printers: click (>>) Click here to select . . . to open the Print Setup dialog box shown in Figure 12-6, select your printer from the Name drop-down list box, and then click OK.**

   The two generic printer drivers — MS Publisher Imagesetter and MS Publisher Color Printer — appear on the drop-down list of printers, along with any additional printers that you have installed. If you select a generic printer, Microsoft Publisher 97 posts a dialog box asking whether you really want to use the generic printer driver.

Figure 12-6:
The Print Setup dialog box.

7. **Click Next so that you can view the** Step 3: What printing options do you want? **dialog box, as shown in Figure 12-7.**

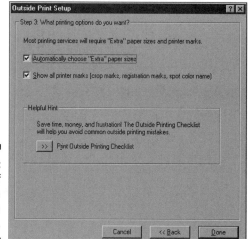

Figure 12-7:
Step 3 of
the Outside
Print Setup
wizard.

Step 3 is the last dialog box in the sequence; it offers three selections:

Automatically choose "Extra" paper sizes. This option automatically prints your publication to larger sizes so that bleeds and printer marks appear on the page. A *bleed* is a color that prints right to the edge of the page (as far as the printer permits).

Show all printer marks (crop marks, registration marks, spot color name). This option prints marks for trimming the printed page and for aligning color separations.

Print Outside Printing Checklist. When you click this button, Microsoft Publisher 97 prints Part A and Part B of the "checklist for outside services." Part A is a sheet of questions that you can ask to screen outside printing services. Part B is a four-page set of requirements for your document and print job.

8. **Click Done to complete your selections.**

If you choose the spot-color option, Microsoft Publisher 97 tells you that it may be more economical to select process colors (cyan, magenta, yellow, and black) rather than two other colors. Our experience suggests that you shouldn't worry about this problem until you select more than two additional colors beyond black. Also, if you choose spot-color printing, you see only those spot colors and their tints in color selection dialog boxes. See Chapter 10 for more about colors.

Avoid using two spot colors in gradient fills, in which the two colors are blended. That configuration prints poorly, if at all. You can use either spot color blended with white or with black, however.

Outside printer printing

When you want to specify a print job to an outside printer, make sure that a check appears in the Print to file check box of the Print dialog box. If checked, the program prints to a disk file that you can take to your outside printing service. Otherwise, Microsoft Publisher 97 uses this printer driver to try to print to your current printer (which may or may not work, depending upon its type).

As with any printer, you should visit the printer's Properties dialog box to see what's there before you do your printing. The MS Publisher Imagesetter and MS Publisher Color Printer have identical Properties dialog boxes. Ask your outside printing service for guidance on making these selections.

You may notice that the About dialog box for the Properties dialog box tells you that the generic drivers were developed jointly by Adobe and Microsoft. On any certified Postscript imagesetter, you should get good results with these drivers because most professionally used print output devices are Adobe Postscript certified.

The Book Printing Options

You may discover the Book Printing Options button at the bottom of the Print dialog box; Figure 12-8 shows the Book Printing Options dialog box. This option lets you Print one page per sheet as its default. You should use the default when your publication uses page sizes that are the same size as the sheets of paper that you are using. When you can print a publication as a two-page spread, the Print as book option not only prints your pages two to a sheet (that is, two letter size pages 8 $\frac{1}{2}$" × 11" on an 11" × 17" page), but also does so consecutively, placing numbered pages in the correct order.

Proof Printing

If you select an outside printer, your Print command on the File menu becomes a Print Proof command. Use that command or the Ctrl+P keystroke to print a *proof* with your inside printer. Then you can send the proofs to your outside printer or service bureau.

When you set up to print to an outside printer, Microsoft Publisher 97 changes the way that it interprets print jobs on your desktop printer to reflect the settings that you made in the Outside Print Setup dialog box.

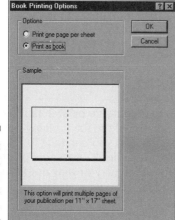

Figure 12-8:
The Book
Printing
Options
dialog box.

Your responsibility is to provide the correct instructions and files to your outside printer. If you don't, you may pay for printing a second time.

Selecting Paper

Selecting paper for your publication's printing is a sensual experience that is rare in computer-land. Paper has texture, heft, thickness, color, shine, brightness (due to fluorescent chemicals), and even smell. We get excited just thinking about it. (Some would say it's because we've been locked up in an office writing this book, but we would disagree.) We love paper — especially the green kind with presidents' portraits on it.

Paper makes up 30 to 50 percent of the total cost of a print job, depending upon the number of copies printed and the type of paper stock chosen. Therefore, you can greatly affect the cost of printing your publication by carefully selecting print stock. Your outside printing service can be a big help in selecting the right paper for your publication. Most printers keep sample stock around for you to look at and, in some cases, to test print. Commercial printers have a great deal of experience with various types of paper and can tell you how well a paper takes ink, folds, or reproduces graphics. Nearly all the larger paper companies distribute sample paper stock kits or paper stock selectors that are strips of sample paper.

Starting your own sampler collection is not a bad idea. PaperDirect is one paper company that will sell you a paper sampler and refund the money on your first order. Other paper manufacturers sell, or more likely give away, their samplers upon request.

Paper as a design element

When you choose paper for your publication, you must match the paper's characteristics to your publication. Paper size, weight, thickness, and methods of measuring these elements vary with the various types of paper. A paper's features related to color, texture, and finish are important to consider when you are deciding on your publication's best presentation. Please note that paper quality is a design element that makes a substantial impression upon the reader.

✔ Buy heavier, better paper when your publication will be handled several times — as will a company's annual report, for example. If your publication will be looked at briefly and then thrown away, you can get by with a lightweight, cheaper paper.

✔ Choose paper color to enhance your publication. The most readable text is printed on a soft, yellowish-white paper. For the best accuracy with process colors, use neutral white paper. Brighteners added to paper stock as fluorescent dyes also alter color fidelities. Be aware that the color of your paper affects how your ink color will appear on the finished product. To avoid unpleasant surprises, you may want to test how the ink color you choose will look when matched with your paper color.

✔ Print on the side of the paper recommended by the paper manufacturer. Paper has a grain that makes one side better for printing; reams of paper have a grain indicator on their wrapping with an arrow to indicate which side you should print on. When printing pages, try to have the grain parallel to the binding edge to help your readers turn pages and to keep your pages lying flat.

✔ Choose paper stock weight and thickness that is appropriate for your printing device. Laser printers typically have a limit of 60-pound stock. If you put heavier paper through a laser printer, you can damage it. Check your printer's documentation for its requirements. If you are printing on two sides of the paper, make sure that your paper is heavy enough that the type from one side doesn't show through to the other side. This is called *bleedthrough* and can make your publication unattractive and difficult to read.

✔ Select a coated paper (at a little more expense) if you need opacity and better resolution for your printing. This is particularly important if you are printing in color or using photographs. You can buy paper stock that's coated on one side (C1S) or on two sides (C2S). C1S is used for labels, packaging, and covers; C2S is used in books or commercial publications. Coated paper withstands higher ink coverage and results in blacker blacks, better color fidelity, and higher resolution. Please note that the coated paper smudges more and may require *varnish* to keep the color from coming off on readers' hands. Also, note that coated paper exhibits less of the printed image showing through to the opposite side of a page.

Special papers from PaperDirect

Microsoft has teamed up with PaperDirect, a direct-mail special paper supplier, to incorporate the special papers that they sell into some of the PageWizard's designs. Microsoft Publisher 97 can display several PaperDirect patterns on your screen (provided that you have not set up your publication to print to an outside printer). To display special paper on-screen, choose View⇨Special Paper and select a design in the Special Paper dialog box (shown in Figure 12-9).

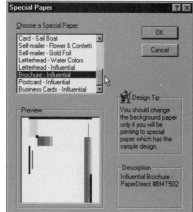

Figure 12-9:
The Special
Paper
dialog box.

You can see these special papers on your screen, but they don't print. To achieve this on-screen effect when you print, you must use the special paper that PaperDirect sells.

We find the PaperDirect catalog to be a treat, even if it seems to show up in our mailboxes every other week. To see what PaperDirect offers, purchase its PaperKit, which contains a sample of each of the pages in the catalog. The phone number is 1-800-A-PAPERS.

PaperDirect also has matching envelopes, business cards, brochures, and postcards for its stationery sets, as well as computer templates, frames, certificates, theme and fun papers, laser foils, and other resources for the desktop publisher.

More Printing Resources

Printing is a big topic, and we've only touched upon the subject here. Fortunately, some great resources are out there to help you. The best book on working with the printing industry, how printers (both mechanical and human) work, and the process of working with printers and graphic arts suppliers is *Getting It Printed,* by Mark Beach, Steve Shepro, and Ken Russon (Coast to Coast Press, Portland, OR, 1986). The book should be a standard reference for any desktop publisher.

Another place to read about printing is the more condensed (and dense) book, *Pocket Pal,* from International Paper. You can buy this book at any graphics supply house. This book gives you many pages of technical details on printing, paper selection, printing inks, type, copy preparation, and dozens more subjects. It is particularly valuable for giving you a detailed, high-level view of the printing industry; we just couldn't do without it.

Part VI
Publishing on the Internet

The 5th Wave   By Rich Tennant

Principal

"I found these two in the multimedia lab morphing
faculty members into farm animals."

In this part . . .

These days, everyone seems to be talking about the Internet and the World Wide Web. You rarely see a television commercial, magazine ad, or billboard that doesn't have a Web site address plastered on it somewhere (you know, http://www.givemeyourmoney.com). The two chapters in this book will help you to create a Web site of your own and publish it to the World Wide Web. After all, if we didn't help you publish your work, we may as well call the book *Microsoft's Create Some Nice-Looking Stuff on Your Computer and Not Let Anyone See It For Dummies.*

Chapter 13

Weaving a Web Page

- -

- -

*Y*ou don't know how to write HTML code, but you want to create professional-looking Web pages? Microsoft Publisher 97 can help. In fact, if you can click a few buttons, you can create some great-looking Web pages in minutes! How? Read on.

What are Web pages?

A Web page is simply a document encoded using HTML (hypertext markup language) to describe its appearance. An HTML document can have hyperlinks — graphics or text that you can click to move to other documents or other parts of the current document. A Web site is one or more Web pages published on a Web server. A Web server is a computer connected to the Internet running Web server software. For more in-depth information on all this World Wide Web stuff, pick up a copy of *Desktop Publishing & Design For Dummies,* by John R. Levine & Carol Baroudi (published by IDG Books Worldwide, Inc.).

Using the Web site PageWizard

As we mention in Chapter 1, the easiest way to create a publication in Microsoft Publisher 97 is to use a PageWizard. Creating a Web site is no exception. Can you create a Web site from scratch using Microsoft Publisher 97? Sure. Would you want to? Probably not. To use the Web site PageWizard, just double-click its icon on the PageWizard tab of the Task Launcher. If the Task Launcher is not visible, you can get it back by choosing File➪Create New Publication. Figure 13-1 shows the Task Launcher with the Web site PageWizard selected.

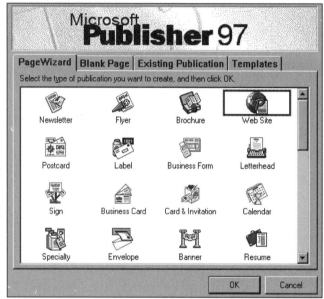

Figure 13-1:
The Task
Launcher
with the
Web site
PageWizard
selected.

After you double-click the Web site PageWizard, Microsoft Publisher 97 displays the first of the Web site PageWizard Design Assistant dialog boxes, as shown in Figure 13-2.

Microsoft Publisher 97 lets you create three different types of Web sites: Corporate, Community, and Personal. Additionally, you have the option of creating a one-page Web site, or a multiple-page Web site. If you create a Multiple-page Web site, Microsoft Publisher 97 creates buttons with hyperlinks to the various pages for you. Click the radio button next to the type of Web site that you would like to create, and then click Next.

No matter which type of Web site you choose, Microsoft Publisher 97 displays another dialog box asking whether you want a one-page site or a multiple-page site, as shown in Figure 13-3.

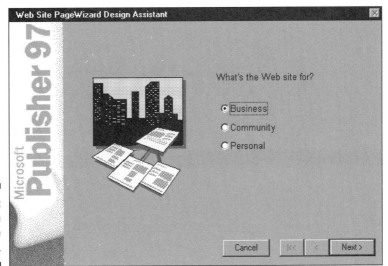

Figure 13-2:
Steps in the
Web site
PageWizard.

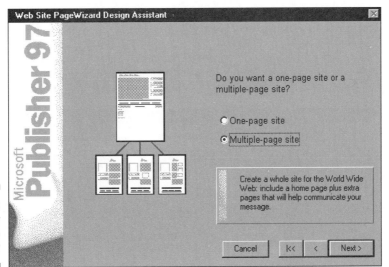

Figure 13-3:
How many
pages do
you want?

Obviously, the simplest Web site would consist of a single page. For now, click the One-page site radio button. You can come back later and create multiple-page sites. If you clicked the One-page radio button, you see the dialog box shown in Figure 13-4, asking you to select a style. If you clicked the Multiple-page radio button, you see a different dialog asking what additional pages you want in your Web site.

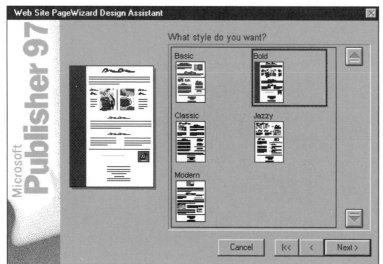

Figure 13-4:
Pick a style,
any style.

Click the style that you find most appealing and then click Next. One of the authors is partial to the Bold style.

Microsoft Publisher 97 displays a dialog box asking you to select a type of background for your Web site, as shown in Figure 13-5.

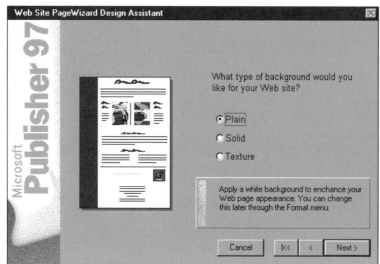

Figure 13-5:
Choose
your
background
wisely.

The Web site PageWizard lets you choose from the following background types:

- ✔ **Plain:** Just a plain white background. This works well for Web pages with lots of text.

- ✔ **Solid:** Microsoft Publisher 97 picks the color for you, but you can change it later.

- ✔ **Texture:** Microsoft Publisher picks the texture for you, but you can change it later.

Click the radio button next to the type of background that you want and then click Next. The dialog box shown in Figure 13-6 is displayed.

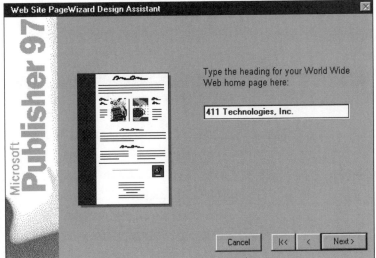

Figure 13-6: Enter a heading for your Web page.

The Web site PageWizard needs to know what you want to call your Web page. This heading will show up at the top of the Web page. Type a heading and click Next.

A dialog box asking whether you would like to add your postal or street address to your Web site appears, as shown in Figure 13-7.

Go ahead and click the radio button next to Yes, please! You can always remove the address later. Click Next.

The dialog box shown in Figure 13-8 is displayed.

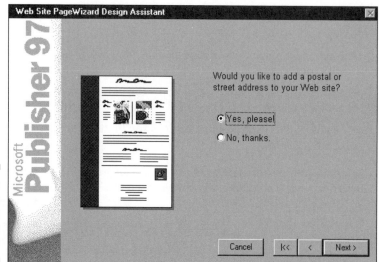

Figure 13-7:
Would you
like an
address
with that?

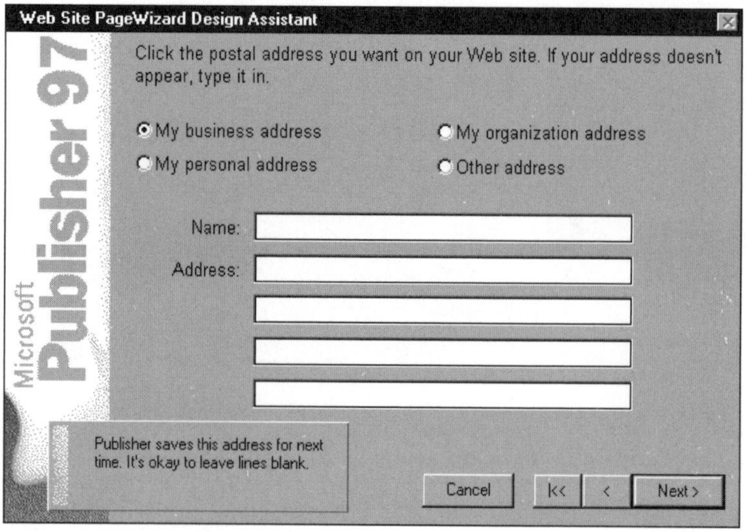

Figure 13-8:
Enter your
address.

Select the type of address that you want to include. You may select only one. If the address that appears is not correct, you may edit it before clicking Next. Click Next (you knew that, didn't you?).

You are almost finished. The dialog box shown in Figure 13-9 is displayed, allowing you to include your phone number, fax number, and e-mail address.

When you click the check boxes, the Web site PageWizard displays a text box under the option so that you can enter the desired information. If you enter an e-mail address, the PageWizard creates a hyperlink so that a person viewing your Web site can click the hyperlink to send you e-mail.

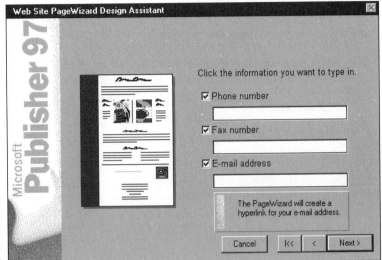

Figure 13-9: Include your phone and fax numbers, and e-mail address.

Enter the desired information and click Next. Finally, Microsoft Publisher 97 shows you the last of the Web site PageWizard dialog boxes, informing you that it has all the information it needs to create your Web site. Click the Create It! button and Microsoft Publisher 97 goes to work. It generally takes less than one minute to create the Web site on our PC, but as they say, "results may vary" depending on your configuration.

That's all there is to it. Now you can edit the text and picture frames to personalize your Web site.

Adding text or picture objects

Adding text or pictures to your Web site is pretty simple. In fact, if you have added text or pictures to a Microsoft Publisher 97 publication, you already know how to add them to your Web site. If you used the Web site PageWizard to create your Web site, you probably have several text and picture frames in your publication. Did we call your Web site a publication? Guess so.

We strongly recommend that you use the Web site PageWizard to create your Web site. It is much easier, in our opinion, to create the site using the PageWizard and change what you don't like than it is to create the Web site from scratch.

Adding text

To change the place holder text that the PageWizard put in your publication, just highlight the text and start typing.

If you don't have any text frames or don't want to change the text in an existing text frame, just create a new one. You remember how.

1. **Click the Text tool.**

2. **Draw the text frame.**

3. **Start typing.**

We think that the Web site PageWizard does a reasonably good job of designing the Web page, but feel free to add, delete, or move objects as you see fit.

Adding pictures

To change a picture on your Web page, follow these steps:

1. **Double-click the picture.**

   The Microsoft Gallery appears and you can select a new picture for your Web page.

2. **Click on the image that you want and click Insert.**

   The Import Picture dialog box shown in Figure 13-10 will probably appear.

3. **Select the Change The Frame To Fit The Picture radio button.**

4. **Click OK.**

   Choosing Change The Frame to Fit The Picture will display the picture best, but you may need to resize the frame to fit your layout.

If you want to add a new picture, follow these steps:

1. **Click the Picture tool.**

2. **Draw a frame for the picture.**

3. **Choose Insert➪Picture File from the menu.**

4. **Click the desired file and click OK.**

5. **Choose an option in the Import Picture dialog box (either Change The Frame To Fit The Picture or Change The Picture To Fit The Frame) and click OK.**

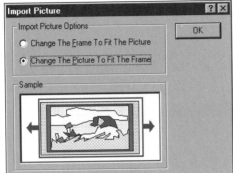

Figure 13-10:
The Import Picture dialog box.

Adding and removing hyperlinks

Hyperlinks allow the person viewing your Web site to click an object (text or a graphic) and jump to another document on your Web site or elsewhere on the Internet, and to send an e-mail.

Adding hyperlinks

Several ways are available to add a hyperlink to an object on your Web page. You add hyperlinks to text, pictures, WordArt, and even the contents of table frames. To add a hyperlink to text or a table frame, you must first select the individual text that you want to hyperlink. Selecting just the text or table frame will not work. Follow these steps to create a hyperlink:

1. **Select the object to which you want to add a hyperlink.**

2. **Select Insert⇨Hyperlink, select Hyperlink from the context menu, click the Hyperlink button on the toolbar, or press Ctrl+K.**

3. **Select the type of hyperlink that you want from the Hyperlink dialog box.**

4. **Fill in the Hyperlink Information section of the Hyperlink dialog box and click OK.**

As shown in Figure 13-11, you can create four types of hyperlinks:

- ✔ **A document already on the Internet:** You need to supply the URL (uniform resource locator or address) of the document the hyperlink connects to.

- ✔ **An Internet e-mail address:** You need to supply an e-mail address.

- ✔ **Another page in your Web site:** Select the appropriate page in your Web site.

- ✔ **A file on your hard disk:** You need to supply the path to the file to which you want to link. This file will be published along with your Web site.

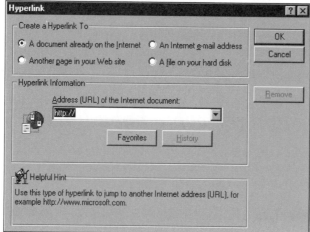

Figure 13-11:
The
Hyperlink
dialog box.

Removing hyperlinks

Removing a hyperlink from an object is a snap:

1. **Select the object from which you want to remove a hyperlink.**

2. **Select Insert⇨Hyperlink, select Hyperlink from the context menu, Click the Hyperlink button on the toolbar, or press Ctrl+K.**

3. **Click the Remove button in the Hyperlink dialog box.**

Adding color and texture to the background

Although we usually prefer a white background for our Web sites, you can produce dramatic effects by applying texture and/or color to the page background. The easiest way to do this is to select Solid or Texture from the

Web site PageWizard dialog box. If you didn't select one of these options, or just want to change the color or texture that you are currently using, you need to use the Background and Text Colors dialog box.

Adding color to the background

To add or change the color of the background, do the following:

1. **Select View⇨Go to Background or press Ctrl+M.**

   All your objects disappear. Do not be alarmed. They are still on the foreground layer where you left them.

2. **Select Format⇨Background and Text Colors.**

   The Background and Text Colors dialog box shown in Figure 13-12 is displayed.

3. **Click the Custom tab.**

   The Custom tab of the Background and Text Colors dialog box shown in Figure 13-13 is displayed.

4. **Click the down arrow next to the Color option and select a color.**

5. **If necessary, click the No Texture button.**

6. **Change the Custom Text Colors options as desired.**

7. **Click OK.**

8. **Select View⇨Go to Foreground or press Ctrl+M.**

   You are returned to the foreground view of your publication. Marvel at your sense of color for three minutes.

Adding texture to the background

To add or change the texture of the background, follow these steps:

1. **Select View⇨Go to Background or press Ctrl+M.**

   All your objects disappear. Do not be alarmed. They are still on the foreground layer where you left them.

2. **Select Format⇨Background and Text Colors.**

   The Background and Text Colors dialog box shown in Figure 13-12 is displayed.

3. **Select a texture from the Available Selections list.**

   Microsoft Publisher 97 automatically changes the text colors to coordinate with the selected background texture.

4. **Click OK.**

5. **Select View⇨Go to Foreground or press Ctrl+M.**

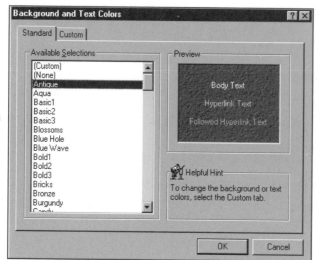

Figure 13-12:
The
Standard
tab of the
Background
and Text
Colors
dialog box.

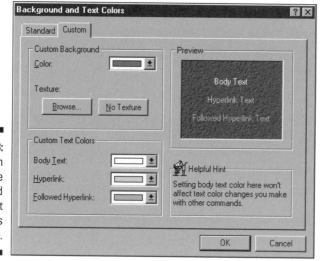

Figure 13-13:
The Custom
tab of the
Background
and Text
Colors
dialog box.

We are all for fancy backgrounds with bright colors for Web pages that have little text, but a plain white background works best for Web pages with lots of text.

Chapter 14

Getting Published (On the Internet)

• •

• •

So, you have created a stunning Web site and you are wondering what you should do with it. Well, you have come to the right place. In this chapter, we discuss previewing your Web site in your Web browser and publishing your Web site.

Previewing a Web Site

After you have created your Web site, you probably want to preview it to make sure that it meets with your expectations before you go through the trouble of publishing it for the entire world to see. You want to make sure that it looks the way you intended and that all the hyperlinks function. You must have Web browser software installed and configured in order to preview a Web site.

To preview your Web site, select File⇨Preview Web Site or press Ctrl+Shift+B. Microsoft Publisher 97 opens your default Web browser and displays the first page of your Web site. Click the hyperlinks to make sure that they function properly, and view the other pages (if any) of your Web site. When you are finished viewing your Web site, close your Web browser. You return to Microsoft Publisher 97.

Publishing Your Web Site

What's the difference between previewing your Web site and publishing it? When you preview your Web site, Microsoft Publisher 97 opens the Web site on your computer and shows you how it will look when it is published on the Internet. Publishing a Web site entails copying it to a computer running Web server software.

Microsoft Publisher 97 gives you three options for publishing your Web site:

- ✔ Publish to a folder on your PC
- ✔ Publish to a local network drive
- ✔ Publish to the Internet

The first two options are quite similar. Why would you go through the trouble of creating a Web site and not publish it on the Internet? Perhaps you are working off-site and do not have a connection to the Internet. Publishing to a folder on your PC or to a local network drive causes Microsoft Publisher 97 to create all the HTML and image files that make up your Web site on a local drive so that you can copy them to your Web server at a later time.

The last option lets you connect to the Internet from within Microsoft Publisher 97 using the Microsoft Web Publishing Wizard and guides you through the steps of posting your Web site.

The Microsoft Web Publishing Wizard is a work in progress. As this book goes to press, version 1.1 is current. We have no way of knowing what version you will have when you read this book, so keep in mind that the figures shown in this chapter may not accurately reflect what you see on your screen. In our opinion, publishing your Web site to a local drive and copying it to your Web server is much easier using FTP software than using the Web Publishing Wizard. If you don't know how to use FTP, pick up a copy of *Internet For Dummies* by John R. Levine & Carol Baroudi (published by IDG Books Worldwide, Inc.) for the low-down.

Publishing to a folder on your PC

After you have created your Web site, publishing it to a folder on your PC is a breeze:

1. **Choose File⇨Publish Web Site to Folder.**

   The Select a Folder dialog box, shown in Figure 14-1, appears.

2. **Select the folder to which you would like to publish your Web site and click OK.**

   Microsoft Publisher 97 creates the HTML and image files and places them in the selected folder. We told you it was a breeze.

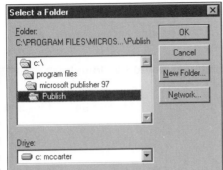

Figure 14-1:
Select a
folder for
your Web
site.

Publishing to a local network drive

After you have created your Web site, publishing it to a local network drive
is almost as easy as publishing to a folder on your PC. If you are already
connected to the network drive that will store your Web site, follow these
steps:

1. **Choose File⇨Publish Web Site to Folder.**

   The Select a Folder dialog box shown in Figure 14-1 appears.

2. **Select the folder to which you would like to publish your Web site
   and click OK.**

   Microsoft Publisher 97 creates the HTML and image files and places
   them in the selected folder. Now that didn't hurt, did it?

If you are not connected to the network drive that will store your Web site,
follow these steps:

1. **Choose File⇨Publish Web Site to Folder.**

   The Select a Folder dialog box shown in Figure 14-1 appears.

2. **Click the Network button.**

   You are prompted for a drive letter and path, as shown in Figure 14-2.

Figure 14-2:
Select a
drive letter
and enter
the path.

Map Network Drive		? |X|
Drive:	E:	OK
Path:		Cancel
☐ Reconnect at logon		

3. **Enter the drive letter and path and click OK.**

   You may be prompted for a username and password, depending on your network configuration.

4. **Select the folder to which you would like to publish your Web site and click OK.**

   Microsoft Publisher 97 creates the HTML and image files and places them in the selected folder.

Publishing on the Internet

As we mention earlier in the chapter, we think that publishing your Web site to a folder on your PC and copying it using FTP software is the easiest way to go. To publish your Web site on the Internet using the Microsoft Web Publishing Wizard, you must have Internet access. Most people access the Internet from home by dialing into an *Internet Service Provider* (ISP). If you do not have access to the Internet, you can still publish your Web site to a local drive or to a network. This creates all the HTML (*hypertext markup language*) documents and image files, allowing you to copy the files to the Internet at a later time.

If you have not installed the Microsoft Web Publishing Wizard and wish to do so (though we can't imagine why you would) follow these steps:

1. **Select File⇨Publish to Web.**

   You see the Publisher dialog box shown in Figure 14-3.

Figure 14-3:
Click Yes to connect to the Internet and download the Microsoft Web Publishing Wizard.

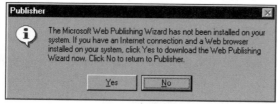

Publisher

The Microsoft Web Publishing Wizard has not been installed on your system. If you have an Internet connection and a Web browser installed on your system, click Yes to download the Web Publishing Wizard now. Click No to return to Publisher.

Yes   No

2. **Click Yes to have Microsoft Publisher 97 automatically connect you to the Internet.**

3. **Follow the instructions on the Microsoft Web site to download and install the latest version of the Microsoft Web Publishing Wizard.**

   Doing so took us just over 12 minutes to download the software using a 28.8 Kbps modem.

We do not recommend downloading any version of software that has the word "Beta" in the title.

If you have already installed the Microsoft Web Publishing Wizard, follow these steps to publish your Web site to the Internet:

1. **Select File⇨Publish to Web.**

   You see the first of the Web Publishing Wizard dialog boxes shown in Figure 14-4.

Figure 14-4:
Click the
New button
to add your
Web server
to the list.

2. **Click the New button to add your Web server to the list.**

   You see the dialog box shown in Figure 14-5.

3. **Type a name for your Web site and select your Internet Service Provider (ISP) from the list.**

   Select <Other Internet Provider> if your ISP is not listed.

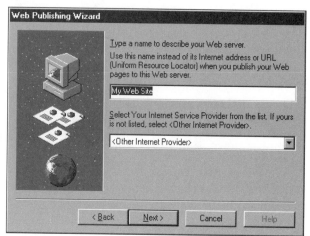

Figure 14-5:
Select your
Internet
Service
Provider.

4. Click Next.

You see the dialog box shown in Figure 14-6.

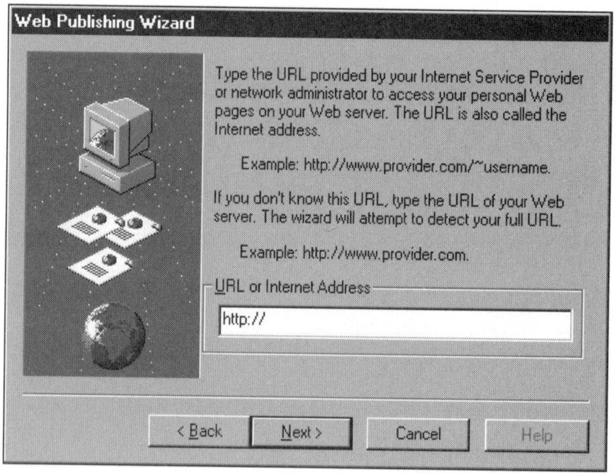

Figure 14-6:
Type your
Internet
address.

5. **Type the URL or Internet address of the Web server that will host your Web site, and click Next.**

6. **The Web Publishing Wizard connects you to the Internet and prompts you to select the type of connection to your Web server, as shown in Figure 14-7.**

Figure 14-7:
Select a
connection
type.

7. **Select a connection type (most likely the dial-up connection) and click Next.**

You are prompted to enter a Username and Password, as shown in Figure 14-8.

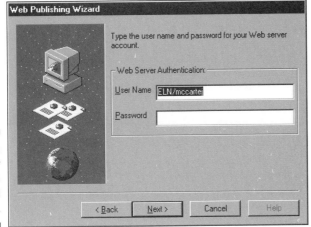

Figure 14-8:
Enter your
Username
and
Password.

8. **Enter your Username and Password and click Next.**

9. **Click Next again to start the authentication process.**

10. If you see the dialog box shown in Figure 14-9, you have incorrectly entered some required information.

The most likely culprits are the Username and Password. Click the <u>B</u>ack button to correct this information and try again.

Figure 14-9:
The Wizard
could not
post your
Web site.

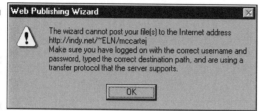

> **Web Publishing Wizard** ☒
>
> ⚠ The wizard cannot post your file(s) to the Internet address
> http://indy.net/~ELN/mccartej
> Make sure you have logged on with the correct username and
> password, typed the correct destination path, and are using a
> transfer protocol that the server supports.
>
> [OK]

11. If you see a message stating that you have successfully posted your Web site, you are finished.

Take the rest of the day off with pay.

Part VII
The Part of Tens

The 5th Wave   By Rich Tennant

HOPING TO CASH IN ON THE WEALTH OF OUT-OF-WORK LOOMERS, CLUNK CORP CONVERTS TO THE CONTROVERSIAL "PEDA-TRACK-BALL" SYSTEM AT THEIR PLANT IN OHIO.

In this part . . .

*E*verybody needs lists to get them through the day. We give you ten things on various topics to help you create publications that get you through the night.

Chapter 15
Ten Great Design Ideas

Consider these ten general design tips for all your publications.

Borrow the best ideas of others

Ideas are not copyrightable, but designs are. The more people you borrow from, the more original it makes you!

Design your piece with your audience in mind

Your audience will be more likely to read your work if they like its design.

Use a design grid

Create a design grid and align your page elements to it. Doing this imposes consistency on your pages. See Chapter 4 for information on how to work with grids.

Use pictures well

Pictures are attention getters. If your picture tells your story, then your reader will get the point quicker if they see the picture. Give the picture an appropriate caption and group the two (picture and caption) together. It's a great way to get your story read.

Check out the Design Gallery

The Design Gallery has many attractive page elements and other great stuff that you can use: headlines, sidebars, pull quotes, ornaments, tables of contents, and so on, in several great styles. Use these elements and the Fancy First Letter feature to break up your pages and make them interesting. Don't find what you like? Try creating your own Design Gallery category and storing your own favorite design elements.

Put repeating design elements onto your backgrounds

If you put items on the background, you don't have to repeat them on every page, and you can't mistakenly delete them or move them about. Chapter 4 tells you how to make the most of background pages.

Keep It Simple, Stupid!

KISS is a guiding design principle. Simplicity is elegant and lets the reader focus on your message. Make your design consistent and simple to follow by using repetitive elements well.

Create templates and use the PageWizards

Any design that stands up to time deserves repeating. Save your work as templates and then use these as your starting places. We love the PageWizards (see Chapter 1), and we are not proud.

Use multicolumn text frames

If you use multicolumn text frames rather than lots of single-column text frames, you have fewer objects on your layout to worry about. Text autoflows easily, columns align without strife, and your life flows as smoothly as water flows downhill to the sea.

Live with your designs a while

Revisiting the scene of the crime is an excellent way of improving your publication; go back and take another critical look at your work. If you can, show your publication's page proofs to others and get some comments.

Chapter 16
Ten Design Blunders

*B*e on the lookout for these ten design blunders in all your publications.

Not designing your publication for the right audience

Not designing your publication for the right audience is the design-blunder equivalent of sending an invitation to file your publication in the circular file (the wastebasket, that is). For example, if you are creating a corporation's annual report, whimsical display fonts are inappropriate.

Not talking to your printer early in the project

You can prevent a whole range of design blunders by consulting with your printer, consultant, or service bureau from the beginning of your project. For example, some print colors may not be available from your printer.

Using the wrong printer driver

Congratulations! Using the wrong printer driver during your design process gives you the opportunity to reformat your entire document.

Using too little white space

Well-designed publications use 50 percent of the page for white space. Using less makes your publication seem busy and hard to read.

Making your publication too complicated

A busy page with many different design elements can distract your reader from the important points of your message. Highlight the important parts of your publication so that your readers look at what you want them to see. A common problem is using too many fonts, giving your page a "ransom note" feeling.

Making your pages too boring!

Spice up your pages — add contrast. Add graphics, drop or raised caps, color, rules, and other design elements meant to break up a repetitive page design. This is particularly important for long publications that use similar page styles.

Printing too many or too few copies

Printing too many or too few copies of your publication is easy to do, but either case can cause you grief. Try hard to print the right amount of your piece. Think hard about just how many copies of a publication are required for your work. For example, try to figure out how many people going by your trade show booth are likely to pick up your flyer or how many copies of the brochure you're really going to mail out.

Designing a publication that is too expensive

It's easy to run over your publication's budget. When you're designing your piece, try to substitute less-expensive elements or processes. For example, don't use process color if you can't afford it or don't need it. Use spot colors instead.

Don't violate copyright laws

Know the source of your graphics, designs, and text, and know your rights to use them. Refer to a text like *The Desktop Publisher's Legal Handbook,* by Daniel Sitarz, Nova Publishing, Carbondale, IL, to help you stay out of trouble.

Scanning your files at the wrong resolution

Be resolution appropriate. Don't waste disk space and processing time by scanning a graphic at a high resolution when you are printing at a low resolution. But don't scan your graphic at a low resolution when you are printing at a high one; this makes your image look coarse and inappropriate.

Chapter 17

Ten Text Tips

These tips on text can save you time, aggravation, and even embarrassment!

Use the keyboard shortcuts

Become familiar with and use the text-navigation and text-formatting keyboard shortcuts (see Tables 17-1 and 17-2) — they save you time.

Table 17-1	Helpful Keyboard Shortcuts for Text Navigation	
Press the Key(s)...	**Or, the Key(s) (on Numeric Keypad with Num Lock Off)**	**To Do This...**
Home	[7]	Go to the beginning of current text line
End	[1]	Go to the end of current text line
Up-arrow	[8]	Move up one text line
Down-arrow	[2]	Move down one text line
Right-arrow	[6]	Move right one character
Left-arrow	[4]	Move left one character
Ctrl+Home	Ctrl+[7]	Go to the beginning of current text frame
Ctrl+End	Ctrl+[1]	Go to the end of current text frame
Ctrl+Up-arrow	Ctrl+[8]	Go to the beginning of current paragraph
Ctrl+Down-arrow	Ctrl+[2]	Go to the beginning of next paragraph
Ctrl+Right-arrow	Ctrl+[6]	Move right one word
Ctrl+Left-arrow	Ctrl+[4]	Move left one word

Table 17-2	Helpful Keyboard Shortcuts for Text Formatting
Press These Keys...	*To Format Selected Text Like This...*
Ctrl+B	Bold
Ctrl+I	Italic
Ctrl+U	Underline
Ctrl+=	Superscript
Ctrl+Shift+=	Subscript
Ctrl+Shift+K	Small caps
Ctrl+Spacebar	Plain text (to remove all style formats from selected text)

Zoom in and out of your text block

Use the F9 keystroke to zoom in and out of your text block. By changing the on-screen size of the elements that you're viewing, you can work on your text (and other objects) at the 100% view without having to go blind, and then you can quickly get an overview of the results.

Show those special characters

Choose View⇨Show Special Characters from the menu or press the Ctrl+Shift+Y keystroke combination.

Check your spelling and then proofread

Spell checkers correct stupid spelling errors. Proofreading your document corrects stupid spell checkers. Misspelled words show that you are careless, and misused words can be very amusing. Both distract from your message.

Use the Format Painter

This handy-dandy tool copies the format of any object that you select and lets you apply that format to any other object. The Format Painter works as well for circles and lines as it does for text.

Use autoflow

Use Microsoft Publisher 97's autoflow feature to pour your text from frame to frame. With autoflow, you can manage your stories, add continuation notices, and not worry about leaving out text.

Hyphenate justified text

Justified text can leave rivers of white space running through it, especially when the text is in narrow columns. Hyphenation can help eliminate the excess white space and makes justified text seem appropriate. For text that is left or right justified, hyphenation reduces the ragged-edge look of the text.

For the sake of appearance, make sure that you don't have hyphens that appear at the end of the line on more than two consecutive lines.

Use the text frame's context-sensitive menu

Don't forget that any text frame has a context-sensitive menu. It contains many valuable commands that you use for working with your text frames (and other objects on your layout). Context-sensitive menus are just a right-click away; that is, right-click and the menus appear.

Use typographers symbols and conventions

Using typographer's symbols and conventions gives your publication polish. When appropriate, use the following: ' ' and " " in place of ' ' and " "; the symbols for en dashes –; em dashes —; real fractions $1/4$, $1/2$, $3/4$; the symbols ™, ©, and ®; properly accented characters such as À, Ñ, à, è; and ligatures such as æ and Æ.

The Insert Symbols dialog box can help you find and use these special symbols.

Replace two spaces after a sentence with a single space.

Use your word processor to edit your stories

If your word processor is Microsoft Word, you can use the Edit Story in Word command to edit your text. If you use another word processor, edit your text in it. If you use your word processor for the majority of your text work, you'll find that you write your text faster, you have better tools to work with, and you'll basically be a happier camper.

Chapter 18

Ten Type Tips

*L*ook to these type tips to help you get a smooth, attractive publication.

Use fonts sparingly

Too many fonts are distracting and they make your publications look like ransom notes.

Use appropriate fonts

In general, use sans serif fonts for headlines and serif fonts for body text. Sans serif fonts are clear but harder to read. Use them in short spurts. Serif fonts give the readers' eyes something to follow and improve comprehension.

Create a style sheet

Using consistent text styles while you design your publication can help you save time and give your readers a sense of familiarity with your work. That is, if readers can recognize a text style as a particular kind of headline, they can go right to it. To save you time, style sheets let you make wholesale changes to your text formatting without you having to change each individual text frame, thus saving you much hair pulling. (We don't have that much hair left, anyway.) You can create styles by using the Text Styles dialog box from the Format menu. That dialog box also lets you import a style sheet from another document. Chapter 7 describes working with styles.

Collect fonts in families

Having an extensive collection of styles in a single font is better than having a single style in many different fonts. With the single font collection, you can provide contrast on your page without distracting the reader with many different looks.

Use the WordArt program to create fancy headlines

Why not? You can get some great effects that way. Among the effects that you can get in the WordArt program is text that looks like a fish, flows along a wave shape, or is rotated through any angle.

Yearn to kern your headlines

Microsoft Publisher 97 makes letter spacing and line spacing too darn big. The larger the letters you use, the worse the problem gets, and it is execrable for serif fonts. Use Microsoft Publisher 97's kerning feature to adjust the line spacing of your headlines. Use small caps in headlines; they look way cool. Leave more line spacing above a headline and less below to have a headline appear to *belong* to the text to which it applies.

Use table frames to present tabular data

Tabular data is best when presented in table frames (see Chapter 6). Microsoft Publisher 97 helps you set up table frames with its regular array of cells, column and row headings, and other special formats. Word even has a table auto-formatting feature that lets you instantly choose and create attractive layout styles. Table frames are also useful for making tables of contents and for formatting regular arrays of data (like graphs).

Use bulleted and numbered Lists

Use Microsoft Publisher 97's bulleted and numbered lists features to automatically create and format your lists. They're fast, they're neat, and they're easy. Use the Bulleted or Numbered Lists button on the Format toolbar, or choose the Indents And Lists command on the Format menu.

Wrap text around your graphics

Wrapping text around your graphics provides a very pleasing design effect. In Microsoft Publisher 97, text wrapping is easy to do and you get to choose from several different ways of doing it. Chapter 5 talks about text wrapping in detail.

Use ruler settings to make your tabs

Don't use tabs to indent paragraphs; use ruler settings instead. You'll find that working with ruler indents is easier than with tabs if you change your mind about using or removing these elements. See Chapter 7 for a discussion on how to use the ruler to set these features.

Chapter 19

Ten Ways to Use Color

*W*e've come up with the following cool color ideas for your consideration.

Use color sparingly

Use color sparingly; too much color distracts from your message. Stick to a couple of spot colors and use colors for design elements on your page in a consistent fashion. For example, make all headlines in your newsletter the same color so that your readers can quickly spot a headline.

Highlight important information

Because color is one of the first things that your readers notice, use it to highlight your most important information first. That way, your readers see what you want them to see. For example, use shading to make your sidebars, tips, or other elements stand out.

Create a color scheme and stick to it

A color scheme reinforces your design and makes it easier for a reader to find elements on the page. For example, use a dark or black font on a light background for the bulk of your text that the reader sees.

Consider using process color

Use process color if you are considering using two or more spot colors, because in this case, using process color may be cheaper. Chapter 10 explains the difference between spot and process colors and their uses.

Use complementary colors

Try using one dominant color and shades or tints of its complementary color. Of all color schemes, those based on complementary colors attract the most attention. Red and green are complementary colors. Chapter 10 tells you how to pick pairs of complementary colors by using the Windows Color selector.

Use culturally appropriate colors

Use culturally appropriate colors in your publications. That is, don't make your stop signs green and your go signs red. Doing so may cause your readers to be confused and misread your signs (or your publication).

Use a colored page as a design element

Try using color for an entire page for a change. Why not? You've already paid for the paper.

Use a color for your text

Your text doesn't always have to be black; try using a color instead. But before you do, make sure that the combination of your ink color and the printed page has good contrast and is readable.

Use spot colors appropriately

If you use two spot colors, don't mix them together. Blend your spot colors with black or white to create shades or tints and use gradients to create interesting patterns; see Chapter 10 for "how-to" instructions. You can get a lot of mileage out of spot colors.

Use the Microsoft Publisher 97 color-matching system

To get more consistent results, why not use Microsoft Publisher 97's color-matching system? The Windows Image Matching System provides a way to remove colors that won't print on your printer, or to match colors between your screen and printer. Chapter 10 tells you how to get consistent color from your color monitor and your printer.

Chapter 20

Ten Things to Check Before Printing

· ·

*T*o make your printing process roll smoothly, check out the following things before you try to print.

Give page proofs to your outside printer

Print a set of page proofs for your publication and give it (set) to your outside printer. To do this, set up your publication to print to an outside printer and choose File⇨Print Proof to print the proofs on your local printer. Here's the routine: Print a proof, correct your document, print a proof, correct your document…. Give your printer your final page proofs and don't leave the results that you want up to his or her imagination.

Show your page proofs around

Show your page proofs to several people. The more eyes that see them, the greater the chance that mistakes will get noticed.

Include all your files and fonts on your submission disk

When you turn in your disks to your outside printer or service bureau, make sure that all of your files and fonts are on the disks. Your service bureau may need your fonts, and it certainly needs all the files that you reference in your publication. If you neglect to include all the files, you may see blank boxes where your graphics should be!

Give your service bureau all original materials

Make sure that you have all the original materials that your publication needs collected with your submission. If your service bureau requires a photograph or drawing for reference, don't forget to include it.

Give the Microsoft Publisher 97 Infosheet to your outside printer

The Infosheet helps you determine what files and fonts you need to give to your printer, so including a printed copy of the Infosheet with your submission is a good idea. Choose File⇨Print Infosheet to print the Infosheet; this command appears on the File menu only when you set up your publication to print to an outside printer.

Use the Microsoft Publisher 97 checklist

Print the checklist for outside printing and fill it in. To print the checklist, click the Print Outside Printing Checklist button in the Outside Print Setup wizard. Use the questions in Part A to screen your potential printers; use the answers to see whether you want to work with them. Then, fill in Part B and give it to your printer. Now, doesn't that feel good?

Run the Design Checker

We don't like hidden objects, empty frames, and other things that we put on a page that aren't going to print properly. And we have a devil of a time finding them without this nice tool. Choose Tools⇨Design Checker to run the Design Checker.

Specify the correct printer driver

Check that you have specified the correct printer driver for your publication and your printer. In other words, make sure that you are submitting the print job formatted for the printer that will print it. The current printer driver shows up in the Name list box of the Print Setup dialog box.

Use printing marks on your master copies

Make sure that your master copies have crop marks and other printing marks, such as registration marks, on them. These marks help your printer greatly in preparing the final printed matter quickly and correctly. Printing marks are detailed in Chapter 12.

Check for the end of the story

As you reformat text frames, moving text at the end of your story so that it is out of view is easy. To keep this from affecting your final publication, check that all your story endings are properly included on the last connected text frame. One way to do this is to check the continuation mark on the last frame of a story.

Chapter 21

Ten Questions for Your Service Bureau

A sk the following questions as you screen and select an outside printer or service bureau.

Are you comfortable working with Windows files?

Many shops are Mac-only shops in the desktop publishing game. Although the differences in quality and capabilities between the Macintosh and Windows operating systems and graphics programs have narrowed, some shops are still Macintosh only. Try to use a shop with PC experience.

How do you want to receive my files?

Can they work with Microsoft Publisher 97 files, or do they need or want EPS files? A service bureau can work with Microsoft Publisher 97 files only if it has a copy of the program on hand. Many service bureaus don't keep Microsoft Publisher 97 around. Therefore, you can give shops without Microsoft Publisher 97 an EPS file that they can print as is, without the program on hand. The disadvantage of using an EPS file is that the service bureau cannot make changes to the file if a problem arises.

What is your usual turnaround time?

When do you need it, and what will they charge you if you need it quicker? This question helps you plan your production and submission schedule.

What kind of imagesetter do you use?

This question tells you the particular printer driver to use. Microsoft Publisher 97 has a generic imagesetter driver called MS Imagesetter. If you know the particular imagesetter that your service bureau has, however, using the real printer driver (for that imagesetter) will give you superior results and fewer errors.

What kind of equipment do you have in your shop?

Does the printer have a high-quality scanner, a Xerox DocuTech Publisher high-volume printer, or a color laser copier? The type of equipment that the printer has available factors into the price and the kind of work that the service bureau can do.

Do you have the fonts in my publication?

If not, you need to supply the fonts or avoid using what they don't have. Without all your required fonts available, the service bureau may give you printed output that has substitute fonts in place of the ones that you specified in Microsoft Publisher 97.

Do you have the creator applications for the EPS graphics that I create?

Without the creator application (the one that saved the EPS file to disk), your service bureau cannot correct any problems in your files. The printed results are your responsibility. See Chapter 9 for a discussion of EPS graphics.

How much do you charge?

Get a quote in writing — it's your insurance that you pay for what you get and get what you pay for.

Can you outsource the work that you can't do?

If your service bureau works with commercial printers and other businesses, you can use that one source to manage your entire print job and save you hassles and headaches.

Can you give me some references?

Who are the service bureau's clients? Are they happy with the work? Ask the shop to show you some samples of the printed work.

Chapter 22

Ten Ways to Save Money Printing

*L*ook over these money-saving tips for ideas to help you save on your printing expenses.

Talk to your printer

Printers know how to save you money. Tell them what your budget is and then ask them how to meet it. Ask them what else you can do to lower your costs.

Choose an appropriate printer

Get recommendations for a printer from others and choose a printer appropriate to the kind of printing that you do. Each printing establishment specializes in a particular kind of printing. Some are good at low- or high-volume printing; others specialize in careful color work. Select your printer accordingly.

Solicit three written bids for a print job

Get competitive bids for your print job. Make the process meaningful by providing a complete disclosure of your printing requirements. Select the printer whose bid seems the most reasonable, and get everything in writing: deadlines, delivery, and storage costs, for example. Don't necessarily select the cheapest bid, but don't overpay.

Make a careful paper selection

You can find paper bargains out there if you try. Let your printer help you make a paper selection.

Provide master print copy to your printer

The further that you can go in the printing process, the less you pay and the fewer variables there are in things that can go wrong. If you can, supply the film that is used to make the printing plates to your commercial printer. Chapter 12 tells a little more about the source of film and master copy.

Ask for a cash discount

If you pay immediately with cash, you should pay less. Hey, it's worth a try.

Don't print close to your deadline

Don't cut your deadline too close; leave some time for back-and-forth discussions between you and the printer. For example, if you have enough time, you can request a press proof and examine it. That way, you see a page printed with the inks and press that will run the whole print job, and you can check it carefully for errors.

Use special paper to print in color without having to print in color

Although the paper from PaperDirect (800-A-PAPERS) is more expensive than common stock, you can run its colored designs through an ink jet or laser printer and do short-run printing. You can get outstanding results, and only other desktop publishers know that you did it. (And we won't tell.)

Use a print broker for large and/or expensive print jobs

Is your print job especially large or expensive? Using a print broker can save you money if your job falls into one of these two categories.

Minimize the amount of setup work that your printer must do

If your printer has a three-color printing press, don't use four colors. That requires an extra print run and will cost you more money.

Chapter 23

Ten Resources You Should Know About

W e recommend these additional sources of good information on desktop publishing.

Desktop Publishing & Design For Dummies, by Roger Parker, IDG Books Worldwide, Inc.

Our hero, Roger Parker, tells it like it is and like it should be. This book gives you sensible advice that can improve your desktop publishing efforts. Roger doesn't mind if you steal his ideas, as long as you buy his books.

The PC Is Not a Typewriter, by Robin Williams, Peachpit Press

Short, sweet, and to the point. The most sensible, easy-to-read desktop publishing style guide around by one of the clearest-headed people we know. Tastes great, less filling.

Pocket Pal, 14th Edition, International Paper

The definitive small reference to printing and print technology. It's loaded with facts, and its overview of the industry just can't be beat.

The Illustrated Handbook of Desktop Publishing & Typesetting, 2nd Edition, by Michael Klepper, Windcrest Books

Klepper is a graphic-design professional, and this large book collects many techniques, products, and history of the industry. It's a definitive piece of work that can serve as both a textbook to learn the field of desktop publishing and as a reference. It is also available in CD-ROM format.

Technique Magazine, Boston, MA

Technique Magazine presents the technology and practice of desktop publishing to a broad audience from beginners to old hands. The magazine is attractively published and illustrates what's possible when DTP professionals put their minds to it. Barrie's column on "Electronic Print Technology" appears in this magazine on a bimonthly basis.

Windows 95 For Dummies, by Andy Rathbone, IDG Books Worldwide, Inc.

Microsoft Publisher 97 is a Windows 95 program, after all. If you need help getting started, start here. Other books that we like are *Real Life Windows 95,* by Dan Gookin, and *Windows 95 Uncut,* by Alan Simpson, both from IDG Books Worldwide, Inc.

The Macintosh Font Book, 3rd Edition, by Efert Fenton, Peachpit Press

Fenton's book may be Macintosh oriented but it's a great place to go to learn about fonts and how to use them.

Getting It Printed, by Mark Beach, Steve Shepro, and Ken Russon, Coast to Coast Press

These authors tell you how to talk to your printer and how to get the best results from the process.

Real World Scanning and Halftones, by David Bladner and Steve Roth, Peachpit Press

This book is the best introduction to digital imaging technology out there. Martin Nyman's *Four Colors/One Image,* also by Peachpit Press, is another outstanding book on this general subject, with more of a focus on image editing and color output. Both are beautiful pieces of work.

Font and Function, Adobe Systems

Adobe's fonts are as good as anyone's in the industry, and no collection is larger and better. Although many other vendors, such as Bitstream, are equally good, Adobe's quarterly magazine is a resource that shouldn't be missed for selecting and working with type.

Index

•𝒱•

The Internet For Macs® For Dummies® 2nd Edition	by Charles Seiter	ISBN: 1-56884-371-2	$19.99 USA/$26.99 Canada
The Internet For Macs® For Dummies® Starter Kit	by Charles Seiter	ISBN: 1-56884-244-9	$29.99 USA/$39.99 Canada
The Internet For Macs® For Dummies® Starter Kit Bestseller Edition	by Charles Seiter	ISBN: 1-56884-245-7	$39.99 USA/$54.99 Canada
The Internet For Windows® For Dummies® Starter Kit	by John R. Levine & Margaret Levine Young	ISBN: 1-56884-237-6	$34.99 USA/$44.99 Canada
The Internet For Windows® For Dummies® Starter Kit, Bestseller Edition	by John R. Levine & Margaret Levine Young	ISBN: 1-56884-246-5	$39.99 USA/$54.99 Canada

MACINTOSH

Mac® Programming For Dummies®	by Dan Parks Sydow	ISBN: 1-56884-173-6	$19.95 USA/$26.95 Canada
Macintosh® System 7.5 For Dummies®	by Bob LeVitus	ISBN: 1-56884-197-3	$19.95 USA/$26.95 Canada
MORE Macs® For Dummies®	by David Pogue	ISBN: 1-56884-087-X	$19.95 USA/$26.95 Canada
PageMaker 5 For Macs® For Dummies®	by Galen Gruman & Deke McClelland	ISBN: 1-56884-178-7	$19.95 USA/$26.95 Canada
QuarkXPress 3.3 For Dummies®	by Galen Gruman & Barbara Assadi	ISBN: 1-56884-217-1	$19.99 USA/$26.99 Canada
Upgrading and Fixing Macs® For Dummies®	by Kearney Rietmann & Frank Higgins	ISBN: 1-56884-189-2	$19.99 USA/$26.99 Canada

MULTIMEDIA

Multimedia & CD-ROMs For Dummies® 2nd Edition	by Andy Rathbone	ISBN: 1-56884-907-9	$19.99 USA/$26.99 Canada
Multimedia & CD-ROMs For Dummies® Interactive Multimedia Value Pack, 2nd Edition	by Andy Rathbone	ISBN: 1-56884-909-5	$29.99 USA/$39.99 Canada

OPERATING SYSTEMS:

DOS

MORE DOS For Dummies®	by Dan Gookin	ISBN: 1-56884-046-2	$19.95 USA/$26.95 Canada
OS/2® Warp For Dummies® 2nd Edition	by Andy Rathbone	ISBN: 1-56884-205-8	$19.99 USA/$26.99 Canada

UNIX

MORE UNIX® For Dummies®	by John R. Levine & Margaret Levine Young	ISBN: 1-56884-361-5	$19.99 USA/$26.99 Canada
UNIX® For Dummies®	by John R. Levine & Margaret Levine Young	ISBN: 1-878058-58-4	$19.95 USA/$26.95 Canada

WINDOWS

MORE Windows® For Dummies® 2nd Edition	by Andy Rathbone	ISBN: 1-56884-048-9	$19.95 USA/$26.95 Canada
Windows® 95 For Dummies®	by Andy Rathbone	ISBN: 1-56884-240-6	$19.99 USA/$26.99 Canada

PCS/HARDWARE

Illustrated Computer Dictionary For Dummies® 2nd Edition	by Dan Gookin & Wallace Wang	ISBN: 1-56884-218-X	$12.95 USA/$16.95 Canada
Upgrading and Fixing PCs For Dummies® 2nd Edition	by Andy Rathbone	ISBN: 1-56884-903-6	$19.99 USA/$26.99 Canada

PRESENTATION/AUTOCAD

AutoCAD For Dummies®	by Bud Smith	ISBN: 1-56884-191-4	$19.95 USA/$26.95 Canada
PowerPoint 4 For Windows® For Dummies®	by Doug Lowe	ISBN: 1-56884-161-2	$16.99 USA/$22.99 Canada

PROGRAMMING

Borland C++ For Dummies®	by Michael Hyman	ISBN: 1-56884-162-0	$19.95 USA/$26.95 Canada
C For Dummies® Volume 1	by Dan Gookin	ISBN: 1-878058-78-9	$19.95 USA/$26.95 Canada
C++ For Dummies®	by Stephen R. Davis	ISBN: 1-56884-163-9	$19.95 USA/$26.95 Canada
Delphi Programming For Dummies®	by Neil Rubenking	ISBN: 1-56884-200-7	$19.99 USA/$26.99 Canada
Mac® Programming For Dummies®	by Dan Parks Sydow	ISBN: 1-56884-173-6	$19.95 USA/$26.95 Canada
PowerBuilder 4 Programming For Dummies®	by Ted Coombs & Jason Coombs	ISBN: 1-56884-325-9	$19.99 USA/$26.99 Canada
QBasic Programming For Dummies®	by Douglas Hergert	ISBN: 1-56884-093-4	$19.95 USA/$26.95 Canada
Visual Basic 3 For Dummies®	by Wallace Wang	ISBN: 1-56884-076-4	$19.95 USA/$26.95 Canada
Visual Basic "X" For Dummies®	by Wallace Wang	ISBN: 1-56884-230-9	$19.99 USA/$26.99 Canada
Visual C++ 2 For Dummies®	by Michael Hyman & Bob Arnson	ISBN: 1-56884-328-3	$19.99 USA/$26.99 Canada
Windows® 95 Programming For Dummies®	by S. Randy Davis	ISBN: 1-56884-327-5	$19.99 USA/$26.99 Canada

SPREADSHEET

1-2-3 For Dummies®	by Greg Harvey	ISBN: 1-878058-60-6	$16.95 USA/$22.95 Canada
1-2-3 For Windows® 5 For Dummies® 2nd Edition	by John Walkenbach	ISBN: 1-56884-216-3	$16.95 USA/$22.95 Canada
Excel 5 For Macs® For Dummies®	by Greg Harvey	ISBN: 1-56884-186-8	$19.95 USA/$26.95 Canada
Excel For Dummies® 2nd Edition	by Greg Harvey	ISBN: 1-56884-050-0	$16.95 USA/$22.95 Canada
MORE 1-2-3 For DOS For Dummies®	by John Weingarten	ISBN: 1-56884-224-4	$19.99 USA/$26.99 Canada
MORE Excel 5 For Windows® For Dummies®	by Greg Harvey	ISBN: 1-56884-207-4	$19.95 USA/$26.95 Canada
Quattro Pro 6 For Windows® For Dummies®	by John Walkenbach	ISBN: 1-56884-174-4	$19.95 USA/$26.95 Canada
Quattro Pro For DOS For Dummies®	by John Walkenbach	ISBN: 1-56884-023-3	$16.95 USA/$22.95 Canada

UTILITIES

Norton Utilities 8 For Dummies®	by Beth Slick	ISBN: 1-56884-166-3	$19.95 USA/$26.95 Canada

VCRS/CAMCORDERS

VCRs & Camcorders For Dummies™	by Gordon McComb & Andy Rathbone	ISBN: 1-56884-229-5	$14.99 USA/$20.99 Canada

WORD PROCESSING

Ami Pro For Dummies®	by Jim Meade	ISBN: 1-56884-049-7	$19.95 USA/$26.95 Canada
MORE Word For Windows® 6 For Dummies®	by Doug Lowe	ISBN: 1-56884-165-5	$19.95 USA/$26.95 Canada
MORE WordPerfect® 6 For Windows® For Dummies®	by Margaret Levine Young & David C. Kay	ISBN: 1-56884-206-6	$19.95 USA/$26.95 Canada
MORE WordPerfect® 6 For DOS For Dummies®	by Wallace Wang, edited by Dan Gookin	ISBN: 1-56884-047-0	$19.95 USA/$26.95 Canada
Word 6 For Macs® For Dummies®	by Dan Gookin	ISBN: 1-56884-190-6	$19.95 USA/$26.95 Canada
Word For Windows® 6 For Dummies®	by Dan Gookin	ISBN: 1-56884-075-6	$16.95 USA/$22.95 Canada
Word For Windows® For Dummies®	by Dan Gookin & Ray Werner	ISBN: 1-878058-86-X	$16.95 USA/$22.95 Canada
WordPerfect® 6 For DOS For Dummies®	by Dan Gookin	ISBN: 1-878058-77-0	$16.95 USA/$22.95 Canada
WordPerfect® 6.1 For Windows® For Dummies® 2nd Edition	by Margaret Levine Young & David Kay	ISBN: 1-56884-243-0	$16.95 USA/$22.95 Canada
WordPerfect® For Dummies®	by Dan Gookin	ISBN: 1-878058-52-5	$16.95 USA/$22.95 Canada

For scholastic requests & educational orders please call Educational Sales at 1. 800. 434. 2086

FOR MORE INFO OR TO ORDER, PLEASE CALL ▶ 800. 762. 2974

For volume discounts & special orders please call Corporate Sales, at 415. 655. 3000

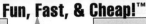

IDG BOOKS WORLDWIDE

Order Center: **(800) 762-2974** *(24 hours a day, seven days a week)*

Quantity	ISBN	Title	Price	Total

Shipping & Handling Charges

	Description	First book	Each additional book	Total
Domestic	Normal	$4.50	$1.50	$
	Two Day Air	$8.50	$2.50	$
	Overnight	$18.00	$3.00	$
International	Surface	$8.00	$8.00	$
	Airmail	$16.00	$16.00	$
	DHL Air	$17.00	$17.00	$

*For large quantities call for shipping & handling charges.
**Prices are subject to change without notice.

Ship to:

Name _____

Company _____

Address _____

City/State/Zip _____

Daytime Phone _____

Payment: ☐ Check to IDG Books Worldwide (US Funds Only)

       ☐ VISA   ☐ MasterCard   ☐ American Express

Card # _____ Expires _____

Signature _____

Subtotal _____

CA residents add
applicable sales tax _____

IN, MA, and MD
residents add
5% sales tax _____

IL residents add
6.25% sales tax _____

RI residents add
7% sales tax _____

TX residents add
8.25% sales tax _____

Shipping _____

Total _____

Please send this order form to:
**IDG Books Worldwide, Inc.
Attn: Order Entry Dept.
7260 Shadeland Station, Suite 100
Indianapolis, IN 46256**

*Allow up to 3 weeks for delivery.
Thank you!*